C1 Advanced Trainer

Six practice tests with answers

WITH RESOURCES
DOWNLOAD

2

Cambridge University Press
www.cambridge.org/elt

Cambridge Assessment English
www.cambridgeenglish.org

Information on this title: www.cambridge.org/9781108716512

© Cambridge University Press and Cambridge Assessment 2020

This publication is in copyright. Subject to statutory exception
and to the provisions of relevant collective licensing agreements,
no reproduction of any part may take place without the written
permission of Cambridge University Press.

First published 2020

20 19 18 17 16 15 14 13 12 11 10 9 8 7 6 5 4 3 2 1

Printed in Dubai by Oriental Press

A catalogue record for this publication is available from the British Library

ISBN 978-1-108-71651-2 Student's Book with answers with Resources Download
ISBN 978-1-108-71652-9 Student's Book without answers with Audio Download

Cambridge University Press has no responsibility for the persistence or accuracy
of URLs for external or third-party internet websites referred to in this publication,
and does not guarantee that any content on such websites is, or will remain,
accurate or appropriate. Information regarding prices, travel timetables, and other
factual information given in this work is correct at the time of first printing but
Cambridge University Press does not guarantee the accuracy of such information thereafter.

It is normally necessary for written permission for copying to be obtained
in advance from a publisher. The answer sheets at the back of this book are
designed to be copied and distributed in class.

The normal requirements are waived here and it is not necessary to write to the
publishers for permission for an individual teacher to make copies for use
within his or her own classroom. Only those pages that carry the wording
'© Cambridge University Press and Cambridge Assessment 2020 Photocopiable' may be copied.

Contents

Acknowledgements

Our highly experienced team of Trainer writers, in collaboration with Cambridge Assessment English reviewers, have worked together to bring you *C1 Advanced Trainer 2.*

We would like to thank Carole Bartlett (writer), Tom Bradbury (writer), Annie Broadhead (writer), Lynda Edwards (writer), Marla Del Signore (writer), Helen Chilton (reviewer), Thorkild Gantner (reviewer), Howard Goodison (reviewer), Susan Kingsley (reviewer), Peter May (reviewer) and Angela McCarthy (reviewer) for their work on the material.

The authors and publishers acknowledge the following sources of copyright material and are grateful for the permissions granted. While every effort has been made, it has not always been possible to identify the sources of all the material used, or to trace all copyright holders. If any omissions are brought to our notice, we will be happy to include the appropriate acknowledgements on reprinting and in the next update to the digital edition, as applicable.

Text

Key: T = Test

T1: Text adapted from 'Chrissie Hynde: 'It's hard work being alone. Paintings are an outlet' by Jude Rogers, *The Guardian*, 04.11.2018. Copyright © 2018 Guardian News & Media Ltd. Reproduced with permission; Text adapted from 'No Man's Sky developer Sean Murray: It was as bad as things can get' by Keza MacDonald, *The Guardian*, 20.07.2018. Copyright © 2018 Guardian News & Media Ltd. Reproduced with permission; Text adapted from 'Science's search for a super banana' by Nic Fleming, *The Guardian*, 05.08.2018. Copyright © 2018 Guardian News & Media Ltd. Reproduced with permission; Text adapted from 'Skating on thick ice: touring Sweden's frozen lakes' by Seán M Williams, *The Guardian*, 10.02.2018. Copyright © 2018 Guardian News & Media Ltd. Reproduced with permission; Text adapted from 'How to focus – tips from a Cambridge don, London cabbie and others' by Will Coldwell, *The Guardian*, 13.10.2018. Copyright © 2018 Guardian News & Media Ltd. Reproduced with permission; **T2:** Text adapted from 'Finding a tenor on the floor: when audience members save the day' by Tim Dowling, *The Guardian*, 24.07.2018. Copyright © 2018 Guardian News & Media Ltd. Reproduced with permission; Text adapted from 'Into the dark: what's it like working through the night?' by Michael Segalov, *The Guardian*, 11.11.2018. Copyright © 2018 Guardian News & Media Ltd. Reproduced with permission; Text adapted from 'Gastrophysics: The New Science of Eating by Charles Spence – review' by Bee Wilson, *The Guardian*, 23.03.2017. Copyright © 2017 Guardian News & Media Ltd. Reproduced with permission; Text adapted from 'The surprising nation that loves bees more than anywhere else in the world' by Chris Leadbeater, *The Telegraph*, 19.05.2017. Copyright © 2017 Telegraph Media Group Limited. Reproduced with permission; Text adapted from 'The yoga industry is booming – but does it make you a better person?' by Brigid Delaney, *The Guardian*, 17.09.2017. Copyright © 2017 Guardian News & Media Ltd. Reproduced with permission; **T3:** Text adapted from 'Stradivarius violins really do match a sweet voice' by Tom Whipple, *The Times*, 22.05.2018. Copyright © 2018 The Times/News Licensing. Reproduced with permission; Text adapted from 'The great learning curve: how to improve your study habits' by Gavan Naden, *The Guardian*, 22.03.2018. Copyright © 2018 Guardian News & Media Ltd. Reproduced with permission; Text adapted from 'Climbing has gone from niche sport to worldwide sensation. What is its dizzying appeal?' by Phil Daoust, *The Guardian*, 12.08.2018. Copyright © 2018 Guardian News & Media Ltd. Reproduced with permission; Text adapted from 'Monkeying around in Borneo: a voluntourism trip with a difference' by Alex Lane, *The Guardian*, 01.11.2017. Copyright © 2017 Guardian News & Media Ltd. Reproduced with permission; **T4:** Text adapted from 'Teens get a bad rap: the neuroscientist championing moody adolescents' by Decca Aitkenhead, *The Guardian*, 17.08.2018. Copyright © 2018 Guardian News & Media Ltd. Reproduced with permission; Text adapted from 'Hours from rescue, I knew we were about to flip: Levison Wood rafts through the Grand Canyon' by Levison Wood, *The Telegraph*, 19.07.2018. Copyright © 2018 Telegraph Media Group Limited. Reproduced with permission; Text adapted from 'The secret life of an extra: don't talk, don't eat and don't go home till 2am', *The Guardian*, 26.12.2016. Copyright © 2016 Guardian News & Media Ltd. Reproduced with permission; **T5:** Text adapted from 'Why being bilingual works wonders for your brain' by Gaia Vince, *The Guardian*, 07.08.2016. Copyright © 2016 Guardian News & Media Ltd. Reproduced with permission; Text adapted from 'Southdale Center: America's first shopping mall – a history of cities in 50 buildings, day 30' by Colin Marshall, *The Guardian*, 06.05.2016. Copyright © 2016 Guardian News & Media Ltd. Reproduced with permission; Text adapted from 'When 26.2 miles just isn't enough – the phenomenal rise of the ultramarathon' by Adharanand Finn, *The Guardian*, 02.04.2018. Copyright © 2018 Guardian News & Media Ltd. Reproduced with permission; **T6:** Text adapted from 'How to get just the right amount of exercise for your body (and mind)' by Luke Mintz, *The Telegraph*, 10.08.2018. Copyright © 2018 Telegraph Media Group Limited. Reproduced with permission; Text adapted from '"We've got to open minds": meet the composers reshaping opera' by Flora Willson, *The Guardian*, 08.06.2018. Copyright © 2018 Guardian News & Media Ltd. Reproduced with permission; Text adapted from 'How we grin to bear it – the science of smiling' by Richard Stephens, *The Guardian*, 22.12.2014. Copyright © 2014 Guardian News & Media Ltd. Reproduced with permission; Text adapted from 'How art detectives hunt down fakes' by Jonathan Eley, *Financial Times*, 22.12.2019. Used under licence from the Financial Times. All Rights Reserved.

Photography

All the photographs are sourced from Getty Images.

T1: Image Source; Leonard Mc Lane/DigitalVision; Chris Whitehead/DigitalVision; Thomas Northcut/DigitalVision; petek arici/E+; Image Source/DigitalVision; Westend61; Betsie Van der Meer/DigitalVision; Maskot; Tom Werner/DigitalVision; ullstein bild; FatCamera/E+; **T2:** Hero Images; DAJ; Nicolas Holtzmeyer/EyeEm; SolStock/E+; Kris Ubach and Quim Roser/Cultura; Dougal Waters/DigitalVision; Jetta Productions Inc/DigitalVision; Plume Creative/DigitalVision; Monty Rakusen/Cultura; Crezalyn Nerona Uratsuji/Moment Open; **T3:** NicolasMcComber/E+; Tanya Little/Moment; GCShutter/E+; Hero Images; Paul Bradbury/OJO Images; SOPA Images/LightRocket; **T4:** Emma Kim/Image Source; Monty Rakusen/Cultura; John Slater/DigitalVision; Michael H/DigitalVision; Hero Images/Digital Vision; **T5:** sturti/E+; Hero Images; Petri Oeschger/Moment; Dougal Waters/DigitalVision; Robert Daly/Caiaimage; Hero Images; **T6:** Hero Images; Image Source/DigitalVision; Elena Peremet/Moment; Image Source/DigitalVision; Glow Images; Zero Creatives/Cultura.

Front cover photography by Fabrizio Zampetti/EyeEm/Getty Images.

Audio

Audio recordings by DN and AE Strauss Ltd. Engineer: Neil Rogers; Editor: James Miller; Producer: Dan Strauss. Recorded at Cambridge Assessment, Cambridge.

Introduction

Who is *C1 Advanced Trainer 2* for?

This book is suitable for anyone who is preparing to take *C1 Advanced*. You can use *C1 Advanced Trainer 2* in class with your teacher or on your own at home.

What is *C1 Advanced Trainer 2*?

C1 Advanced Trainer 2 contains six practice tests for *C1 Advanced*, each covering the Reading and Use of English, Writing, Listening and Speaking papers. The first two tests are 'guided tests', which means that they contain extra training and support to help you with each of the tasks in the exam. Tests 3–6 are purely practice tests. All six tests are at *C1 Advanced* level and match the exam in format and standard.

Test 1 consists of a Training section and an Exam Practice section for each part of each paper. The training sections give information about each part of the exam and provide advice and practice to help you prepare for it. They focus on grammar, vocabulary and functional language directly relevant to particular task types. This is supported by work based on correcting common grammar and vocabulary mistakes made in the exam by *C1 Advanced* candidates, as shown by the **Cambridge Learner Corpus**. (For more information on the Cambridge Learner Corpus, see page 6.) The exam practice sections consist of the test itself accompanied by an Action plan, giving step-by-step guidance for each task, with tips on general strategy and advice linked to the specific questions. A follow-up task at the end of the exam practice section invites you to reflect on the task and consider how you could improve your performance.

Test 2 also consists of a Training section and an Exam Practice section for each part of the exam. The training sections are shorter than those in Test 1. They review the information provided in Test 1 and also include further practice for that part of the test. The exam practice sections provide additional tips and advice.

Tests 3–6 are complete practice tests without advice or training. They give you the opportunity to practise the skills you have acquired while working through Tests 1 and 2.

There are explanatory Keys (see opposite) for all tests.

Features of *C1 Advanced Trainer 2*

- Full-colour **visual material** for the Speaking paper in all six tests.
- **Explanatory Keys** for the Training and Exam Practice sections, not only giving information about which answers are right, but also, where appropriate, explaining why certain answers are correct and other options are not.
- **Notes** in the **Keys** for all Writing tasks to explain what is required and **model answers** for each task type.
- **Downloadable resources** consisting of audio recordings for the six Listening tests, as well as keys and audioscripts. These resources can be downloaded from http://esource.cambridge.org
- **Audioscripts** for all recordings. The scripts for Listening tests have underlining to indicate the sections that give the answers to the questions.
- **Photocopiable answer sheets** for the Reading and Use of English and Listening papers. Before you take the exam, you should study these so that you know how to mark or write your answer correctly. In the Writing exam, the question paper will have plenty of lined paper for you to use for your answers.

How to use *C1 Advanced Trainer 2*

Test 1 Training

- For each part of each paper, you should begin by studying the **Task information**, which tells you the facts you need to know, such as what the task type tests and the kinds of question it uses.
- Throughout Test 1, you will see information marked **TIP**. These tips give you practical advice on how to tackle each task type.
- In all papers, training exercises help you develop the skills you need (e.g. working out meaning from context) by working through example items.
- Answers to all the training exercises are in the **Keys**.
- Throughout Test 1, there are **Useful language** sections, which present and practise grammatical structures, vocabulary or functional expressions that are often tested by particular task types.

- Many exercises involve focusing on and correcting common language mistakes made by actual *C1 Advanced* candidates, as shown by the **Cambridge Learner Corpus** (see opposite 6).

- In **Listening**, you are prompted to use the downloadable audio, with the track number clearly identified:

   You will also need a watch or clock to make sure that you keep to the time allowed for each part of the test.

- In **Writing**, the Keys contain **model answers** for the tasks. Although there are many different ways of answering each question, it is worth studying these and thinking about the structure and language of each of the answers provided.

- In **Speaking**, you are sometimes prompted to use the audio recordings and do tasks as you listen. You can practise speaking on your own, with a partner or in a group of three, using what you have learnt in **Useful language** and in **Tips**.

Test 1 Exam Practice

- Look first at the **Action plan**, which gives you clear step-by-step guidance on how to approach each task type.

- Read any further **Tips** for that part of the exam.

- Work through an exam-style task, following the **Action plan** and making use of the **Advice** boxes, which suggest ways of dealing with specific items.

- Answers to all items are in the **Keys**. For **Listening**, the parts of the **Audioscripts** which identify the correct answers are underlined.

- After doing the exam task, look at the **Follow-up** task and consider how you can do better in this part of the exam in future.

Test 2 Training

- Answer the questions in the **Review** section, as these will remind you about this part of the exam. If you need to, use the cross-reference to the **Task information** in Test 1 to check your answers.

- Look at the **Tips** and work through the exercises, which focus on other useful exam techniques and language to help with this part of the exam.

- There is further work based on mistakes frequently made by *C1 Advanced* candidates, as shown by the Cambridge Learner Corpus.

Test 2 Exam Practice

- Think about the **Action plan** in Test 1 for each part of the exam. Use the cross-reference if you need to.

- Use any **Tips** on strategy and **Advice** relating to specific questions to help you work through the exam task.

- Do the task under exam conditions if possible, i.e. not using a dictionary and spending an appropriate amount of time on the task.

- Check your answers in the explanatory **Keys**.

Tests 3–6 Exam Practice

- In Tests 3, 4, 5 and 6, you should apply the skills, techniques and language you have learnt in Tests 1 and 2.

- You can do these tests and the four papers within them in any order, but you should always try to keep to the time recommended for each paper.

- It will be easier to keep to the exam instructions if you can find somewhere quiet to work and ensure there are no interruptions.

- For the Speaking paper, it is best if you can work with a partner or in a group of three, but if that is not possible, you can follow the instructions and do all four parts on your own.

- You can check all answers for them, and also study the Listening audioscripts, after you have completed the tasks.

Audio

For Listening papers, you will always hear the recordings played a second time with full instructions and appropriate pauses, as in the exam.

The Cambridge Learner Corpus (CLC)

The CLC is a large collection of exam scripts written by candidates taking Cambridge English exams around the world. It currently contains over 55 million words and is growing all the time. The CLC is error coded to show the mistakes students tend to make and also what they tend to do well. It forms part of the Cambridge English Corpus (CEC) and it has been built up by Cambridge University Press and Cambridge Assessment English. The CLC currently contains scripts from:

- over 220,000 students
- 173 different first languages
- over 200 different countries.

Exercises in *C1 Advanced Trainer 2* which are based on the CLC are indicated by this icon: ⊙ Find out more about the Cambridge Learner Corpus at www.cambridge.org/corpus.

Level of *C1 Advanced*

- *C1 Advanced* is at Level C1 in the Common European Framework of Reference for Languages (CEFR). Achieving this level means that your English is good enough for you to study or work in most situations where English is the main language used.
- A pass mark at *C1 Advanced* is given a grade: A, B or C.
- Achieving a grade A means that your English is considered to be at Level C2 on the CEFR.
- If you do not get enough marks for a grade C in the examination, you may get a certificate stating that your English is at Level B2, provided you have demonstrated that is the case.

Grading

- The overall Cambridge English Scale score that you receive for the exam is the average of the separate scale scores you receive for each of the four skills and Use of English.
- The overall score determines your grade and CEFR level.
- There is no minimum score for each paper, so you don't have to pass all four papers to pass the exam.
- Candidates whose performance is below Level C1 but falls within Level B2 receive a Cambridge English certificate stating that they have demonstrated ability at Level B2.
- Whatever your grade, you will receive a Statement of Results. This includes your overall scale score, your scale score in each of the four skills and Use of English, your CEFR level and your grade.
- For more information on grading and results, go to the Cambridge Assessment English website (see *Further information* on page 9).

Content of *C1 Advanced*

C1 Advanced has four papers, each with several parts in it. For details on each part, see the page reference under the *Task information* heading in the tables on the following pages.

Reading and Use of English (1 hour 30 minutes)

There are eight parts to this paper and they are always in the same order. Parts 1–4 contain texts with accompanying grammar and vocabulary tasks. Parts 5–8 contain a range of texts and accompanying reading-comprehension tasks.

The texts used are from newspapers, magazines, journals, books, leaflets, brochures, etc.

Part	Task type	No. of questions	Format	Task information
1	Multiple-choice cloze	8	A text with eight gaps, each with four options. This mainly tests vocabulary: idioms, collocations, fixed phrases, etc.	page 10
2	Open cloze	8	A text with eight gaps which must be filled with one word each.	page 14
3	Word formation	8	A text with eight gaps. Each gap corresponds to a word. The stems of the missing words are given and must be changed to form the missing word.	page 17
4	Key word transformation	6	Six questions, each with a gapped sentence which must be completed in three to six words, including a given key word.	page 21
5	Multiple choice	6	A reading text followed by multiple-choice questions.	page 24
6	Cross-text multiple matching	4	Four short texts, followed by multiple-matching questions. You must read across texts to match a prompt to elements in the texts.	page 29
7	Gapped text	6	A text with missing paragraphs. You must choose the correct paragraphs from a list to complete the text.	page 33
8	Multiple matching	10	A text (or several short texts) with multiple-matching questions.	page 38

Writing (1 hour 30 minutes)

You have to do Part 1 (Question 1) plus any one of the Part 2 tasks. In Part 2, you can choose one of questions 2 to 4. The possible marks for Part 1 and Part 2 are the same. In all tasks, you are told what kind of text you must write, who you are writing to, and why you are writing.

Part	Task type	No. of words	Format	Task information
1	essay	220–260	You have to write an essay based on two points in given information. You need to decide which of the two points is more important, and to explain why.	page 42
2	report review letter or email proposal	220–260	You are given a choice of tasks which specify the type of text you have to write, your purpose for writing, and the person or people you have to write for.	page 46

Listening (approximately 40 minutes)

You will both hear and see the instructions for each task, and you will hear each of the four parts twice. You will hear pauses announced and you can use this time to read the questions. There is one mark for each question in this paper. At the end of the test, you will have five minutes to copy your answers onto the answer sheet.

If one person is speaking, you might hear an announcement, radio broadcast, speech, talk, lecture or anecdote, for example. If there are two speakers, you might hear a radio interview, discussion or conversation, for example.

Part	Task type	No. of questions	Format	Task information
1	Multiple choice	6	You hear three short extracts and have to answer two multiple-choice questions on each. Each question has three options: A, B and C.	page 51
2	Sentence completion	8	You hear a recording and have to write a word or short phrase to complete sentences.	page 54
3	Multiple choice	6	You hear a recording and have to answer multiple-choice questions, each with four options: A, B, C and D.	page 56
4	Multiple matching	10	You hear five short extracts. There are two matching tasks focusing on the gist and the main points of what is said, the attitude of the speakers and the context in which they are speaking, etc.	page 59

Speaking (15 minutes)

You will probably do the Speaking test with one other candidate, although sometimes it is necessary to form groups of three. There will be two examiners, but one of them does not take part in the conversation. The examiner will indicate who you should talk to in each part of the test.

Part	Task type	Format	Task information
1	Short conversations between one of the examiners and each candidate.	The examiner asks you both some questions about yourself and your interests and experiences.	page 61
2	Individual 'long turn' with brief response from partner	You are each given some visual and written prompts; the examiner will ask you to talk about these for about a minute. You are asked to give a short response after your partner has finished their 'long turn'.	page 63
3	Collaborative task	You are given some spoken instructions and written stimuli for a discussion or decision-making task and you discuss these prompts with your partner.	page 65
4	Three-way interaction between candidates and one of the examiners	The examiner asks you and your partner questions relating to topics arising from Part 3.	page 67

Further information

The information about *C1 Advanced* contained in *C1 Advanced Trainer 2* is designed to be an overview of the exam. For a full description, including information about task types, testing focus and preparation for the exam, please use the *C1 Advanced Handbook*, which can be obtained from Cambridge Assessment English at the address below or from the website at www.cambridgeenglish.org.

Cambridge Assessment English
The Triangle Building
Shaftesbury Road
Cambridge
CB2 8EA

TASK INFORMATION

- In Part 1, you read a text which has eight gaps (plus one example).
- For each gap, there is a choice of four words or phrases: (**A**, **B**, **C** or **D**). You need to choose the correct word or phrase to complete each gap.
- The task tests your understanding of the text and your knowledge of vocabulary.
- The gapped word may be part of a collocation (e.g. *pay attention*), phrasal verb or set phrase.
- Sometimes your choice of a word or words for a gap will depend on the meaning of the whole text or a large section of the text, and not just the words immediately around the gap.
- Sometimes your choice will depend on grammatical words that come immediately before or after the gap, such as prepositions. e.g. *He <u>objected</u> to the comments.*

IDENTIFYING COLLOCATIONS

1 ⊙ **Circle the four correct collocations in the following sets.**

1	make	a difference / sense / some research / an exception / trouble / damage
2	do	your best / the shopping / some changes / a reservation / someone a favour / harm
3	have	an experience / an effect / patience / a row / harm / place
4	take	word with someone / notice / something for granted / pleasure / a choice / turns
5	put	pressure on someone / something into practice / a mess / foot on something / an end to something / your mind to something
6	give	a talk / your word / something for granted / credit to someone / use of / someone a chance
7	set	an example / a record / an alarm / an excuse / a fuss / fire to something
8	keep	a promise / pity on someone / a diary / a secret / in touch / an impact on something

TIP A collocation is two or more words that often go together. For example: fast food ✓ and NOT quick food ✗; make a cup of tea ✓ and NOT do a cup of tea ✗. When words collocate, they sound natural together. If they don't collocate, they sound unnatural together.

TIP If you're not sure whether words collocate, you can look them up in learners' dictionaries and in collocation dictionaries.

TIP When you practise doing Part 1 tasks, keep a record of any collocations that are new to you.

2 ⊙ **Choose one of the collocations from Exercise 1 to complete each sentence.**

1 Last year, Amy .... for the fastest-ever 1500 metres run by a student at her school.

2 'Will you .... that you won't tell anyone else about this?' Sarah asked Philip.

3 After Sachiko moved back to Japan from Los Angeles, she .... with her friend Ana by email.

4 Last year, I .... with my neighbour because his motorbike was blocking my front gate, and we didn't speak to each other again for ages.

5 Maria and Pawel .... to cook the dinner; Maria does it one day and Pawel does it the next.

TIP There are several different types of collocations, e.g. verb + noun (make a mistake); noun + verb (dogs bark); adjective + noun (heavy rain); adverb + adjective (fully aware).

6 Whenever Jim really .... learning something new, he usually succeeds.

7 'Robbie, could you .... , please? Could you help me fix my bike?' asked Michael.

8 Kate .... to get her students to work hard but some of them didn't pay much attention to her.

3 ⊙ Choose the correct adverb (A, B, C or D) to complete each gap.

1 Camille was .... *disappointed* when she only came third in the 800 metre race.

   A sharply   B bitterly   C fiercely   D crossly

2 Cliff was .... *moved* by the sad story that his grandmother told him.

   A soundly   B heavily   C widely   D deeply

3 The decision to build a new bridge across the river was .... *controversial*.

   A solidly   B firmly   C highly   D strongly

4 The local newspaper played a .... *important* role in the campaign against poor air quality.

   A vitally   B chiefly   C completely   D principally

5 House prices in the capital city are .... *high*.

   A vastly   B hugely   C extremely   D greatly

6 Public transport in the region is .... *subsidised* by the government, so fares are low.

   A firmly   B heavily   C thickly   D solidly

7 Advice on how to invest your savings is much more .... *available* than it used to be.

   A thoroughly   B largely   C widely   D highly

8 Research suggests that regular exercise and a feeling of being happy are .... *linked*.

   A nearly   B finely   C exactly   D closely

UNDERSTANDING THE PRECISE MEANING OF WORDS

Choose the correct option (A, B, C or D) to complete each gap.

1 Young people in my region used to feel cut off from other young people, but this changed with the .... of social media.

   A design   B issue   C arrival   D result

2 Environmental research shows that much more should be done to .... certain species in the local area which are regarded as endangered.

   A overcome   B protect   C expose   D control

3 It's .... what the key is to achieving success in this type of business. No one seems to know.

   A unbelievable   B unfair   C unclear   D undeniable

4 I took part in a very interesting psychological experiment. I was one of about 100 .... of various ages and backgrounds.

   A members   B participants   C players   D entrants

5 My brother was on the .... of joining the police force, but then he changed his mind.

   A edge   B border   C line   D point

TIP Part 1 questions often test understanding of the exact meanings of words rather than knowledge of collocations. e.g. *The shop manager is concerned about the way her staff are noticed / impressed / treated by certain customers, many of whom can be very rude.* Staff can be *noticed, impressed* and *treated* by customers, so all three words are acceptable collocations. However, *many of whom can be very rude* indicates that the sentence is about the customers' behaviour, so *treated* is the correct option in this sentence.

ACTION PLAN

1 Look at the title and think about what the subject of the text will be.

2 Read the whole text quickly to get a general idea of the topic.

3 Look carefully at the words before and after each gap. Is there a word you can think of that would fit the gap?

4 Look carefully at the options for each question and eliminate those you know are incorrect.

5 The options have similar meanings, so you need to choose the word that combines with the words on either side of the gap.

6 Sometimes only one option is correct grammatically, so look closely at words such as prepositions before or after the gap.

7 If you get stuck on one question, move on to the next one. You may have a better idea if you go back to it after you have completed the whole text.

8 When you have chosen an answer for every gap, read through the text again and make sure that each word makes sense in the context of the text as a whole.

Follow the exam instructions, using the advice to help you.

For questions **1 – 8**, read the text below and decide which answer (**A**, **B**, **C**, or **D**) best fits each gap. There is an example at the beginning **(0)**.

Mark your answers **on the separate answer sheet**.

Example:

0   **A**   suppose   **B**   picture   **C**   conceive   **D**   presume

Would you rather win a silver or bronze medal?

Try to **(0)** .... yourself as an athlete in an Olympic event. We can **(1)** .... assume you'd want to win, and, if that wasn't possible, you'd prefer to **(2)** .... up second rather than third. However, research **(3)** .... that the reality may be different.

In one study, volunteers assessed athletes' faces as they waited for their medals. In particular, they looked out for athletes with a 'Duchenne smile', which is thought to show happiness and is **(4)** .... by a raising of the mouth and a crinkling round the eyes. Gold medal winners were rated as happiest, but those in second place seemed less happy than bronze medallists. Researchers also found that the **(5)** .... by which a medal was won or lost appeared important: silver medallists who **(6)** .... lost out on gold were significantly less happy than those who only just beat the third-placed athlete.

Do silver medallists **(7)** .... on how they might have won gold, whereas bronze medallists just feel lucky to win something? We can't be sure, but researchers think comparative performance may greatly affect the **(8)** .... of happiness.

1	A soundly	B steadily	C safely	D strongly
2	A take	B come	C make	D end
3	A exposes	B suggests	C notifies	D admits
4	A characterised	B featured	C constituted	D specified
5	A distance	B area	C size	D limit
6	A tightly	B finely	C closely	D narrowly
7	A wonder	B reflect	C consider	D evaluate
8	A impact	B conclusion	C feeling	D search

Advice

1 *Only one of these adverbs collocates with 'assume'. It might help to think of the adjectives that these adverbs are formed from – then see which one seems to fit best in this phrase: 'It is .... to assume that ...'.*

2 *One of these phrasal verbs means 'eventually finish'.*

3 *Only one of these verbs is a normal collocation with 'research'.*

4 *Think about the meaning here. The correct word with 'by' means 'has the following typical qualities'.*

5 *One of these words is often used in connection with races.*

6 *Only one of these adverbs collocates with 'lose'.*

7 *Only one of these verbs fits with the preposition 'on'.*

8 *Think about the meaning here. Which of these nouns would you normally think of in connection with the words that come after the gap?*

FOLLOW-UP
Is there anything that you would add to or change in the Action plan?

TASK INFORMATION

- In Part 2, you read a text which has eight gaps (plus one example).
- You have to complete each gap correctly, using one word only.
- The main focus of the task is on grammar and common words and expressions used to structure a text.
- Sometimes more than one answer to a question is possible (for example, both *if* and *whether* may fit). In this case, either response will be marked as correct.
- You must spell each word correctly, but both UK and US spellings are allowed.
- The answer will always be a single word. Remember not to use contractions, as these count as two words. e.g. *doesn't* = two words.

USEFUL LANGUAGE: RELATIVE PRONOUNS

⊙   **Complete each gap in the sentences with an appropriate relative pronoun.**

1 Pete forgot .... he had left his keys and he took ages to find them.
2 We can't understand .... the authorities are so unwilling to change their position.
3 The most memorable part of Jackie's holiday was .... she and her family went on a whale-watching boat trip.
4 Ahmed had problems with the internet connection, at .... point he decided to stop working for the day.
5 The staff in the finance department are eager to find out .... is to be appointed as their new manager.
6 No one expected Terry to win a race this year, but that is exactly .... happened last weekend.
7 As a child, Alison collected sea shells, many of .... she still has at home.
8 I'm not sure .... car that is, but it's been parked in the same place for over a week.

> **TIP** The missing grammatical words could include: prepositions (e.g. *in, with*), articles (*a ,an, the*), pronouns (e.g. *she, them*), determiners (e.g. *this, those*), relative pronouns (e.g. *which, who*), parts of verbs (e.g. *be, been*), modal verbs (e.g. *could, will*), particles of phrasal verbs (e.g. *set up/down*), conjunctions (e.g. *and, although*) and parts of phrases (e.g. *in order to*).

USEFUL LANGUAGE: ADJECTIVE + PREPOSITION

⊙   **Complete the gaps in the sentences with the correct preposition.**

1 Helen has always been very good .... solving problems.
2 Historically, the region has always been associated .... rice-growing.
3 Portugal is renowned .... the quality and beauty of its tiles.
4 Eliana's experiences are very typical .... young people doing internships these days.
5 Local businesses were strongly opposed .... the introduction of a new property tax.
6 My father will soon be eligible .... a pension.
7 The band have received some negative reviews, so they're rather wary .... journalists now.
8 We're very grateful .... all the support we've been given.
9 Faiza was exposed .... lots of different types of music as she was growing up.
10 Gavin has doubts about the project and wasn't convinced .... the latest reports.

USEFUL LANGUAGE: VERB + NOUN + PREPOSITION

 Circle the correct preposition in the following sentences.

1 It was very hard to make sense *in / at / of* what the caller to the radio programme was saying.
2 Fortunately, Suresh made a speedy recovery *from / of / with* his illness.
3 The coaches took great pride *at / in / for* the progress that the team made last year.
4 I have to keep an eye *to / for / on* my sister's flat while she's away.
5 We feel that the company has lost sight *about / from / of* its original objectives.
6 The security staff had to take the blame *for / about / on* the robbery at the shopping mall yesterday.
7 Latecomers aren't usually allowed in, but the staff made an exception *from / for / about* several people today because of the traffic problems.
8 Olaf has been put in charge *of / for / to* the new advertising campaign.

> **TIP**
> In Part 2, gaps often require words that connect different parts of a sentence. e.g. *There were three people helping **but** it still took several hours to clean the house.*

> **TIP**
> After you put a connecting word into a sentence, read the whole sentence again carefully to check that it makes sense.

USEFUL LANGUAGE: CONNECTING WORDS

1 **Put the connecting words from the box into suitable groups in the table below.**

~~when~~	whether ... or not	whereas	either ... or	in case
because	unless	even though	so as not to	whether
before	so as to	neither ... nor ...	in spite of	as ... as

Concession	Time	Condition
although / though	after	if
despite	until	even if
....	*when*	....
....	....	....
Comparison	**Reason**	**Correlation**
than	so that	both ... and ...
rather than	in order to/that	not only ... but (also) ...
....	....	....
....	....	....
	....	....

2 **Use words from the table in Exercise 1 to complete the gaps in the sentences.**

1 It would be nice to go out for a walk but let's wait .... it stops raining.
2 .... was the software quite original, but it was also very useful.
3 .... resubmit his application for a scholarship, Duncan decided to write a completely new application.
4 The football match will start at 8 p.m. .... the weather is so bad that it has to be delayed.
5 .... having a Scottish name, Sonny's mother lived her whole life in India.
6 Matteo found it hard to tell .... or not the lawyer was genuinely interested in helping him.
7 .... the lake looks beautiful from a distance, once you get close up, you can see it's polluted.

ACTION PLAN

1 Look at the title and read the whole text quickly to get a general idea of the topic.

2 Look carefully at the words before and after each gap and decide what type of word each gap needs.

3 Write one word only in each gap. Don't write contractions, as these count as two words.

4 Read the sentences before and after the gapped phrase to check your answer makes sense.

5 Sometimes more than one answer is possible (e.g. *although*, *though*).

6 Make sure you spell the words correctly.

7 If you get stuck on one question, move on to the next one. You may have a better idea if you go back to it when you have completed the whole text.

8 When you have chosen an answer for every gap, read the text again and check that each word makes sense in the context of the whole text.

Follow the exam instructions, using the advice to help you.

For questions **9 – 16**, read the text below and think of the word which best fits each gap. Use only one word in each gap. There is an example at the beginning (0).

Write your answers **IN CAPITAL LETTERS on the separate answer sheet**.

Example: `0` `A` `T`

Blue diamonds

Blue diamonds are the world's most expensive diamonds, with some valued **(0)** .... over 350 million US dollars. However, no one knew **(9)** .... recently precisely where these rare stones came from.

Most diamonds are formed from pure carbon under extreme heat 150 to 200 kilometres underground, and **(10)** .... is thought that volcanic eruptions bring them to the earth's surface. Research by scientists has revealed, however, that blue diamonds were probably formed somewhere **(11)** .... 600 and 800 kilometres down, in a part of the earth's interior known **(12)** .... the lower mantle.

These researchers analysed 46 blue diamonds, all of **(13)** .... contained minerals only found in the lower mantle. **(14)** .... only were these stones formed four times nearer the earth's core **(15)** .... normal diamonds, but they also contain an element called boron that is mostly found on the earth's surface. What seems to have happened, **(16)** .... to the researchers, is that billions of years ago, rocks containing boron were carried down into the lower mantle by movements of the earth's tectonic plates, and were eventually returned to the surface by volcanic action.

Advice

9 Read the whole sentence and think about what word can collocate with 'recently'.

10 This is part of a passive structure. There's no mention of who thinks this about diamonds.

11 The word you need combines with 'and' two words later.

12 Here you need a preposition to go with 'known'.

13 The word here refers back to '46 blue diamonds'.

14 Read the whole of the sentence. The word needed here is part of a structure which holds together the two parts of the sentence.

15 Look at the first half of this sentence, from (14) to 'diamonds'.

16 The word you need here is part of a fixed phrase. You may not think of it as grammar.

FOLLOW-UP

Did you follow all the steps in the Action plan?

TASK INFORMATION

- In Part 3, you read a text which has eight gaps (plus one example).
- You have to complete each gap correctly, using one word only. This word must be formed from a root word, which you will see in capital letters at the end of the line with the gap (e.g. **ENJOY** → enjoyment).
- Part 3 tests your ability to form words using prefixes (e.g. **LIKE** → dislike), suffixes (e.g. **FRIEND** → friendship), and combinations of words to make compound words (e.g. **FEED** → feedback).
- When you read the text, you need to decide what type of word is needed in each gap. It could be a verb, noun, adjective or adverb (e.g. enjoy, enjoyment, enjoyable, enjoyably).
- You might also need to decide if the word is positive or negative (e.g. active or inactive; agreement or disagreement).
- If the missing word is a noun, you need to decide if it should be singular or plural (e.g. scientist or scientists).
- You should also decide on the form of a verb (e.g. replacing or replaced).
- The spelling must be correct. Both UK and US spellings are allowed.

USEFUL LANGUAGE: IDENTIFYING TYPES OF WORDS

1   **Read the following text and decide what type of word is needed in each gap – a verb, noun, adjective or adverb. How do you know?**

My uncle was a **(1)** .... footballer when he was younger. **(2)** ...., he had to retire from the game when he was only 28 years old because of a serious knee injury. He says he can see many **(3)** .... between his life as a player nearly 30 years ago and the lives of players today. For one thing, the players' **(4)** .... levels today are much higher than they were when he was playing. That, together with a good diet and expert medical care, **(5)** .... modern footballers to have longer careers. My uncle says he's quite **(6)** .... of modern players in this respect, as he is of the money they earn. However, he is glad he never had to deal with social media, which he thinks is one of the **(7)** .... of being a well-known player today.

TIP Try to learn 'word families' – e.g. fortune, misfortune, fortunately, unfortunately.

TIP Look at the words before and after the gap to help you decide what type of word you need. For example, a gap between a verb and a noun needs an adjective – it was an **enjoyable** day. A word at the very beginning of a sentence followed by a comma is usually an adverb – **Suddenly**, there was a loud noise.

2   **Use the words from the box below and form new words to fill the gaps in Exercise 1. Remember that you can add prefixes, suffixes or compound words.**

able   fit   envy   fortunate   profession   draw   different

USEFUL LANGUAGE: USING PREFIXES AND SUFFIXES

Complete this table. The first row has been completed as an example. Sometimes more than one word is possible, and sometimes a particular form of the word does not exist.

TIP When you come across a new word, it's a good idea to keep a note of other possible forms of the word. Use a dictionary to help you with this.

Verb	Noun	Adjective	Adverb
create	creation creator creativity	creative uncreative	creatively
intend			
	origin		
		popular	
increase			
please			
		kind	

USEFUL LANGUAGE: UNDERSTANDING SUFFIXES

1 Here are a few suffixes in English. Complete the table where there are dotted lines (.............................).

Suffix	Function	Meaning	Examples
-er, -or	to make a noun from a verb	• person who does something • object that does something	*thinker, boxer, operator ruler, projector,*
-ist	to make a noun, often from another noun	• people in certain professions • people with certain beliefs • some musicians	.... *anarchist, theorist* ....
-tion, -sion	to make a noun from a verb	for many different things	....
....	to make a noun from an adjective	often for feelings, qualities and states of mind	*sadness, kindness, readiness*
-ise / -ize	to make a verb from an adjective	cause to have a quality	*modernise* ....
-ment	to make a noun from a verb	process or result of doing something	*enjoyment* ....
....	to make a noun from an adjective	quality or state of something	*modernity, sensitivity*
-ship	to make a noun, often from another noun	status	*friendship* ....
-ify	to make a verb from an adjective or noun	cause to have a quality	*notify* ....
-ive	to make an adjective from a verb or noun	for many different things	*active* ....

2 Complete the sentences by using the suffixes from the table in Exercise 1 to change the words in capital letters.

1 Craig briefly .... the discussion that had taken place. **SUMMARY**

2 Helen says she learnt Turkish through total .... in the language. **IMMERSE**

3 I was surprised at how reasonable the .... fees at the sports club were. **MEMBER**

4 The team's success last year was all down to their .... **DETERMINE**

5 Yolanda was trained as a classical .... **VIOLIN**

6 One thing that attracts Rosie to physics is the .... of the subject. **COMPLEX**

7 The economy is good and .... prospects for young adults are improving. **EMPLOY**

8 The police are still trying to .... the suspect. **IDENTITY**

USEFUL LANGUAGE: ADJECTIVES AND ADVERBS

1 Look at the two examples and then complete the table.

Noun	Adjective	Adverb
tradition	*traditional*	*traditionally*
energy	*energetic*	*energetically*
function		
drama		
politician		
essence		
sarcasm		
athlete		
emotion		
controversy		
irony		
nutrition		
enthusiasm		
anecdote		

2 Use the word in capital letters to form either an adjective or an adverb to complete the sentence. Look at the table in Exercise 1 to help you.

1 I always get .... when I think about my grandmother. **EMOTION**

2 Grace spoke .... about her experience of travelling in Asia. **ENTHUSIASM**

3 In .... terms, this isn't the best thing to eat, but it's very tasty. **NUTRITION**

4 The information in the study was mostly .... **ANECDOTE**

5 .... , Jenkins was not selected for the national team. **CONTROVERSY**

6 Sven has a tendency to sound rather .... when he speaks. **SARCASM**

ACTION PLAN

1. Look at the title and read the whole text quickly to get a general idea of the subject.
2. Look carefully at the words before and after each gap and decide what type of word each one needs.
3. Sometimes you will need to read a sentence or a longer section to know what type of word is needed.
4. Look at the word in capital letters to the right of the gap and decide whether to add a prefix or suffix or make some other kind of change.
5. You will sometimes need to make more than one change.
6. For nouns, check whether they should be singular or plural.
7. For an adjective or adverb, check whether it should have a positive or negative meaning.
8. Make sure you spell the words correctly.

Follow the exam instructions, using the advice to help you.

For questions **17 – 24**, read the text below. Use the word given in capitals at the end of some of the lines to form a word that fits in the gap **in the same line**. There is an example at the beginning (**0**).

Write your answers **IN CAPITAL LETTERS on the separate answer sheet.**

Example: | 0 | H | I | S | T | O | R | I | C | A | L | L | Y | | | | | | |

Araucaria trees in South America

Large areas of Chile, Argentina and Brazil have **(0)** .... been covered by forests of Araucaria, or monkey puzzle trees as they are often called. A valuable source of timber, fuel, resin and nuts for eating, the Araucaria has played a key role in the cultural and **(17)** .... development of local communities. However, many of the forests are now **(18)** .... by logging and modern farming, and 5 out of the 19 species of Araucaria are **(19)** ....

The fact is that some forests owe their **(20)** .... to humans. A recent study in the region found there had been two major forest **(21)** .... The first, 4,500 to 3,200 years ago, was due to climatic changes and higher levels of **(22)** .... The second, between 1,400 and 900 years ago, coincided with the development of **(23)** .... complex societies in the region. Through excavations and soil **(24)** .... , the researchers found that local populations had modified the land, protected seedlings and even planted trees to help the forests grow. The researchers hope their findings will help efforts to conserve the ancient, partly man-made Araucaria forests.

HISTORY

ECONOMY
THREAT

DANGER

EXIST

EXPAND
MOIST

INCREASE
ANALYSE

Advice

17. What type of word is often needed before a noun?
18. Think about the passive construction in the sentence and what is the appropriate form needed for the word.
19. This word is an adjective and will need a prefix and a suffix.
20. What type of word will follow 'their'?
21. Is a singular or plural word needed here?
22. Do you need a verb or a noun here?
23. The word after the gap is an adjective, so what type of word is needed here? How many changes will you need to make?
24. Here you need a noun that means 'the process of examining something'.

FOLLOW-UP

Did you read through the text at the end to make sure your answers made sense?

TASK INFORMATION

- Part 4 tests your ability to be flexible in your use of English by expressing a message in a different way. At the same time, it tests your ability to use grammatical structures and vocabulary accurately.
- In Part 4, there are six questions (plus one example).
- Each question has an initial stimulus sentence, a key word and a second sentence with a gap in it.
- Your task is to complete the gap, using the key word given, so that the second sentence has the same meaning as the stimulus sentence.
- You must not change the key word at all.
- You will need to write between three and six words, including the key word, to complete the gap. Contractions (e.g. *don't*) count as two words.
- The mark scheme divides your answer into two parts and one mark is given for each part that is answered correctly.
- The spelling must be correct, but both UK and US spellings are allowed.

HOW TO APPROACH PART 4

Read the two sentences and then work through the questions below in order.

Because of the heavy rain, it was decided at the last minute to cancel the match.

MADE

Because of the heavy rain, a last-minute .... off the match.

a How are the words before the gap in the second sentence different from the words in the stimulus sentence?

b How are the words after the gap in the second sentence different from the words in the stimulus sentence?

c Which words and information in the stimulus sentence are missing from the second sentence?

d Which part of the stimulus sentence does the key word relate to: the first part or the second part?

e Can you complete the gap now?

TIP After you have written your answer, read it again to check that it has the same meaning as the stimulus sentence. Does it have all the same ideas?

TIP After you have written your answer, check that it is at least three words and no more than six words long.

APPLYING THE APPROACH TO PART 4

1 **Use questions a – e above to help you complete the sentences. Part of the answer is given.**

1 The last time Janet saw her cousin was three years ago.

SEEN

Janet ..... *hasn't* .... *for* ..... three years.

2 Juan was sorry that he didn't tell Maria where he was staying.

LET

Juan wished .... *Maria know* ... where he was staying.

3 I know it was wrong of me to ignore what Mrs Robertson was saying this morning.

ATTENTION

I know I should .... *to what* ... Mrs Robertson was saying this morning.

2 Read the advice and complete the sentences below.

Advice

Which phrase with AS means 'it was harder?'

1 Finding a place to park the car was harder than I thought it would be.

AS

It wasn't .... a place to park the car as I thought it would be.

Advice

'If the company had offered' is part of a conditional structure. Which conditional is it? What should the verb form be in the first part of the sentence? And which phrasal verb means 'refuse / don't accept' a job?

2 Max didn't accept the job because the company wouldn't offer him a better salary than his current one.

TURNED

Max .... the job if the company had offered him a better salary than his current one.

Advice

Which idiom with EYE means 'look after?'

3 Maggie was quite happy to look after her neighbour's children for a couple of hours.

EYE

Maggie didn't mind .... her neighbour's children for a couple of hours.

MAKING SURE SENTENCES HAVE THE SAME MEANING

Choose the sentence, A or B, that has the same meaning as the stimulus sentence.

1 It's very unusual for Peter to go to bed late.

EVER

A Peter *hardly ever stays* up late.

B Peter *hardly ever gets* up late.

2 Whatever I do to it, my laptop just doesn't work.

GET

A I can't *get my laptop to work, no* matter what I do to it.

B I can't *get a laptop that works, no* matter what I do to it.

3 The beach was much less crowded than it had been the previous year.

NEARLY

A The beach *was nearly as crowded as* it had been the previous year.

B The beach *wasn't nearly as crowded as* it had been the previous year.

4 Apparently, Carol was a really good singer when she was younger.

SUPPOSED

A Carol *is supposed to have been* a really good singer when she was younger.

B Carol *was supposed to become* a really good singer when she was younger.

5 We'll miss the start of the lecture if we don't walk faster.

TIME

A Unless we walk faster, the lecture *will start some time after* we get there.

B Unless we walk faster, the lecture *will have started by the time* we get there.

ACTION PLAN

1 For each question, read both sentences carefully.

2 Look carefully at the words before and after the gap.

3 You will need to make various changes, e.g. negative to positive, active to passive, verb to noun.

4 Include the given word completely unchanged.

5 Make sure you write three to six words.

6 You can use contractions (e.g. *I'm* or *don't*), but remember that these count as two words.

7 Check your spelling carefully.

8 Check that you haven't missed out any ideas from the first sentence or added any new ones.

Follow the exam instructions, using the advice to help you.

For questions **25 – 30,** complete the second sentence so that it has a similar meaning to the first sentence, using the word given. **Do not change the word given.** You must use between **three** and **six** words, including the word given. Here is an example **(0).**

Example:

0 'I'm sorry I got to the party so late,' Joanna said to her friend.

HAVING

Joanna apologised to her friend .... up so late at the party.

The gap can be filled with the words 'for having turned', so you write:

Example: | **0** | *FOR HAVING TURNED* |

Write **only** the missing words **IN CAPITAL LETTERS on the separate answer sheet.**

25 Visiting Tortuga Beach is easier than it used to be.

AS

Tortuga Beach isn't .... it used to be.

26 I'm not in contact with any of my primary school friends.

TOUCH

I've .... my primary school friends.

27 I was surprised when my brother was suddenly promoted.

CAME

My brother's sudden .... to me.

28 I'm sure customers will complain about the new shop layout.

BOUND

There .... from customers about the new shop layout.

29 Kerry only started playing badminton because you suggested it.

NEVER

Kerry .... up badminton if you hadn't suggested it.

30 Everyone I talk to thinks cars should be banned from the city centre.

FAVOUR

Everyone I talk to is .... cars from the city centre.

Advice

25 *Use a comparative structure beginning with 'not' which means the same as 'easier than'.*

26 *Which phrase with 'touch' means 'not stay in contact with'?*

27 *You need an expression with 'came' meaning 'it was surprising'.*

28 *Which idea in the first sentence does the adjective 'bound' relate to? And what verb form follows 'bound'?*

29 *Which phrasal verb with 'up' means 'start playing (a sport)'?*

30 *Which prepositions come before and after the noun 'favour' when it's part of a phrase meaning 'support an idea'?*

FOLLOW-UP

For each question, did you make sure that the second sentence has the same meaning as the first?

TASK INFORMATION

- In Part 5, you read a long text and answer six multiple-choice questions about it. Each question has four options.
- The questions are presented in the same order as the information in the text.

TIP Underline and label the parts of the text that contain the ideas that are in the options (A–D). This will help you to decide what the correct answer is.

- The texts come from a variety of sources. They are often newspaper or magazines articles, but can also be extracts from books, usually non-fiction, but occasionally fiction.
- The texts are on a wide range of topics and they vary in style from more to less formal.
- The questions test your understanding of a variety of things, including the main ideas and details of a text, the views and attitudes expressed in it, ideas which are implied, and features of text organisation, such as reference words and the use of examples.

IDENTIFYING THE IDEAS AND FEELINGS EXPRESSED IN THE TEXT

1 **Read the extract from an article about a woman called Jenny Granger and the question that follows it.**

Jenny Granger, lead singer of the rock band The Traces, has spent most of the last three years painting, and a book showcasing her art has just been published. As one critic recently pointed out, rock stars becoming painters has become quite a regular thing. <u>Given that the Rolling Stones' guitarist Ronnie Wood and the great American singer-songwriters Bob Dylan and Joni Mitchell have all had high-profile exhibitions of their paintings, Granger's career change is perhaps not so surprising</u>. But she has certain doubts. 'There are so many people who've been painting all their lives and they can't get their work into a gallery,' she says. 'Then I play around with some colours for a couple of years and because of who I am, there's a big fancy book of my paintings, and <u>lots of articles and reviews in the press about it</u>! It makes me quite uncomfortable.' She may not be the most technically skilled of artists, but <u>the portraits, landscapes and abstract images that she paints</u> have improved in quality over time. <u>One writer has claimed that she's a phoney</u>, but that's clearly not right. In fact, she's very genuine. 'I have no problems admitting that I'm not a great painter, but I'm serious about what I do,' she says. 'But yeah, my current situation – the focus being on me – is rather embarrassing.'

What does Jenny Granger feel embarrassed about?
A the way people compare her with other rock stars
B the subject matter she chooses for her paintings
C the attention her art is getting
D the criticism she has received

2 **Match the options (A – D) in the question with the underlined sections of text containing similar ideas. Option A has already been done as an example.**

3 **Now, find the place or places in the text which mention Jenny feeling embarrassed. Which option (A – D) does this refer to?**

WORKING OUT THE MEANING OF WORDS FROM THE CONTEXT

Try to work out what the words in bold in the following sentences mean.

Example: *With its beautiful bright cover and over a hundred magnificent reproductions of her paintings inside, Jenny Granger's book is very **eye-catching**.*

The cover is described as *beautiful* and *bright*, and the reproductions inside the book are described as *magnificent*. So, *eye-catching* is likely to be related in meaning – something like *it has an attractive appearance*.

1 Jenny says some artists she knows are always **moaning** about how difficult their lives are, but they forget that things were a lot tougher for most artists in the past.

2 Jenny is very protective of her privacy. She rarely gives interviews and **shuns** publicity as much as possible.

3 After a successful 20-year career in rock music, mixing with all sorts of famous people, Jenny must have some fascinating stories to tell. She is reluctant to **dwell on** the past, however, preferring to talk about her plans for the future.

4 Jenny was initially invited to exhibit her paintings alongside those of another artist whose work she didn't like, but she refused **point-blank**. People who know her well say it's typical of her to say exactly what she thinks.

5 Jenny had no musical training and she wasn't known for her vocal **prowess**, but she sang with great feeling, which largely made up for it.

> **TIP** Texts are likely to contain some words that you don't know. However, in most cases, you should be able to use the context to work out what these words mean.

IDENTIFYING OPINION EXPRESSED IN THE TEXT

1 Read another extract from the article about Jenny Granger. As you read, try to work out what the words in the box mean.

> do justice to   in awe of   conjure up   envisage   with hindsight

> **TIP** Questions in Part 5 often test your understanding of opinions expressed in the text. You may need to decide whether the text is giving factual information, or whether an opinion is being expressed.

In her early twenties, Jenny went to art school, but dropped out before completing her degree. 'I was spending all my time playing music, and I wasn't **doing justice to** the art course,' she says. 'But I hung out with a group of young artists. I remember being very impressed with them. In fact, I was really **in awe of** how clever and cool some of them were.' Jenny also recalls that they were dedicated to self-improvement. '<u>They seemed to have been born with perfect technique</u> – they could **conjure up** a brilliant painting or sculpture out of nothing almost overnight. <u>But they were very disciplined too – they worked at getting better</u>.' So did Jenny **envisage** successful artistic careers for any of her friends? 'I didn't think about it at the time,' she says. 'But **with hindsight**, 20 years later, I can see that <u>their ideas actually weren't very radical or new. They did pretty much what they were told to do</u>. That hasn't stopped a few of them doing very well for themselves, though. In fact, <u>a couple of them are now world-famous artists and their paintings sell for millions of pounds</u>.'

> **TIP** In answering opinion questions, you should ask yourself questions about each option such as: *Is the opinion expressed in the option the same as an opinion in the text? Is it the writer's opinion or someone else's opinion? Is the opinion what the writer thought in the past or what the writer thinks now?*

2 Read the following question about the text above, and match the options (A – D) with the underlined sections of text containing similar or connected ideas.

Looking back at the artists she knew in her early twenties, Jenny's view now is that

   A they didn't have much natural talent.

   B they focused too much on making money.

   C they were rather conventional in their thinking.

   D they didn't spend enough time developing their skills.

3 The question in Exercise 2 asks what *Jenny's view now is* about the artists she knew in her twenties. Look at the text again, and for each option (A – D) answer the following questions:

   • Do we know what Jenny's view in the past was?

   • Do we know what Jenny's view now is?

   • Has Jenny's view changed over time?

4 Which option (A – D) reflects what Jenny's view now is?

ACTION PLAN

1 Read the instructions at the top of the page, the title of the text and the sub-heading (if there is one). These will tell you what the subject of the text is.

2 Read the text quickly to gain a general understanding of what the text is about. Don't worry about words and phrases you don't understand on first reading.

3 Read each question quickly, highlight the key words and find out which part of the text each question relates to.

4 Read each question carefully and look in the relevant section of text for a suitable way to answer the question.

5 Read the question and its options together with the related section of text, and identify the correct answer. Rule out options that you think are wrong.

6 Don't leave any questions without an answer. If you're not sure what the answer is, guess as best you can.

Follow the exam instructions, using the advice to help you.

You are going to read an article about a man called Gerry Wilson who developed a video game called *Way Beyond*. For questions **31 – 36**, choose the answer (**A**, **B**, **C** or **D**) which you think fits best according to the text.

Mark your answers **on the separate answer sheet**.

Way Beyond – what went wrong and how to put it right

Kaya Reed meets Gerry Wilson, the creator of the notorious video game Way Beyond

It is hard to blame Gerry Wilson for being hesitant about talking to the press. It's partly what led to the difficulties he faced after the launch two years ago of the first version of his controversial space exploration video game *Way Beyond*. As the public face of the development studio which created *Way Beyond*, he had talked up the game and its enormous ambitions in interviews before its release. As a result, he was the target of much of the anger when features promised during development were not present when the game came out. One online commentator drew up a list of everything Wilson had said in interviews about *Way Beyond*, cross-referenced with what was actually in the game. The results were not flattering, and the subsequent criticisms on the internet left Wilson and his colleagues stunned and concerned.

The stance that newspapers and magazines took was interesting. Most reviewers noted that the game felt a little empty, but they also praised its lonely mood, its weirdly beautiful aesthetic qualities, and the astounding technical feat of generating an entire universe of planets, each with its own ecosystem. But unintentionally, they gave the critics ammunition. After a couple of weeks, many disappointed players simply moved on to other more conventional games, while a significant number of others voiced their anger on social media and across various gamers' forums.

TIP Questions follow the order of the text, and many questions contain obvious clues about the part of the text that they relate to – e.g. 'in the third paragraph', 'in line 57'.

TIP There may be words and phrases in the text that you don't know, but usually it's possible to work out what they mean from the surrounding text.

Gerry Wilson is reluctant to relive the particulars of what happened in the weeks and months following *Way Beyond*'s release, but it involved a lot of online criticism of people who'd worked on the game. 'A lot of it was very personal,' he says. 'We'd obviously messed up the launch and people were entitled to point out where we went wrong. But the way they did it was so unfair and over the top. We really felt that all of our hard work hadn't been recognised, and some of the criticism was unreasonable.'

But Wilson and his team didn't give up. Instead, they decided to keep working on *Way Beyond*, and concentrate on what the people who were actually playing it wanted, rather than the people who were angry about it. 'We did something that I've always done, when I look back at my life,' says Wilson. 'When I dealt with problems when I was kid, moving between lots of schools, or when I've had nasty bosses later in life, I basically just got my head down and worked. I just focused on making games, doing cool creative things. The rest of the team wanted to do that too.'

The latest version of *Way Beyond* has just been released. It's still recognisable as the lonely, abstractly beautiful space-exploration game from two years ago. But three big updates have added a lot more – and one is particularly crucial. It is now definitely a better game, with much *line 41* more to do and a clearer structure. You could always fly around the universe, explore planets, craft equipment to make survival easier, trade with aliens, and answer the call of a mysterious galactic intelligence. Now you can also construct bases, drive around in vehicles and – and this is the key one – invite other players to explore with you, in groups of four. You can crew a freighter together, or colonise a planet with ever-expanding constructions.

Wilson is happy with *Way Beyond* as it is now. 'We've kept the feeling we always wanted to have of landing on a planet that no one's ever been to before – the sense of loneliness, but also the calmness,' says Wilson. He's also pleased with the public reaction to it: 'We listened to the people who stuck with the game from the start and tried to respond to their requests and suggestions, and what they're saying now is incredibly gratifying.' Despite the controversy, and contrary to what one might assume, *Way Beyond* has sold extremely well right from the very start. 'I'm really proud of what we've achieved,' says Wilson. 'Basically, six of us managed to produce a supercool, innovative game that's unlike anything else. That's less than a tenth of the number of people who usually work on something of this scale.'

TIP The options are unlikely to contain key words that are in the text. If you do find a key word from the text in one of the options, don't assume that option is the answer.

TIP Options often express ideas that might be true in the real world. However, an option can only be a correct answer if it expresses the same meaning as something that is stated in the text.

31 What does the writer say about Gerry Wilson in the first paragraph?

   A He created false expectations about *Way Beyond*.

   B His comments on *Way Beyond* were misrepresented.

   C He put too much faith in his ability to promote *Way Beyond*.

   D His understanding of what gamers wanted from *Way Beyond* was flawed.

32 How did the press respond to the first version of *Way Beyond*?

   A It exaggerated the game's weaknesses.

   B It encouraged comparison with other games.

   C It questioned the ability of the game's designers.

   D It drew attention to the game's unusual atmosphere.

33 How does Wilson feel looking back on the period after the first release of *Way Beyond*?

   A surprised at how much events affected him

   B bitter about the lack of protection offered to him

   C resentful about the nature of the criticism he received

   D unsure about what motivated the behaviour of some people

34 What is the writer's main purpose in the fourth paragraph?

   A to highlight the pressures involved in games development

   B to give an insight into people who work in the games industry

   C to provide some information about Wilson's background

   D to explain how Wilson handled a difficult situation

35 The words 'one that is particularly crucial' in line 41 refer to being able to

   A play the game with other people.

   B move through space more freely.

   C create more significant settlements.

   D use a greater number of resources.

36 What does the writer think may surprise some people about *Way Beyond*?

   A how small its development team was

   B how much commercial success it's had

   C how influential gamers' feedback has been for it

   D how closely it matches the developers' original concept for it

FOLLOW-UP

How could you help yourself to get better at doing this part of the test?

TASK INFORMATION

- In Part 6, you read four short texts on the same subject.
- There are four questions about the texts. To answer the questions, you need to read across all the texts.
- The questions will require you to find opinions in the texts and decide whether the opinions are similar or different.
- The texts are extracts from longer texts and are written by four different people. They are usually written in an academic style, but you do not need specialist knowledge to understand them.

SUMMARISING OPINIONS IN THE TEXTS

1   Read the texts and write brief notes below to summarise what each expert says regarding question 1 below. The relevant parts of the texts are underlined with the number 1 in the margin next to them, and expert D's view has already been summarised.

Which expert

1   shares expert D's view regarding whether public libraries should continue to collect books and other printed materials?

D   *Libraries should stop collecting printed products.*

> **TIP** Summarising experts' opinions is a way of making sure you have fully understood what they think. It can also help you decide which views are similar and which are different.

2   Now answer the question: Who shares expert D's view?

LOOKING FOR PARAPHRASES TO IDENTIFY OPINIONS IN THE TEXTS

1   Which of the phrases below might the experts use to express their views about *public libraries bringing people together*?

- They're places where people can meet.
- You can make useful contacts there.
- You can concentrate there because they're quiet.
- They connect communities.
- Anyone can go to a public library – they're not exclusive places.

> **TIP** The words in the questions are not usually the same as the words in the texts. Look for paraphrases of key words in the questions.

2   Underline the parts of each text relating to question 2 below. The opinion in Text A has already been underlined. Which text (A – D) is the answer to question 2 below?

Which expert

2   takes a different view from the others regarding the importance of public libraries for bringing people together?

READING THE TEXT CAREFULLY

1   Read what expert B says about question 3 (lines 3 to 5 in Text B). Which phrase means *very expensive to run*? Which phrase means *important for companies?*

> **TIP** Sometimes experts begin by referring to the opinions of other people and then they give their own, very different opinion. Read carefully to make sure you know exactly what that expert thinks.

Which expert

3   shares B's view regarding the extent to which public libraries are good for a country's economy?

2   Does B think public libraries are good or bad for the economy? What does B say other people think?

3   Look at Texts A, C and D and find phrases in them which mean:

- libraries help the economy to grow
- it's not clear if libraries make economic sense
- libraries are too expensive to run

4   Which text, A – D, is the answer to question 3?

Do we need public libraries today?

A

A recent study found that 75% of public libraries in the USA assist library users with job applications, while 48% of them provide entrepreneurs and small business owners with considerable assistance. In other words, libraries contribute significantly to local wealth creation. Their contribution is not just financial, however. As places where people meet up, seek information and advice, and borrow and read books, magazines and other reading materials, 2 they connect the communities in which they are located in a way that benefits everyone. The digital revolution has, of course, had an enormous impact. Alongside a massive increase in the volume of information available digitally, more books are being printed than ever before. Public libraries have to find efficient ways of building up their stocks 1 of print-based books as well as their digital resources. Libraries need more government support than they currently receive to deal with this challenge.

B

Public libraries are a vital feature of the towns and cities where we live. As we spend more and more time alone with our electronic devices, libraries are a reminder that life is not just about ourselves, but about other people too. It is sometimes argued that public libraries are a drain on public finances. However, by providing support, including free internet access, to jobseekers, and training in essential work skills, libraries play a key role in ensuring that employers have the staff they need, and so provide a vital service to the business sector. Public libraries are also crucial as sources of objective information; they offer as wide a range of information on important issues as possible. This is very different from the internet where, because of commercial pressures, the information we receive tends to be highly selective. Having said that, is it sensible for public libraries to go on purchasing books, journals, magazines and 1 newspapers in their traditional printed formats rather than digitally? Because of costs, storage and the preferences of younger generations, I don't see how it can be.

C

Whether it's a child looking for a fun story, an immigrant in need of language-learning materials, a student wanting a place to study, or a pensioner seeking company, we can all go to one place: the local library. Also, many libraries play a useful role in supporting people who are looking for employment, although whether this is a cost-effective service is open to question. What we can say with confidence is that public libraries are vital in giving the general public free access to information that can be trusted. We are in the midst of a technological revolution, of course, and many people nowadays do most of their reading on electronic devices. Nevertheless, readers of all ages still prefer print-based materials, and public libraries have a duty to supply them with what they want. Therefore, public libraries will 1 need to maintain and add to their collections of books.

D

Supporters of public libraries claim that librarians are gatekeepers of the truth who use their positions to filter and organise resources so that citizens can access authentic, accurate information. The reality, however, is that the information you find in libraries is not necessarily any more credible than what you can find online. It is also inevitable that, in the long term, print will become obsolete. Digital products are cheaper, quicker and easier to store and access, 1 so the logical thing is for libraries to stop acquiring printed products. Libraries may once have been essential to our towns and cities; places where we could not only seek information and educate ourselves, but also find company with others. But life doesn't stand still. The internet, shopping malls, gyms and cafés are where most of us go these days. Perhaps in an ideal world, every district would have a well-equipped public library. In an age when state sector spending has to be cut back drastically, however, it is a luxury we cannot afford.

ACTION PLAN

1. Read the instructions at the top of the page, the title and the sub-heading (if there is one). These will tell you what the subject is of the four texts.

2. Read the four questions and highlight the key words in each one.

3. Read the first text carefully and highlight the sections of the text that relate to each question. Write the relevant question numbers next to each of these highlighted sections.

4. Do the same for each text.

5. Compare the highlighted sections in the four texts which relate to question 37. Read the opinions carefully and decide which are similar and which are different. Then choose the answer to question 37.

6. Do the same for the other three questions.

Follow the exam instructions, using the advice to help you.

You are going to read four extracts from articles in which experts give their views on home schooling, the practice of educating children at home rather than at school. For questions **37 – 40**, choose from the experts **A – D**. The experts may be chosen more than once.

 TIP As an additional technique, you may find it useful to use four different colours to highlight the relevant sections of text for each question. For example, highlight question 37 and the sections in the four texts that relate to that question in yellow. Do the same for question 38 in green, and so on.

Home schooling

In some countries, particularly the USA, increasing numbers of parents are choosing to educate their children at home rather than send them to school. Is this a positive development?

A

Once only the wealthy could afford the resources that schools could offer, but more widespread affluence and ready access to the internet means the balance has changed and, in many ways, learning works better from a kitchen table than in an institutional setting. Massive changes in technology, communications and work practices have had a huge impact on home life, with parents and children often spending very little time together. So if a decision is taken for one parent, or both parents, to educate their children in person, this tends to lead to much healthier relationships. Parents' understanding of their children and commitment to their best interests will usually make up for whatever specific expertise they may be short of. The contention that being home-schooled engenders isolation, overlooks the array of clubs, groups and associations in which home-schooled children participate no less than any of their peers, and where they mix with a wide spectrum of people.

B

A conventional school is a microcosm of the wider society that students will become members of. Learning how to get on with other pupils and staff is invaluable preparation, and something that cannot be achieved outside school. Because schools have to deal with large numbers of pupils, however, their focus tends to be on the group rather than the individual and, as a consequence, only limited individual attention can be given to the particularly gifted or to those with special learning needs. For such pupils, education in the responsive setting of the home may well be a desirable alternative, given adequate professional support. The majority of adults are ill-equipped to provide their offspring with the in-depth cross-curricular knowledge that pupils need. I could help my daughter through the history curriculum, but I couldn't do much for her in other subjects. Also, although we love each other, I would fear for what being in each other's company constantly would do to our relationship – and I doubt we're unusual in that respect.

C

The claim that home schooling enhances the family has plausibility. If parents deliver their own children's education, with all the time and emotional investment that entails, the chances are that their close family ties will be reinforced. That said, the home is where you eat, sleep and play, and is therefore not particularly conducive to the concentration needed to absorb certain types of knowledge. Of course, education is not just about knowledge acquisition; it's also about the development of the whole person, including what it takes to live alongside and communicate effectively with individuals of all kinds. Mainstream schools tend to excel at this, whereas home schooling falls short. Once children are mature enough, most will gain more educationally from being in class with a trained professional than alone with a loved one who lacks the requisite skills.

D

High-calibre teachers will often be the first to admit that their know-how largely comes from doing their jobs rather than being instructed in how to do them, and similarly, the majority of parents who are motivated enough to tutor their own sons and daughters full time will become proficient through practice. The process is also likely to be immensely helpful in terms of bonding, and thus runs counter to what, unfortunately, is happening in much of society – the fragmentation of traditional interpersonal structures. Education at home also means children can avoid being subjected to peer pressure, bullying, rowdiness and other aggravations that school pupils have to deal with and which get in the way of education. Another common misconception is that keeping young people out of 'normal' school removes them from society. Home educators actually go to great lengths to involve their children in an impressive diversity of cultural and social contexts.

Which expert

shares A's view regarding the variety of interaction that is possible for home-schooled children? **37** ☐

expresses a different view from the other three experts regarding the likely impact of home schooling on the family unit? **38** ☐

shares B's view on how well-suited parents are to teach their children? **39** ☐

has a different view from A on whether the home is a suitable environment for academic learning? **40** ☐

FOLLOW-UP
Did you follow all the steps in the Action plan?

Advice

37 What does A think about the variety of interaction that is possible for home-schooled children? Does A think the variety of interaction is good or limited?

38 Remember that the writers may not use the actual word 'family'.

39 First, check what B says about parents teaching their own children. Does B think they are well-suited or not?

40 Does A think the home is a suitable environment for learning?

TASK INFORMATION

- Part 7 has one long text from which six paragraphs of roughly equal length have been removed. The six gaps are numbered **41 – 46**. The extracted paragraphs are in jumbled order after the text, together with a seventh paragraph which does not fit any of the gaps. These seven paragraphs are labelled **A – G**.
- You have to decide which paragraph (**A – G**) fits each of the gaps (**41 – 46**) in the base text.
- The task tests your understanding of the way the text as a whole is organised and structured, how ideas are developed within the text and the way paragraphs are connected.
- The text has a title and often some general information about the content of the text under the title.

FINDING THE LINKS BETWEEN THE PARAGRAPHS

1 Read the following two paragraphs from a text about bananas and answer questions a – c below them.

Some experts suggest the banana is in danger of extinction. A disease called *fusarium wilt*, more popularly known as Panama disease, is spreading, wiping out banana plantations that provide a staple food for hundreds of millions of people and a livelihood for hundreds of thousands more.

1	

So, which of the two theories should we believe? Can banana growers stay one step ahead of the disease, or is its further spread inevitable? And is this the first time that the banana has been under such a threat?

a Find and underline in the first paragraph:
- a word that means people who know a lot about a specific subject
- words relating to the idea that something is disappearing or being destroyed.

b Find and underline in the second paragraph:
- a word that means sets of ideas

c Read the first sentence of the second paragraph again and decide what you think the topic of the removed paragraph might be.

2 Read paragraphs A, B and C below, and underline words and phrases that could link to a paragraph coming before or after them. In paragraph A, words in the first sentence are underlined as examples.

A

In fact, that last point is relatively easy to answer. An earlier form of the disease was reported in Australia, Costa Rica and Panama in the late 19th century. It spread across Latin America, devastating production of the Gros Michel, a sweet and creamy banana that dominated the export market. But what can we learn from this?

B

What followed was mass unemployment and huge economic losses. The banana industry took several decades to recover. By the 1960s, however, the Cavendish banana, which is resistant to the fungus, had replaced the previously successful Gros Michel banana. Today the Cavendish accounts for 99% of global exports.

C

Others say such talk of disaster is exaggerated, however. They point out that bananas are as cheap and abundant as ever in our shops. The fungus causing the disease has been advancing steadily for three decades, yet global production has continued to rise. Latin America – where some 80% of exported bananas are grown – has so far managed to keep the disease away.

> **TIP** The first sentence of a paragraph often links back to an idea or particular words in the previous paragraph.

> **TIP** The links between paragraphs might be: connected ideas; related vocabulary (e.g. *cars* and *buses* in one paragraph and *vehicles* in the other); reference words, e.g. *this, she, her*; linking words and phrases, e.g. *therefore, on the other hand*.

3 Which of the three paragraphs (A – C) fits best between paragraphs 1 and 2 in Exercise 1? Look for links with the words that you underlined in paragraphs 1 and 2.

4 Put words from the box into the appropriate group below.

moreover	question	these	he	similarly	one of them	on the other hand
developments	it	differences	as a result	there	interestingly	issue	later on

Reference words	Linkers	Content words / ideas
this	however	points

5 Read another part of the article about bananas. Choose from the paragraphs D – G the one which fits each gap 2 – 4. There is one extra paragraph which you do not need to use. Use the underlined words and phrases to help you work out how the paragraphs are connected.

The new strain of the Panama disease, known as TR4, is particularly deadly. Apart from the Cavendish banana, it also affects other varieties that together make up 80% of bananas grown worldwide. While other major banana diseases can be controlled if enough pesticides are used, scientists have not yet come up with a chemical fix for TR4.

> **2**

That's how plant diseases often advance, but the particular fear in this case is that the frequent movement between continents of banana industry staff will cause TR4 to eventually reach South and Central America. 'It's only a matter of time,' says Dr Miguel Dita, a plant disease specialist in Brazil. 'Many banana companies have operations in Asia, Latin America and the Caribbean.'

> **3**

Either way, the implications are extremely serious. While bananas represent a cheap, nutritious snack or dessert in the West, more than 400 million people in Africa, Latin America and Asia rely on them as staple foods, and farming them provides employment for hundreds of thousands more. Clearly something needs to be done to combat the disease. But what?

> **4**

Another way to slow the spread of the disease could be to support and strengthen banana plants' natural resistance to disease. Certain bacteria and fungi that live inside banana plants can make them stronger, and scientists are currently investigating how they might be able to take advantage of these natural protection processes.

D One approach is to introduce measures restricting the movement of people, equipment and plant material. These have helped in some places such as Australia, as have practices including treating shoes, farm vehicles, machinery and tools with disinfectants.

E Dr Charles Staver, an agricultural scientist based in Montpellier, France, agrees: 'It could be a tourist that brings in an ornamental plant. Banana industry technicians travel around the world, so there's also a high risk of them bringing it in.'

F What researchers have discovered is it gets into the banana plant's roots and blocks the supply of water and nutrients, eventually killing it. It is thought to spread through infected plant parts and soil attached to shoes, tools, vehicles, planting materials and water.

G None of the options tried so far, however, look likely to eradicate the new destructive variety of the fungus. Research published last year, nevertheless, suggests a scientific solution is close.

ACTION PLAN

1. Read the instructions at the top of the page, the title and the sub-heading (if there is one). These will tell you what the subject of the text is.

2. Read the main text quickly to get a general idea of what it is about.

3. Read the extracted paragraphs A–G to get a sense of what each one is about.

4. Look at the words before and after the gaps in the main text. Look for links between these words and words at the start and end of each of the paragraphs A–G. Remember that one paragraph will not be used.

5. If you can't find the paragraph for one gap, move on to the other gaps.

6. Don't leave any gaps blank.

7. When you have finished, read through the completed text to make sure that the paragraphs all connect logically and naturally.

Follow the exam instructions on pages 36–37, using the advice to help you.

You are going to read a magazine article about skating on frozen lakes. Six paragraphs have been removed from the article. Choose from the paragraphs **A – G** the one which fits each gap (**41 – 46**). There is one extra paragraph which you do not need to use.

TIP Look for words that connect ideas, e.g. related vocabulary, pronouns, linking words and phrases ('however', 'for this reason', 'similarly', etc.).

Mark your answers **on the separate answer sheet**.

Wild skating in Sweden

The setting sun was reflected on the frozen lake as we skated under the watchful gaze of our guides, Björn and Jan. The profound silence was only interrupted by the noise of our skates gliding and scratching across Östjuten Lake. Even animal sightings were rare in this isolated landscape, though we passed tree trunks gnawed by beavers.

41

Over four days and 125 km of 'wild' skating in south-east Sweden, I learned that skating on natural ice is full of contradictions of this kind. I learned to be attentive, not so much to the setting – the forested shores of the lakes didn't vary much – but to noises coming from the ice, and its colour and texture. One day it was covered in a layer of water; the next it had a light dusting of snow.

42

On the first day, my group were briefed on safety precautions like this, and then skated 10 km for practice. On the subsequent days, we covered up to 40 km, in two-hour spurts, before stopping to refuel with bread, cheese and salami. As dusk fell, we returned to our two minibuses, parked by what in summer are wild swimming areas. The region has hundreds of lakes and every day we drove out from our base in search of the best ice.

43

Not that skating is an inherently unsociable activity. Our guides were very friendly, as were the other people in my group. These included Singaporean ice-hockey enthusiasts, a Spanish fan of figure skating, seasoned German and English skiers and a French roller-blader. There was also an Australian who'd only been skating on a public ice rink.

44

This is difficult to imagine nowadays. Warmer temperatures mean that rivers in Britain, France and Germany rarely freeze solidly enough for wild skating to be feasible on them, and it's only in the Scandinavian countries that it's possible to skate regularly on natural ice.

45

In Sweden, these are a legal requirement: if you fall through into the water, you drive them into the ice and haul yourself out. Fortunately, no one in my group ever had to do that. In fact, probably the trickiest part of being on the ice was bending down to clip the blades on to the boots without falling over. I must admit I needed help with this at first.

46

The trip ended with me having one more lesson on what you can do on ice. As the sun went down, our guides built and lit a fire and started roasting marshmallows. The heat from the fire rises, so it doesn't burn a hole in the ice. As I sat on the frozen lake with my muscles aching, I felt oddly cosy and relaxed; yet another intriguing contradiction in that icy setting.

A Skating has evolved in other ways as well. While skaters were once advised to carry a fireman's ladder and a rope in case of emergency, we were kitted out with a rope in a bag, a rucksack that doubled as a floatation device, and two safety 'ice nails'.

B I'd expected to come across other skaters who would tell us where to find it. However, it was only on the third day, a Saturday, when we finally saw any other skaters out on the lakes. They were weekend day-trippers and we just glided past crying 'Hej hej!'.

C All that physical exercise also gave us an appetite. Although the cost of food was included in the trip, we decided to visit a nearby supermarket to gather cuts of reindeer meat, fish fillets and other ingredients. We cooked together, and packed our daily lunches.

D That was the extent of my experience too. The idea for the trip had come when I was doing some research on the late 18th century. I'd read how the industrial revolution led to the development of steel skates, and how wild skating had been popular all over northern Europe.

E This strange peace was suddenly broken by what sounded like thunder beneath our feet. I tensed, and the skaters behind me shrieked. But, as we'd been told, a loud 'boom' isn't necessarily bad: it can tell you the ice is thick. It's the beautiful-sounding 'singing' ice that's the thin, scary stuff.

F By the fourth day, however, I had the hang of it, along with basic wild skating techniques. The skates are longer than those for figure skating or hockey, extending beyond the front and back of the foot. Also, you push sideways more, and with fewer movements, than in other skating.

G Such changes affect your speed and route. We snaked across large lakes, looking out for cracks, small ridges and water holes. Our guides stabbed their sticks into the ice, testing its depth. We stuck to ice that was between 10 cm and 15 cm thick, though 5cm would still be adequate.

Advice

41 In the first sentence after the gap, the writer says: 'I learned that skating on natural ice is full of contradictions of this kind'. The words 'contradictions of this kind' must refer back to something in the missing paragraph.

42 In the first sentence after the gap, the writer says: 'my group were briefed on safety precautions like this'. The words 'safety precautions like this' must refer back to something in the missing paragraph.

43 In the first sentence after the gap, the writer says: 'Not that skating is an inherently unsociable activity'. This suggests that the missing paragraph refers to something that might be considered unsociable.

44 In the first sentence after the gap, the writer says: 'This is difficult to imagine nowadays'. This suggests that the missing paragraph probably refers to something in the past.

45 In the first sentence after the gap, the writer says: 'In Sweden, these are a legal requirement'. What might 'these' refer back to?

46 The paragraph after gap 46 doesn't have an obvious link backwards. So, do the ideas in the paragraph before the gap – e.g. the difficulty of clipping blades onto boots – connect with an idea in any of the paragraphs A–G?

FOLLOW-UP

Which gaps were the easiest to find the answers for and which ones were the hardest?

TASK INFORMATION

- In Part 8, there are ten questions which you have to match with the relevant information in a text or texts. The questions always come before the texts.
- The texts are either one long text divided into four sections (**A – D**), or a group of (usually) four shorter texts (**A – D**) on a common topic.
- For each of the questions, you have to find the section or short text which contains the answer, and you write the letter (**A**, **B**, **C** or **D**) of this section or text next to the question. There is only one possible answer for each question.
- The questions focus on understanding specific details, opinions and attitudes and they test your ability to find the answers quickly across the texts.
- The four sections or texts will be on a common topic so some ideas will be present in more than one section or text. For each question you need to decide which section or text contains the precise answer to the question, and why the other options should be ruled out.

PARAPHRASING

1 The words and phrases (A – J) in the box paraphrase parts of the questions below. Match the paraphrases with the correct questions. Paraphrase A has been matched with question 2 as an example.

> **TIP** The words in the questions are unlikely to appear in the texts. This is why it is often helpful to think about how words in the questions can be paraphrased.

A	~~a strong sense of shame (2)~~	**F**	being persuasive and believable
B	a suggestion that isn't very helpful	**G**	think you're more important than you really are
C	an incorrect message	**H**	create targets
D	things that you don't do very well	**I**	a significant difference
E	make someone lose concentration	**J**	use certain techniques in another situation

Which writer mentions

1 the challenge of expressing ideas in a convincing way?
2 a moment of <u>acute embarrassment</u>? A *a strong sense of shame*
3 a deliberate attempt to cause distraction?
4 the pleasure that can be derived from setting short-term goals?
5 being given advice of doubtful value?
6 the need to be aware of your own limitations?
7 a difficulty caused by having to deal with inaccurate information?
8 being able to transfer skills to a very different activity?
9 the benefit of not taking yourself too seriously?
10 an important distinction?

2 Underline the key words and phrases in the questions 1 – 10 in Exercise 1.

> **TIP** When you read the questions, underline the key words. This will help you to understand and remember what you need to look for.

READING TASK

Now read the texts **A – D** opposite and answer the questions 1 – 10 from Exercise 1.

Concentration

Four people explain why they need to concentrate in their different jobs.

 TIP Start by reading Text A. Then go through the ten questions and write A next to any questions that you find the answers for. After that, go through the same process with Texts B, C and D.

 TIP Sometimes it seems possible that a question could be matched with more than one text. For example, all four writers mention difficult situations, so you might think that they could all be answers to question 2. However, only one of the four texts refers to *acute embarrassment*.

A The professional cartoonist

I sometimes get asked to give a talk about my work. To get over my nerves I usually tell myself that it will all go well, so long as I concentrate. On one occasion, I was in a theatre dressing room, preparing to give a talk to about 200 people, when I suddenly realised there was something wrong with the microphone clipped to my collar. I started to panic: 'The mic's not working and I'm going to lose track of what I'm saying.' Then I caught sight of myself in the mirror and I couldn't help but laugh because, for some reason, my reflection seemed so absurd. That put everything into perspective: in the bigger picture, my talk about being a cartoonist had very little significance – and the talk went well. When I'm drawing cartoons and have a tight deadline to meet, I often focus by playing games with myself. For example, I might give myself a target of doing two cartoon pictures every 40 minutes. It makes the whole process more enjoyable. If I don't win the challenge, I can always try it again another time.

B The actor

When I'm preparing for a play, I fix a time by which I must know my lines off by heart. I won't get it done otherwise. When I was starting out as an actor, someone suggested I put scripts under my pillow at night – I would supposedly learn the lines in my sleep. I'm sure that's just a myth. What I do find effective, though, is to learn lines as soon as I get up in the morning. The process of learning lines for a play is significantly different from learning them for a film. With films, you learn intensively for just one day's work, whereas in theatre, you need the lines for an extended period, and you can't make things up. I remember one occasion when I was on stage in a major production. I was in the middle of a speech that I'd done many times before when my mind suddenly went blank, and there was this agonising silence which seemed to go on forever. Then I said out loud: 'What now?' And my memory instantly returned and I carried on with the scene. It was both weird and stressful.

C The taxi driver

Believe it or not, passengers often get into my cab without knowing the address or even the name of their destination. Getting them to the right place requires huge concentration. Cab drivers in London have to take a tough exam called the Knowledge, which requires you to know where thousands of different streets and locations are, and routes between them. There are countless individual oral tests in which you have to prove your detailed knowledge of the city. The examiners try to put you off. One examiner, for example, started shouting at me when I was trying to answer a question. The justification is that cabbies need to be able to concentrate in highly stressful situations. We use various techniques to remember details. For example, in one central district of London, there are four streets called Walpole Street, Anderson Street, Sloane Avenue and Pelham Street, and to remember the order they come in I think of them as WASP, the first letters of their names. I find mental devices like that very effective and I've actually used them to learn words and phrases in foreign languages when travelling abroad.

D The lawyer

Concentration underpins a wide range of things that I have to do in my job. Whether I'm speaking to a client, making an appeal to a judge, writing a legal document for someone or giving support to junior colleagues, I have to focus on engaging their interest and on getting them to believe that the point I am trying to convey is significant and correct. The complexity of the content means that it's often demanding work, and it's important to be able to recognise when it's time to get away from it for a while. Just carrying on eventually becomes counterproductive for concentration. From time to time, I find myself working on a problem in a way that simply isn't working, even though I'm directing my full attention to it. Like many people, I don't like admitting defeat. However, I've learned from experience that rather than muddling through, it's sometimes better to abandon what I've been doing and to adopt a completely different approach.

ACTION PLAN

1 Read the instructions at the top of the page, the title and the sub-heading (if there is one). These will tell you what the subject of the text is.

2 Read the whole text quickly to gain a general understanding of what the text is about. Don't worry about words and phrases you don't understand on first reading.

3 Read each question, highlighting the key words.

4 Read section A carefully. Underline the parts of the text which contain answers to the questions. Note the number of each question next to the part of text it relates to and write the letter A in the box for that question.

5 Then do the same for the other texts – B, C and D.

6 Remember to check your answers. Check the questions against the text(s).

Follow the exam instructions, using the advice to help you.

You are going to read an article about a transport revolution led by a man called Jaime Lerner in the Brazilian city of Curitiba. For questions **47 – 56**, choose from the sections (**A – D**). The sections may be chosen more than once.

Mark your answers **on the separate answer sheet**.

TIP

The questions usually don't contain exactly the same words as the texts where the answers can be found. Most questions use paraphrasing.

In which section is the following mentioned?

how Curitiba's bus system became a victim of its own success — **47**

initiatives taken that were unrelated to transport — **48**

the importance of Curitiba's bus system for the city's identity — **49**

Lerner's skills as a negotiator — **50**

why the Curitiba transport model works better in some places than others — **51**

the innovations which made Curitiba's bus system a world leader — **52**

an aspect of transport in Curitiba that is surprisingly underdeveloped — **53**

the expectations that certain people had of Lerner as mayor — **54**

how Curitiba inspired changes elsewhere — **55**

why Lerner decided to develop Curitiba's bus system rather than other forms of transport — **56**

Advice

47 Think about the meaning of 'a victim of its own success'.

48 The 'initiatives' here refer to developments in the city. What could have been developed in a city like Curitiba that has nothing to do with transport?

49 A city's identity is to do with the way residents think about the city and the way people outside think of it.

50 Lerner was the mayor of Curitiba. Scan the texts quickly for references to his name.

51 Look for sections where the writer mentions the Curitiba transport model being used in different cities and countries.

52 Look for another way of expressing the idea of 'a world leader'.

53 Look for words in the texts which express the idea of something being surprising.

54 Scan the texts for references to Lerner. Look for words that express the idea of what people might expect from him.

55 Look for mentions of other places.

56 Look for references to other forms of transport.

A transport revolution in Curitiba, Brazil

A

For the first few hundred years of its existence, Curitiba, the capital of the state of Paraná in southern Brazil, was a sleepy, smallish town. But by the 1960s, its population had grown to about 360,000, and the city was facing overcrowding, serious traffic congestion and other problems that afflict many fast-growing cities around the world. In line with the orthodox thinking of the time, the authorities began to draw up plans to widen avenues, demolish historic buildings and adapt the city centre so that cars could become the primary mode of transport. In 1971, they appointed a young architect called Jaime Lerner as city mayor, confident that he would implement the planned changes. Lerner almost immediately shook things up, however. Instead of widening avenues, he created a pedestrian mall in the city centre. And rather than building more roads, he created parks and gardens, and protected the city's rivers from being turned into concrete drainage canals. His most memorable contribution, however, came in his ideas for the city's bus network.

B

Besides calling for wider streets for cars, planners advocated the building of subway train lines. The problem with this was that construction would be costly and lengthy. Lerner instead decided to integrate dedicated bus lanes along the city's main arteries, allowing buses to run at speeds comparable to those of light rail. A determined and clever deal-maker, Lerner persuaded private bus operators to provide the vehicles while he would pay for the new infrastructure. With this trade-off, the first rapid bus lanes cost 50 times less than rail lines. Improvements were then made over time and by the 1990s, the buses were carrying 1.5 million passengers a day. In fact, high ridership created problems, with long queues waiting to board buses and pay fares. Lerner, by now in his third term as mayor, came up with an elegant solution. He called for longer buses, faster boarding through multiple doors, fares paid for before entering the bus and a single fare covering the entire network. Lerner also gave the bus stops, or 'stations', a distinctive look by placing them in futuristic glass tubes. With these additions, the city gained the first bus rapid transit (BRT) network on the planet.

C

Curitiba's bus rapid transit now began to attract attention from other cities in Latin America. Bogotá, the capital of Colombia, a much bigger city with a population of 8 million people, had crippling traffic problems. Seeing how well the Curitiba BRT seemed to be working, the authorities in Bogotá borrowed and added to many of Lerner's concepts to build a viable larger BRT network of their own called the Transmilenio. The 'stations', which feature many of the key functional elements that Lerner first developed, contributed to its success. From there, BRT's influence continued to grow, spreading as far as the United States, South Africa and China. However, it's in Latin America where BRT systems have particularly taken off. 'There's no doubt that's where BRT systems carry the most people of any region in the world,' says one planning expert. 'It's probably down to the similar language and cultural context.'

D

But as the BRT concept spread internationally, it faced problems back in Curitiba. Although ridership remained high, it was declining, while car usage climbed. There were complaints of overcrowding on buses and the tubular bus stops failing to protect passengers from extreme temperatures and heavy rain. Curitiba now has 1.8 million people and mobility remains an issue. Plans have now been made for the creation of a subway system, a form of transport Lerner did his best to avoid as mayor. Another potential solution being considered is the bicycle. Contrary to what one might assume of a city known for sustainability, Curitiba has only recently begun to take cycling seriously. There are plans to develop cycle lanes and to integrate them with the bus system, though this is still in the early stages. Despite these issues, however, BRT has become a cultural touchstone, Curitiba's answer to the freewheeling carnival spirit of Rio and the fast-paced, business-dominated lifestyle in São Paulo. As if to remove any doubt about its symbolic status for the city, the airport gift shop is built in the shape of a life-size BRT station.

FOLLOW-UP

Which do you think it's best to read first, the questions or the texts?

TASK INFORMATION

- The Part 1 task is compulsory. It is always an essay. You have to write between 220 and 260 words.
- The question gives you different information to read: a statement about the topic; three bullet points related to the topic; and three quoted opinions, each referring to one of the bullet points.
- You must write about two of the bullet points in the question. You may use the opinions given, or your own ideas.
- You must explain which of your two bullet points you feel is most important / effective / useful, etc. (depending on the question) and you must give reasons for your choice. Use your own words as far as possible.

MEETING THE TASK REQUIREMENTS

1 Assessment of your writing covers several areas and you need to consider all of these to achieve a high score. Look at this quote from an examiner and complete the gaps.

control	common	content	effect	range	organisation	complex

When we are marking writing, one of the first things we look at is the **(1)** .... of the text. Does it include all the points needed for the reader to be fully informed? We also look at how these points are covered, thinking about what **(2)** .... the writing will have on the reader, whether the ideas are easy to follow, whether the style and text type are appropriate. All this is assessed under Communicative Achievement. We look at the **(3)** .... of the text to see how effectively the ideas are connected, for example by use of paragraphs and linking words. And of course, we look at the language used. Has the writer used a **(4)** .... of vocabulary and grammatical structures, including words and expressions which are less **(5)** .... and structures which are more **(6)** ....? And has this language been used with **(7)** .... , or are there a lot of language errors?

2 **Look at the sample task below and answer these questions to help you plan your answer.**

1 What is the topic of your essay?
2 How many of the bullet points do you have to write about?
3 What other idea do you need to include in your answer?

 TIP You can use a system like this to structure your essay:

- Answer question 1 in your introduction.
- Discuss each bullet point in a separate paragraph.
- Use the concluding paragraph to explain your decision regarding these bullet points.

Your class has been watching a television debate about measures that could improve people's health and well-being in modern society. You have made the notes below:

> **Measures to improve health and well-being**
> - advertising
> - education
> - laws

> Some opinions expressed in the discussion:
>
> "Advertising is everywhere, so it should be used wisely."
>
> "People don't always know how to have a healthy mind and body."
>
> "Governments should find ways to force everyone to take care of themselves."

Write an essay discussing **two** of the measures in your notes. You should **explain which measure you think is most effective, giving reasons** in support of your answer.

3 Remember to support your choices with reasons and examples. Write your ideas for the exam task in the table below. The first section has been completed with the correct quote.

	Which quote relates to this point?	Do you agree with the opinion?	Your own ideas
Advertising	"Advertising is everywhere, so it should be used wisely."		
Education			
Laws			

TIP Practise doing this for other topics. Brainstorm opinions and examples / reasons to justify them.

TIP You need to give a detailed response to the topic. If you find it difficult to come up with ideas for one of the bullet points, it's best not to write about it – choose the other two instead.

USEFUL LANGUAGE: EXPRESSING REASONS

1 Look at the following ideas related to the essay question in Exercise 2 and underline the reason given in each one. The first one has been done for you.

1 I say taxes need to be increased. It will never be popular, but would it be effective? Certainly. <u>It is the only way to reverse the effects of our modern lifestyle</u>.

2 We're all responsible for our own lives. No one else. That's why I say it's up to us to take control.

3 Given that we spend more time alone than with other people, individual choice has to be the key factor.

4 Obviously, these days, when most people spend all day sitting at a computer, the media – including social media – are likely to have the biggest impact on people's choices.

5 A further argument for not forcing people to do exercise by law is that people have enough rules in their work life: they don't want them in their free time as well.

TIP Notice that reasons can be given before or after the ideas expressed. It's a good idea to vary the word order as a way of expressing your ideas in more complex ways.

2 Each of the sentences below expresses a reason. Identify and correct the error in each sentence.

1 the popularity of the media, this has to be one of the best ways of influencing people's behaviour.

2 The negative effect of modern lifestyles on our well-being is largely due for the popularity of technology.

3 People spend less and less time looking after themselves because of they are overwhelmed by the pressures of their daily lives.

4 So tempting advertisements for unhealthy food and drink are everywhere, we buy things we shouldn't without even realising.

5 Should we look after our own health and well-being? Of course we should, as for we are the ones who benefit from doing this.

6 Since that exercise is a key factor in keeping fit and healthy, the government should provide free, or at least subsidised, sports facilities in all towns and cities.

3 Use the guidance above and your notes to write an answer to the sample question in Exercise 2. Remember to discuss two of the bullet points, select one as the most effective and give reasons for your choice.

ACTION PLAN

1 Read the whole question carefully. Highlight all the significant points you must include in your answer.

2 Allow enough time to plan your answer.

3 Choose two of the three listed points to write about.

4 Think about how you can expand each of these two points. The opinions from the discussion may help to give you ideas, but you don't have to use them. You may prefer to use your own ideas.

5 Think about how you are going to compare these two points, and which you will say is more important and why.

6 Remember that you are writing an essay, so your style of writing should be neutral or formal.

7 Organise your essay into clear paragraphs.

8 Write 220–260 words. If you write less, you probably will not deal with all the aspects of the question or show an adequate range of language.

9 If you want to make a correction, do so as neatly as possible.

10 Leave yourself some time to check your essay.

1 **Answer these questions about the task on page 45.**

   1 What are the main content points the examiners will look for?

   2 What kind of text do you have to write?

   3 What are the conventions of this text type which you should follow in your answer?

   4 What register will you need to use?

   5 How many paragraphs might you use? What would the topic of each paragraph be?

   6 What effect will you aim to have on the target reader?

2 **How could you express these phrases from the input text in other words? Remember to use a register which is appropriate for your essay.**

   1 spend money on

   2 is really important

   3 having good food

3 **What examples could you give to illustrate why governments should spend money on research in each of these areas?**

   1 space exploration

   2 green energy

   3 human eating habits

4 **Which two of these areas do you think it will be easiest for you to deal with in your answer? Which can you write about most effectively?**

5 **Now write your essay.**

Follow the exam instructions, using the advice to help you.

You **must** answer this question. Write your answer in **220 – 260** words in an appropriate style on the separate answer sheet.

1   Your class has watched a television discussion on the areas of research that governments should spend money on. You made the notes below:

> ### Areas of research that governments should spend money on
>
> - space exploration
> - green energy
> - human eating habits

> Some opinions expressed in the discussion:
>
> "Space research is really important for the future."
>
> "Only governments have enough money for energy research."
>
> "People's health depends on having good food."

Write an essay discussing **two** of the areas of research in your notes. You should **explain which area of research is more important** for governments to spend money on, **giving reasons** to support your answer.

You may, if you wish, make use of the opinions expressed in the discussion, but you should use your own words as far as possible.

FOLLOW-UP

Did you read the question carefully? Did you discuss <u>two</u> areas of research that governments should spend money on? Did you make it clear <u>which</u> <u>area you think is more important</u>?

Advice

Look at the exam question. Think about the topic as it is presented in the question, the notes and the opinions. Which of the three areas would you find hardest to write about? Don't attempt it – focus your plans on the other two instead.

Can you think of specific examples that would illustrate the importance of governments spending money on the two areas you have chosen?

You may find it hard to decide which area of research you think is more important for governments to spend money on. However, remember that the most important thing is to write well. Choose either one and make a strong argument to support your choice.

You should aim to spend about 45 minutes on your answer, including time for planning and checking.

 TIP It is a good idea to write your answer on alternate lines on the answer page, so that you can make corrections more easily.

 TIP Make it easy for the examiner to see where one paragraph ends and the next begins. You can either indent or leave an extra line between the paragraphs.

TASK INFORMATION

- There are three tasks in this section. You have to choose one of them.
- The tasks will be a letter or email, a review, a report or a proposal.
- You have to write between 220 and 260 words.
- The questions give you three key pieces of information: what to write, why you are writing and who you are writing for.

IDENTIFYING THE READER

1 **All tasks on the Writing paper specify who you are writing for, known as the target reader. Look at the extracts from sample tasks and identify the target reader.**

1 You have received an email from an English-speaking friend.

> …
> Everyone's telling me that going to university is the best thing to do. Some are even saying it's the only option, but I'm not so sure. What are your thoughts? Could there be any disadvantages to going to university and what are my alternatives? What should I do?

 TIP Always check who you are writing for. This information affects choices you make about register, format, vocabulary and grammatical structures in your writing. Will your writing get the response that you need?

2 An international wildlife organisation is holding a photography competition for a new calendar. The advertising manager, Mrs Johnson, has posted a message on their website, asking people to submit a nature photo they think should be included on the calendar. Write a letter to accompany your choice of photo.

Your letter should give a brief description of the photo, including details of when and where it was taken. You should also say why you think it should be chosen.

3 The council where you live has received funding to provide new facilities in the town. You decide to write a proposal to the head of the council recommending two facilities that could be provided. Your proposal should include details of who would use them and how they would benefit the town as a whole. You should also say which of the two facilities you believe would be most popular with residents.

4 The editor of an entertainment magazine has asked readers to write reviews of TV series. You decide to write a review in which you compare two TV series you have watched, one you enjoyed and one you didn't. In your review, briefly describe the two series, explain why one was better than the other and suggest ways in which the other one could be improved.

5 There have been a number of complaints from students about the catering facilities at the college where you study. You have decided to write to the college principal outlining the problems. Your letter should give details of your personal experience of using the facilities and to what extent they meet the needs of the students. You should explain what improvements need to be made and how these can be implemented.

2 Knowing who you are writing for helps you choose a suitable register for your text – formal, neutral or informal. Look back at the sample tasks in Exercise 1. What register would be suitable for each?

3 Look at these extracts from answers to the tasks in Exercise 1. Match them with the tasks and decide if the register is appropriate. If any are not appropriate, suggest ways to improve them.

   a It was so awful, I gave up watching it after the second episode. You're crazy if you like that sort of stuff!

   b I would say this is one of the best pictures I've ever taken. It really does capture the sense of light and space you get when you are out on the water, far from the noise of other people. I hope you agree.

   c The lack of tables and chairs in the canteen is problematic at lunchtimes. It is simply not possible for everyone to sit down and eat together, so I would recommend giving this issue your urgent attention.

   d The recommended course of action is to draw up a list of arguments in favour of and against going to university before you commit to anything.

   e Where can young people spend time together? Nowhere! A new park with shelter, please!

USEFUL LANGUAGE: USING A GREATER RANGE OF VOCABULARY

You should aim to use your own words as far as possible, rather than 'lifting' the words used in the question. Look at words 1–6, which are commonly used in Part 2 questions, and complete the table with alternative words and expressions from the box.

appreciate	be unsure	complaint	concern	dilemma
downside	drawback	enhance		get pleasure from
go for	have doubts	issue	opt for	select	upgrade

1 be not so sure	
2 disadvantage	
3 choose	
4 improve	
5 enjoy	
6 problem	

TIP Including complex ideas in your writing engages the reader's interest in the text, which can help improve your mark for communicative achievement.

USEFUL LANGUAGE: COMMUNICATING IDEAS USING COMPLEX LANGUAGE

In the following sentences, the ideas are expressed clearly but in quite simple ways. Use the given word to communicate similar ideas using more complex expressions and structures. Several answers may be possible. The first one has been done for you.

1 It's difficult to get around town at night because there aren't enough lights on the streets.

LACK

The lack of street lighting makes it difficult to get around town at night.

2 No one can get anywhere on Sundays. There's no bus service.

INTRODUCING

3 The swimming pool had not been regularly maintained, so it closed down.

MAINTENANCE

4 The cycle paths are in good condition in some areas and bad in others.

VARIES

5 I feel that offering more sports facilities and more frequent bus services are both good ideas.

EQUAL

6 The council needs to do better at keeping the parks clean.

IMPLEMENT

7 The council closed one of the car parks last year. Now people have to drive around for ages looking for somewhere to park.

HADN'T

> **TIP** Remember that the language assessment considers range <u>and</u> control. To get higher marks for language, you need to demonstrate that you can use a range of vocabulary and grammatical structures with few errors.

USEFUL LANGUAGE: WRITING WITH CONTROL

⊙ Look at the sentences from answers to Part 2 tasks, each of which contains a common error. Identify the error and correct it. The first one has been done for you.

1 Regarding the facilities that need the most urgent attention, I'd opt for the seating and the lighting. First is old and uncomfortable and second is not bright enough.

Regarding the facilities that need the most urgent attention, I'd opt for the seating and the lighting. <u>The</u> first is old and uncomfortable and <u>the</u> second is not bright enough.

2 I suggest recruiting more well-known performers to attract the people's attention.

3 I'm glad you've asked my advice. Unfortunately, is not an easy decision to make.

4 As soon as I arrived for university, I knew I had made the right choice.

5 I am confident this picture would attract lot of attention.

6 Although I know a lot of people enjoy this programme, I will not say it appeals to a wide audience.

7 I trust the same situation won't occur it again.

8 Another issue is that the canteen opening hours is very limited, only until 3 p.m. What about students who are studying later in the day?

ACTION PLAN

1 Read all three tasks and choose the **one** that you think you can write the best answer to.

2 Look at the question very carefully, underlining the key points.

3 Think about **what kind of text** you have to write (email, letter, report, proposal or review) and follow the English conventions for that type of text.

4 Think about **who** you are writing for (e.g. a principal, a manager, a friend). This will help you decide if your language should be formal, informal or neutral.

5 Think about **why** you are writing and how this will affect your response. For example, are you writing to persuade, to inform, to complain, or something else?

6 Spend some time planning before you start writing.

7 Organise your answer in clear paragraphs. Think about what the topic of each paragraph will be.

8 Make a quick list of the types of structures and vocabulary you can use. Aim to use a wide range of these.

9 Write 220–260 words.

10 Aim to spend about 45 minutes on your answer, including planning and checking time.

Follow the exam instructions on page 50, using the advice to help you.

 TIP You can write in either British or American English, but keep to one or the other. Don't write, for example: 'Blue is my fav<u>our</u>ite col<u>or</u>.'

Write an answer to **one** of the questions **2 – 4** in this part. Write your answer in **220 – 260** words in an appropriate style.

2 You study at an international college and are involved with improving the college's website. You think it would be a good idea to add to the website with short videos of current students talking about their college experiences. You decide to write an email to all students, in which you describe your idea and encourage students to get involved. You should explain how doing this will benefit the college and the students involved.

Write your **email**.

3 You see this advertisement on an English-language website that you enjoy:

> **Are you a student?**
> **Do you use phone apps to help you with your studies?**
> **If so, send in a review of an app!**
>
> Your review should briefly describe what the app does and how it helps you.
>
> What type of students you would recommend it to?
>
> Also, don't forget to tell us how the app could be improved.
>
> The best reviews will be posted on our website.

Write your **review**.

4 You work for an international company which has had a very successful year. Now the director of the company has invited all staff to make suggestions for ways to celebrate this success. You decide to write a proposal, outlining two ideas for how to do this and explaining how the company can benefit from them. You should also say which idea you would recommend more strongly.

Write your **proposal**.

FOLLOW-UP
Did you check your work for errors?

 TIP Choose the question that you feel gives you the best opportunity to use your English effectively. This may not be the question that interests you most.

Advice

2 This is an open email to all students, so it needs to appeal to everyone. It should inform the readers and persuade them to take part.

3 Even if you choose to describe a phone app that you think is perfect, you need to make at least one suggestion for improvement. Remember that the important thing is that you write well, so it doesn't matter if the information is not strictly true. For instance, you could say that the app costs too much, even if it is actually quite reasonably priced.

4 Don't forget that you are making a proposal to the company director, so use a style which is appropriate to the workplace.

TASK INFORMATION

- Part 1 is a multiple-choice task.
- In Part 1, you will hear three short conversations. The conversations are called Extract One, Extract Two and Extract Three on your question paper and the recording.
- The conversations are about different topics and are not connected to each other in any way.
- The conversations are often between a man and a woman so that you can easily identify the speakers.
- Each conversation is about 1 minute long and you will hear each conversation twice.
- You have to answer two multiple-choice questions on each conversation.
- You have to choose the correct answer, A, B or C.
- You have to answer questions about different things, for example, a detail or the main message of the conversation, how the speaker is feeling or what their attitude to something is. You may also have to answer questions about the speakers' opinions or what they agree about.

UNDERSTANDING WHAT IS BEING TESTED

1 **Listen to the recording and answer these questions about it.**

1 **Attitude:** What is the man's attitude to the job interview?

    A He's sure he will do well.

    B He's going to do his best to get the job.

    C He's keen to find out if the job really suits him.

2 **Function:** What is the woman doing?

    A suggesting ways to prepare for the interview

    B warning the man of potential difficulties in the interview

    C giving the man information about the company

3 **Detail:** What does the man think is the best way for him to prepare for the interview now?

    A to do background research on the company before the interview

    B to think about what they might ask him at the interview

    C to act out the interview with someone

4 **Opinion:** The woman thinks the job ad provides

    A some unexpected information.

    B some unhelpful information.

    C some confusing information.

5 **Gist:** How does the woman's viewpoint change during the conversation?

    A She questions the man's motives less.

    B She doubts the man's abilities more.

    C She understands how she can help the man better.

2 **Listen again. Why are the other options incorrect?**

TIP Questions can test different things. If you think about what each question is testing, it will help you focus on the relevant part of the recording while listening.

TIP You will hear information about all three options, but only one option will answer each question correctly.

ACTION PLAN

1 You will have some time to read the questions before you hear the conversations. Use this time to think about what is being tested.

2 You may find it useful to underline the most important words in the questions.

3 Try to answer the questions when you hear the conversations for the first time.

4 Finalise your answers when you hear the conversations for the second time and answer any questions you didn't answer the first time.

5 If you're still not sure about the correct answer after you've heard the conversation twice, make a guess.

6 At the end of the whole test, you have time to transfer your answers to the answer sheet. Make sure you do this carefully.

Follow the exam instructions, using the advice to help you.
You will hear three different extracts. For questions **1 – 6**, choose the answer (**A**, **B** or **C**) which fits best according to what you hear. There are two questions for each extract.

Extract One

You hear two neighbours, Adam and Juliet, talking about living in Montreal, Canada.

1 What attracted Adam to living in Montreal?

A the change in weather from winter to summer

B the feeling of close community evident there

C the value inhabitants place on tradition

2 What do they both say about accommodation in Montreal?

A The frequency with which people move house is above average.

B Central apartments are rarely available for purchase.

C Renting is a comparatively inexpensive option.

Advice

1 *Listen to the whole conversation before you answer either of the questions about it.*

2 *The word 'both' is important in question 2 – both Adam and Juliet must say this.*

Extract Two

You hear two students, a girl called Soraya and a boy called Halim, talking about an essay they have to write on the topic of plastic.

3   What is Soraya doing?

    A   acknowledging the benefits of plastic as a material

    B   assessing the accuracy of information written about plastic

    C   clarifying reasons for a change in people's attitudes to plastic

4   What does Halim say about the documentary he saw?

    A   It failed to offer a balanced argument.

    B   It exaggerated the conclusions it drew.

    C   It omitted some significant points.

Extract Three

You hear a psychologist, Dr Jane Blake, and a journalist, Ed Regas, discussing the teenage years.

5   According to Dr Blake, what mistake do some parents make?

    A   They misinterpret their teenagers' behaviour.

    B   They want to protect their children for too long.

    C   They fail to recognise that their children's needs have changed.

6   Which aspect of adolescence particularly interests Ed Regas?

    A   the role played by gaming in teenagers' lives

    B   teenagers' abnormal sleep patterns

    C   the influence of peers on teenagers

FOLLOW-UP
Which point did you find most useful in the Action plan?

Advice

3   Question 3 focuses on function. What does each of the other Part 1 questions focus on – gist, detail, opinion, etc.? Before you listen, think carefully about what the first word in each option in question 3 means.

4   Think of other ways of expressing the opinions in the options. This may help you recognise the correct answer when you hear it.

5   Remember to read the context sentences before the questions. Here you are told that Dr Blake is a woman because her first name is given so you need to listen for what the woman says. In the conversation each person uses the other's first name at the beginning to help you establish and remember who is who.

6   Which word is most important in question 6 and why?

TASK INFORMATION

- Part 2 is a sentence completion task.
- You will hear one person talking (for example, it could be a talk, a lecture or a broadcast). Sometimes the speaker will give facts and at other times express their opinions.
- The recording will be about 3 minutes long and you will hear it twice.
- On the question paper, you will see eight sentences relating to the recording. Each sentence has a gap.
- You have to fill in the gap using a word or short phrase from the recording.
- You will hear the information in the recording in the same order as the sentences you need to complete.
- You are expected to spell the words correctly. Both British and American spellings are accepted.

MAKING SURE THE ANSWER FITS THE MEANING OF THE SENTENCE

1   Look at this question from a Listening task about a woman called Meg who grows flowers for shops. Write down five words that could complete this sentence.

Meg decided to study **(1)** .... at university.

> **TIP**
> Often you will hear several words that could go in the gap, but only one matches the meaning and context of the sentence.

2   Now look at the first part of the audioscript. Which two words could fill the gap in Exercise 1? Which word fits the meaning of the sentence? Why is the other one not correct?

> **Meg:** I knew from quite an early age that I wanted to get involved in my parents' flower growing company and make it my career. When it came to choosing a university course, though, I was torn between two courses: horticulture or business. Both would be enormously useful but I went for the former.

3   Now look at the next two questions. Listen to the recording and note down the answers.

Meg's parents praised her for her ability to **(2)** .... flowers.

03   Meg uses the word **(3)** .... to describe how she felt when she saw her flowers in shops.

4   Listen again and answer these questions.

03   1   Which word(s) could be mistaken for the answer to each question in Exercise 3?
2   Why are those words incorrect?

ACTION PLAN

1 You should read the introduction and the title so that you understand the context and the topic.

2 You will have time to read the questions before you listen. Read the questions very carefully.

3 Think about what sort of word could fill each gap. For example, is it a verb or a noun? If so, what form is it in?

4 Remember that you will hear the answers in the same order as the questions.

5 You will hear a word or phrase in the recording that is the same as a word on the question paper. This helps you know when to listen for the answer to the next question.

6 The answers must be short – often just one word, and no more than three words.

7 Don't make any grammatical changes to what you hear.

8 If you are not sure about an answer, make a logical guess.

9 At the end of the test, you will have time to transfer your answers to the answer sheet. As you do this, check your spelling and grammar and make sure that what you have written makes sense in the context.

 04

Follow the exam instructions, using the advice to help you.
You will hear a citrus fruit grower, called Ben Tyrell, giving a presentation to students. For questions **7 – 14**, complete the sentences with a word or short phrase.

CITRUS FRUIT FARMER

Ben has an organic farm, so he relies primarily on **(7)** .... to assess the health of his trees.

If the **(8)** .... of a tree are the wrong colour, the tree usually requires fertiliser.

When to give trees fertiliser is determined principally by the

(9) ....

To control fungi on the fruit, Ben uses **(10)** .... as an organic fungicide.

Ben only worries about weeds if they are growing near his

(11) .... system.

The **(12)** .... of the fruit is the last criterion to check before picking begins.

The only tool fruit pickers use is **(13)** .... , otherwise fruit may be damaged.

Ben uses the phrase '**(14)** ....' to describe what he aims to teach school children.

FOLLOW-UP

Did you remember to check that the word(s) you wrote fitted grammatically and fitted the meaning of the sentence?

Advice

7 Ben mentions 'synthetic pesticides', 'observation' and 'protection of young trees'. Which is the correct answer and why?

8 Two parts of a tree are mentioned: what are they? Which one tells Ben the tree needs fertiliser?

9 Which word is very important in this question and why?

10 Two things that can control fungi are mentioned but remember, you are listening for what Ben uses.

11 Why is it wrong to include 'setup' in your answer here?

12 Think carefully about the order in which things happen when a question includes a word like 'last'.

13 Check the spelling of this answer carefully.

14 Remember to write the term exactly as you hear it on the recording.

TASK INFORMATION

- Part 3 is a multiple-choice task.
- You will hear a conversation between two or more speakers. It may be an interview or a discussion.
- The recording is about 4 minutes long and you will hear it twice.
- You have to answer six multiple-choice questions, each of which has four options to choose from.
- Some questions will ask about the speakers' feelings, attitudes or opinions in the recording; these may be explicitly stated or implied.
- You may also have to answer questions which focus on understanding a detail or the gist of the conversation.
- The questions follow the same order as the ideas and information in the recording.

UNDERSTANDING DISTRACTION

1 **Study the multiple-choice question and look at the audioscript. Which is the correct option: A, B, C or D? Why might you be distracted by the other options?**

Why does Pedro say he prefers studying at university to studying at school?

- **A** There is more flexibility about deadlines for assignments.
- **B** There are more resources available to support his studies.
- **C** He has more choice about what he studies.
- **D** He finds working with well-known people inspiring.

> **TIP** In multiple-choice questions, there will always be something in the recording that suggests each of the distracting options, but only one option will answer the question correctly.

> **TIP** Listen carefully to everything that the speaker says about each question before choosing your answer. Be careful not to decide on an answer too soon.

Interviewer:	In our programme today, I'm talking to two students, Pedro and Clare, about studying at university. Pedro, how did you find the transition between studying at school and at university?
Pedro:	Well, I chose to study fine art at university and it covers all sorts of areas like sculpture, print-making, and so on. And on the walls of our department, there are even artworks by some famous artists who used to study there – that's awesome. But the big bonus for me at uni is that my tutor isn't too strict about when I hand things in. At school, I always hated having to give the teacher homework when I knew I needed more time to improve it. At uni I spend ages looking at all the examples of, for example, different pottery techniques or the university's online archive of works of art.

2 **Look at the next question and listen to the recording.**

Which skill does Clare say she has improved most since she started at university?

- **A** oral communication
- **B** problem solving
- **C** team working
- **D** giving presentations

3 **Listen again. Why might you be distracted by each of the other options?**

ACTION PLAN

1 You will have some time to read the questions carefully and think about possible answers.

2 You might find it useful to underline key words in the questions or statement introducing the options to help you focus on what you have to listen for.

3 When you listen to the recording for the first time try to answer as many questions as you can.

4 If you miss a question: leave it blank and concentrate on listening for the answer to the next question.

5 When you listen to the recording the second time, finalise your answers. Answer any questions you have missed.

6 Do not leave any answers blank. It is better to guess than to not answer at all.

7 At the end of the test, you will have time to transfer your answers to the answer sheet. Make sure you do this carefully.

06

Follow the exam instructions, using the advice to help you.
You will hear an interview with two trainee teachers, called Amy and John, about students using smartphones in school. For questions **15 – 20**, choose the answer (**A**, **B**, **C** or **D**) which fits best according to what you hear.

15 Amy would like schools to teach students

A to be aware of advertising on smartphones.

B about the effects of overuse of smartphones.

C how to avoid being distracted by smartphones.

D to decide for themselves when to use smartphones.

16 Amy and John both say that some parents

A aren't consistent in applying rules about using smartphones.

B buy smartphones for quite young children.

C fail to set a good example of smartphone use.

D don't know which sites their children use on their smartphones.

17 John approves of students using smartphones in class in order to

A take photos of their work.

B look up information.

C record a conversation.

D use the calculator.

Advice

15 Listen carefully to find out what Amy's opinion is, not other teachers' opinions.

16 The word 'both' is very important here. Make sure you hear both speakers give the same opinion.

17 Think carefully about the meaning of 'approves' and listen for a paraphrase of this in the recording.

18 What happened when smartphones were banned in one school?

    A The police spent less time on smartphone thefts.

    B Teachers spent more time on the content of lessons.

    C Students soon accepted the situation.

    D Most parents welcomed the decision.

19 John mentions workplaces to point out that company rules regarding smartphone use

    A vary according to the type of work done.

    B should be reviewed regularly.

    C are difficult to enforce.

    D acknowledge that phones are valuable tools.

20 What does Amy conclude about the debate on the topic of using smartphones in schools?

    A It shows parents and teachers hold very different views from each other.

    B It is being used to hide more serious matters.

    C It reflects significant changes in society.

    D It will soon seem outdated.

FOLLOW-UP
Which questions did you find easiest and why?

Advice

18 Listen to everything Amy says about this. A speaker may talk about a question over several turns.

19 In this sort of question the answer is implied. Think about what point is John making when he talks about the workplace.

20 All of these ideas are suggested in the recording, but only one is Amy's conclusion.

TASK INFORMATION

- Part 4 is a matching task.
- You will hear five short monologues, each about 30 seconds long.
- You will hear the whole series of five monologues twice.
- The monologues are all on the same theme.
- On the question paper you will see two matching tasks. You should read the question for each task carefully.
- Each question will have a different focus, for example, identifying how the speakers felt about a situation and understanding why they chose a particular course of action.
- For each task you have to match the five speakers with the correct answers from a list of eight options.
- You have to complete both tasks as you listen.
- The answers in each monologue can be in any order; for example, you might hear the answer to Task Two before the answer to Task One.

FOCUSING ON THE MESSAGE

1 **Study the exam task and read the audioscript below. Which are the two correct answers for Speaker 1?**

2 **Which of the other options might some people be distracted by? Why are these options incorrect?**

 TIP Keep in mind what the question in each task is asking. There will be one or two options that distract but are not the right answer as they don't reflect the message of the extract.

You will hear five short extracts in which people are talking about starting a new hobby.

TASK ONE

Choose from the list (**A – H**) the reason each speaker gives for starting their new hobby.

A   to meet new people

B   to get fit

C   to prevent boredom

D   to travel more

E   to keep a promise

F   to enjoy a new challenge

G   to reduce stress

H   to boost confidence

TASK TWO

Choose from the list (**A – H**) what each person found difficult about starting their new hobby.

A   having to practise so much

B   remembering instructions

C   spending so much money

D   lacking natural talent

E   using the equipment

F   neglecting family

G   having patience

H   changing old habits

Speaker 1

I'd just moved to a new town, for my job, and had started making a new circle of friends. It was one of them, a woman called Jane, who got me into playing the guitar. She was going to classes and asked me to come along. I sort of jumped into it without realising what I was letting myself in for. I was useless. I mean I'm not musical by inclination, so what I was thinking I don't know! I guess it's because I'm the sort of person that if someone says something is hard, I want to prove I can do it. When I told my mum and dad they were very amused!

ACTION PLAN

1 You will have some time to read the questions and options for both tasks before you start listening. As you read, try to think about words and phrases a speaker might use to express the ideas in a different way.

2 Don't forget that you have to answer the questions in both tasks.

3 If you are not sure of an answer the first time you hear the recording, don't worry. When you listen for the second time, you may be able to find the answer more easily because you will already have answered eliminated some options.

4 Listen to the whole of each speaker's monologue before you choose your two answers, as the information you need can come at the beginning, middle or end of the extract.

5 You will probably hear different words used to express the ideas in the options, so listen for paraphrases.

6 At the end of the test, you will have time to transfer your answers to the answer sheet. Do this very carefully.

07

Follow the exam instructions, using the advice to help you.

You will hear five short extracts in which young writers are talking about one of their books winning a competition.

TIP Before you listen, think about possible paraphrases of the options in both tasks.

TASK ONE

For questions **21 – 25**, choose from the list (**A – H**) how each person felt when they entered the competition.

TASK TWO

For questions **26 – 30**, choose from the list (**A – H**) the main consequence for each person of winning the competition.

When you listen you must complete both tasks.

A hopeful of winning the cash prize

B terrified at making a speech

C convinced they would not win

D amused by the reactions of friends

E unhappy with the competition rules

F worried about coping with failure

G impressed by the other books

H determined to learn from the experience

Speaker 1   **21**

Speaker 2   **22**

Speaker 3   **23**

Speaker 4   **24**

Speaker 5   **25**

A offers from overseas publishers

B a change in writing style

C opportunities to travel

D contact with readers

E difficulties finding inspiration

F media intrusion

G increased sales of previous work

H a boost to confidence

Speaker 1   **26**

Speaker 2   **27**

Speaker 3   **28**

Speaker 4   **29**

Speaker 5   **30**

Advice

21 and **26**   Remember that the answers to both tasks can be the same letter.

22 and **27**   Remember that the answer to Task Two may come before the answer to Task One.

23 and **28**   Think about whether Speaker 3 is mainly positive or negative in her attitude.

FOLLOW-UP

Did you try to do both tasks during your first listening or did you concentrate on Task One during the first listening? Different people do this task in different ways and there is no one correct way. You just have to find what works best for you. Which questions did you find most challenging and why?

TASK INFORMATION

- All Speaking tests are taken with a partner (or occasionally with two partners). Part 1 lasts 2 minutes.
- There are two examiners in the room. One asks the questions (the interlocutor), and the other listens to you speaking and completes the mark sheet (the assessor).
- When you sit down, the interlocutor will tell you the examiners' names and take your mark sheet.
- In Part 1, the interlocutor speaks to you individually. They will ask questions about yourself and your life.

FOCUS ON ASSESSMENT: HOW YOUR SPEAKING IS ASSESSED

1   **Complete the text about Part 1 with the words in the box. Use the abbreviations in brackets.**

> Grammatical Resource (GR)   Discourse Management (DM)   Lexical Resource (LR)
> Interactive Communication (IC)   Global Achievement (GA)   Pronunciation (P)

The range of grammatical forms and vocabulary, and how accurate and appropriate they are, are assessed as

(1) .... and **(2)** .... The assessor also listens to your **(3)** .... and the sounds, stress and intonation

of your speech. How you use linking words and expressions to organise what you say and avoid too much

hesitation is called **(4)** .... When you speak to the interlocutor and to other candidate(s) – how well you

initiate conversations and respond is assessed under **(5)** .... The interlocutor also listens to how effectively

you communicate overall and gives a **(6)** .... mark.

2   **Look at the quotes from candidates and consider how successful they were for the criteria indicated.**

LR   Tell me about a special meal you have enjoyed.

A: I remember my birthday dinner last year. I went to an Italian restaurant with my family and we had great food, especially the pasta! There was a band playing music and we all danced after the meal.

---

1   Has the candidate used a range of vocabulary?

2   Has the candidate used appropriate vocabulary?

DM   Where 'Where' near you would you recommend visiting?

A: There are not many tourist places in my area, but I like to take visitors to the forest near my house. The forest is not very big, but there are lots different trees and the atmosphere is nice.

---

5   Is the response relevant?

6   Are the ideas connected effectively?

GR   Do you watch TV regularly?

A: Not as much I am used to. I'm not so keen of it any more, because I have my laptop and I can see movies on that. I tend to watching American series in the main, especially the criminal ones.

---

3   Are a range of grammatical forms used?

4   Are the grammatical forms used with control?

IC   Which is your favourite season?

A: There are four seasons in the year in my country. It's autumn at the moment.

---

7   Is the response appropriate?

TIP   You can prepare for Part 1 by brainstorming ideas and vocabulary for common personal topics.

3   **Plan your own response to each of the questions in Exercise 2. How could you improve the candidate's responses?**

ACTION PLAN

1 Smile and be polite and friendly to the examiners.

2 Listen carefully to the questions and ask for repetition if you don't hear them clearly, e.g. *Could you repeat that please? I'm sorry, could you say that again?*

3 The questions will be addressed to you individually, so when you answer look at the interlocutor. Don't try to speak to your partner at this stage.

4 Try to relax. These questions are about you, so you will know the answers.

5 You should give more than just one- or two-word answers, but don't give detailed, long descriptions or accounts.

6 Expand your answers by giving reasons and examples to support what you say.

7 Do not try to memorise pre-prepared answers by heart before the exam. They will not sound natural or fluent.

8 When your partner is speaking, show interest by looking at him/her and nodding or smiling, but don't respond at this stage.

Work with a partner, if possible, and do the exam task, following the instructions below. Take it in turn to act in the role of the interlocutor.

Part 1
2 minutes (3 minutes for groups of three)

The interlocutor asks you some questions about yourself, your home, work or studies and familiar topics.

Good morning / afternoon / evening. My name is ... and this is my colleague ... .

And your names are?

Can I have your mark sheets, please?

Thank you.

First of all, we'd like to know something about you.

- Where are you from?
- What do you do here / there?
- How long have you been studying English?
- What do you enjoy most about studying English?

 TIP Speak loudly enough for the examiners to hear you.

The interlocutor then asks you some questions about one or two other topics, for example:

- Do you think you spend enough time with your family and friends? Why? / Why not?
- How important is sport in your weekly routine? Why?
- Which holiday have you been on recently that was interesting? Why was it interesting?
- What do you think you'll be doing this time next year?

 TIP Remember to give more than just 'yes/no' answers or very brief answers of one or two words.

FOLLOW-UP

How easy were the questions to answer? How could you improve the way you performed in future?

TASK INFORMATION

- In Part 2 you talk for about 1 minute. The interlocutor will not interrupt while you are speaking.
- You are given three photographs, which are all related to the same theme. The interlocutor will tell you what the theme is and you then choose any **two** of the photographs to talk about.
- The interlocutor will ask you to talk about two questions related to the photographs and the theme. These questions are also written above the photographs for you to refer to while you are talking.
- If you are still speaking after a minute, the interlocutor will say 'Thank you' and signal that you need to stop.
- When you have finished speaking, your partner will be asked a follow-up question that is also related to the pictures. They will give a brief answer (about 30 seconds).
- Your partner will then be given a different set of pictures to talk about for one minute.
- You should not interrupt your partner, but you do need to listen to what they are saying. When they have finished, the interlocutor will ask you a short question.

TIP When you answer the follow-up question, it's a good idea to respond to what your partner has said, e.g. 'I have to agree with Maria ...'

USEFUL LANGUAGE: SPECULATING

1 🎧 **You will often have to speculate about what the pictures are showing. Listen to a candidate talking about the first picture on page S1 and complete the gaps in the audioscript below, using the words in the box. Some gaps can be filled by more than one of the words.**
08

| perhaps | reckon | seem | make | suppose | maybe | looks | impression | appears |

My initial **(1)** .... is that she doesn't **(2)** .... too nervous, I mean, she's sitting down,

not pacing round the room like I do when I'm worried about something. She seems lost in thought.

I **(3)** .... she's waiting for her phone to ring, probably with news from someone. **(4)** ....

it's a business call, something about a job offer, maybe. But then again, it **(5)** .... like she's

at home, so I **(6)** .... it's something more personal. She **(7)** .... quite young, and I can't

(8) .... out a ring or anything on her wedding finger, so **(9)** .... she's waiting to hear from

a new boyfriend.

2 **Use some of these expressions to answer the questions about the other two pictures on page S1.**
- It seems to be ... / They seem + adjective
- I think I can make out ...
- I reckon / suppose ...
- It appears to be / looks like ...
- My initial impression is that ...

TIP Don't worry if you don't know what the pictures are showing – this is a good opportunity to demonstrate a range of language of speculation.

KEEP TALKING

1 🎧 **You need to keep talking about the pictures for one minute. Listen to a candidate talking about the first picture on page S2. What extra information does he add to extend his talking time?**
09

2 **Look at all the pictures on page S2. What could you say about what happened before the moment shown in each picture and what might happen after it?**

ACTION PLAN

1 Listen carefully to the interlocutor's instructions.

2 You will be given three pictures and the interlocutor will tell you the link between them, e.g. 'They show people waiting in different places.'

3 You will also need to answer two questions that the interlocutor asks you. They are also written above the pictures.

4 Indicate with a gesture which pictures you will be talking about and say, for instance: 'I'd like to talk about this picture and this one.'

5 Remember that you are asked to **compare two** of the pictures, not describe them in detail.

6 When comparing the pictures you should mention things that are similar in both pictures and things that are different.

7 You need to keep talking for a minute. Try to focus on the questions but don't worry if you don't have time to answer both fully. It is better to speak for a full minute than to stop early.

8 When your partner is speaking, listen but don't interrupt.

9 Be ready to answer a question about your partner's pictures. You will have 30 seconds.

Do the exam task, following the instructions below.

Part 2
4 minutes (6 minutes for groups of three candidates)

Work in groups of three if possible. One of you is the interlocutor and the other two are the candidates. The interlocutor should lead the task using the script below. Refer to the pictures on pages S3 and S4.

Interlocutor   In this part of the test, I'm going to give each of you three pictures. I'd like you to talk about **two** of them on your own for about a minute, and also to answer a question briefly about your partner's pictures.

[Candidate A], it's your turn first. Here are your pictures. They show **people laughing in different situations.** I'd like you to compare two of the pictures and say **what might have caused the people to laugh in these situations and where you think they are**.

All right?

🕐 *After 1 minute*   Thank you.

[Candidate B], **which situation do you think will be most memorable? (Why?)**

🕐 *After 30 seconds*   Thank you.

Now, *[Candidate B]*, here are your pictures. They show **people teaching others different things**. I'd like you to compare two of the pictures and say **how difficult it might be to teach others these things and how much preparation the teachers might have made**.

🕐 *After 1 minute*   Thank you.

Now, *[Candidate A]*, **who do you think will benefit most from the teaching? (Why?)**

🕐 *After 30 seconds*   Thank you.

FOLLOW-UP

Did you deal with both questions? What other points could you have added?

TASK INFORMATION

- In Part 3 you work with your partner(s).
- The interlocutor explains the task to you: you have a question to answer and related prompts to guide your discussion.
- The interlocutor gives you a question and a set of prompts. You have a short time to read through this information before you start talking.
- After you have been talking together for about 2 minutes (3 minutes for a group of three candidates), the interlocutor will stop you and ask another question.
- The second question requires you to talk together to make a decision related to the prompts. You will have about 1 minute (2 minutes for a group of three candidates) to do this.
- Part 3 lasts about 4 minutes in total (6 minutes for a group of three candidates).

USEFUL LANGUAGE: EXPRESSING AND JUSTIFYING OPINIONS

1   **In Part 3, it is important to give reasons for your opinions. Match the opinions below with the reasons given.**

1 <u>Due to</u> the time it takes to drive during rush hour,	a <u>because of</u> their lack of experience.
2 Teenagers shouldn't be allowed to work in positions of responsibility	b <u>due to the fact that</u> they spend too much time using social media.
3 To my mind, being famous is nowhere near as good as people think	c <u>as</u> train stations tend to be on the outskirts.
4 <u>Because</u> the weather is so unreliable,	d I'd say there's a good argument for banning cars completely.
5 Work experience is one of the best things students can do	e people are unlikely to choose to walk to work instead of driving.
6 It's easier to get into the town centre by bus	f <u>since</u> it opens them up to experiences they can't get anywhere else.
7 Young people today often have difficulty meeting new people face-to-face,	g <u>owing to</u> the loss of privacy.

2   **◉ Use the underlined words from Exercise 1 to complete the sentences below. More than one answer is possible in most cases. Note whether the expression is followed by a noun / noun phrase or by a clause (subject + verb).**

1   Water pollution has not been reduced as much as predicted .... a lack of clear action by the government.

2   More people are choosing to study abroad .... the facilities are better there.

3   Crime rates are rising .... the low numbers of police officers on the streets.

4   The populations of cities are increasing. This is .... there aren't so many opportunities in the countryside.

5   Personally, I don't believe that people will stop using plastic completely. This is .... the lack of suitable alternatives.

ACTION PLAN

1 When the interlocutor places the task in front of you, you have 15 seconds to look at it. Use the time to read the question in the centre and the options around the question.

2 Remember that in this task you need to interact with your partner. Listen and respond to each other.

3 There will be five options that you can discuss, but do not discuss all of them too quickly. It's better to talk about a few well, rather than all of them without enough detail.

4 During this part of the test look at each other, not the interlocutor, as it should be a conversation between you and your partner.

5 The decision question often requires you to look again at the options from a different angle, e.g. which might take the longest? / which would be the least interesting? Listen carefully to the question – don't assume that you will always be asked to choose which option is 'the best' or 'the most important / most effective', etc.

6 When you are asked to decide between the options, try not to hurry to make any decisions or reach an agreement.

7 If you have already expressed your view on the decision question, don't worry. Restate your decision and summarise your reasons for this.

8 It is not necessary for you and your partner to agree on the same option. As long as you both give reasons for your decision, it's fine to disagree.

9 You may find that you don't have enough time to reach a decision. This is fine if you are stopped while you are still working towards a decision.

Do the exam task, following the instructions below.

Part 3
4 minutes (6 minutes for groups of three candidates)

Work in groups of three if possible. One of you is the interlocutor and the other two are the candidates. The interlocutor should lead the task using the script below. Refer to the task sheet on page S5. The candidates should discuss this task sheet together.

Interlocutor	Now I'd like you to talk about something together for about two minutes.
	Here are some jobs which some people would like to have and a question for you to discuss. First you have some time to look at the task.
⏱ *After 15 seconds*	Now, talk to each other about **how challenging it might be to become successful in these different jobs**.
⏱ *After 2 minutes*	Thank you. Now you have about a minute to decide **which of these jobs would be most difficult to succeed in**.
⏱ *After 1 minute*	Thank you.

 TIP

Respond to your partner's comments or opinions while you're talking, e.g. 'That's a good point.' / 'I'm not sure about that because ...' / 'Yes, that's interesting.'

FOLLOW-UP

Did you involve your partner by asking for his/her opinions? Did you both talk for about the same length of time?

TASK INFORMATION

- Part 4 continues the topic of Part 3.
- The total time for this part of the test is approximately 5 minutes for two candidates, and 8 minutes for a group of three.
- The interlocutor asks you and your partner questions which broaden the topic from Part 3.
- You may be asked one or more questions.
- You may be asked to answer the questions on your own or to discuss them with your partner.
- Listen carefully when your partner is speaking, as you may be asked to comment on what he/she has said, or to give your own response to the same question.

> **TIP** You can ask the interlocutor to repeat the question if you don't remember it.

USEFUL LANGUAGE: AGREEING AND DISAGREEING

1   In Part 4, you have the opportunity to say whether you agree or disagree with a statement or with what your partner has said. Complete the responses to the comment below. The first letter of each word is given.

All fast food and soft drinks should be banned in schools.

Agreement	Disagreement
I **(1)** c.................. agree more, their impact on the health of young people is terrible.	I think that's a bit extreme. **(7)** W.................. it be better to educate them to make the right choices?
I **(2)** a.................. with you one hundred percent – they do more harm than good.	I **(8)** t.................. your point, but there has to be some choice, don't you think?
That's exactly how I **(3)** f.................. . They are terrible for young people's health.	I beg to **(9)** d.................. . Young people should be allowed to make their own choices.
(4) A..................! Young people need to be healthy.	Not **(10)** n.................. . If you ban them completely, you'll just make people want them all the more.
That's so **(5)** t.................. . They have a terrible effect on health.	I'm not so **(11)** s.................. about that. Won't that just make them more popular outside school?
You have a **(6)** p.................. there. Young people will always be tempted if these things are available.	I'd say the **(12)** e.................. opposite, actually. Keep them in schools, but make them more expensive to put people off.

2   Look at these comments made in response to Part 4 questions on dreams and ambitions. Respond to each of the comments with your own views (agreeing or disagreeing) and give reasons.

- Everyone needs to be ambitious. It's the only way to succeed in life.
- It's more important to be successful academically than to be successful in other areas of life, such as art or sport.
- If it takes a long time to achieve something, it's more worthwhile than something you can do easily.
- Everyone needs incentives, such as the promise of a pay rise at work, to motivate them to achieve their goals.
- Fame is the ultimate sign of success.
- It's impossible to achieve anything if you don't have money.

ACTION PLAN

1 The questions are not written down, so if you don't understand what you're asked, ask for repetition.

2 The interlocuter may address you individually or ask both of you to discuss. If you are discussing the question, remember to interact as you did in Part 3.

3 If your partner is answering an individual question and you would like to comment, you can, but wait until he/she has finished answering.

4 Remember to extend your answer by giving a reason and/or an example.

5 Sometimes you are asked the same question as your partner, so listen carefully even if it is not your turn.

6 If you are not asked as many questions as your partner, don't worry. It is possible that he/she might have given slightly shorter answers during the rest of the test.

7 At the end of the test say goodbye and thank the examiners. Remember that they are not allowed to comment on your performance.

Do the exam task, following the instructions below.

Part 4
5 minutes (8 minutes for groups of three candidates)

Work in groups of three if possible. One of you is the interlocutor and the other two are the candidates. The interlocutor should lead the task using the script below. The interlocutor asks some general questions which follow on from the topic in Part 3.

Interlocutor
- If you had a choice, what would be your ideal job? (Why?)

- Do you think people value a job more if they've had to work very hard to get it? (Why? / Why not?)

- How difficult do you think it is for a person to maintain motivation once he or she has become successful? (Why?)

- Some people find it hard to cope with being famous or successful. Why do you think this is?

- How important do you think it is to have a good balance between your life and work? (Why?)

- What sort of changes to people's working lives might happen over the next ten or fifteen years? (Why?)

- Thank you. That is the end of the test.

TIP There are no right or wrong answers to these questions. They depend on your opinions. The examiners will not judge your ideas.

FOLLOW-UP

What examples did you give to extend your answers?

Which question was most difficult to answer? Look at it again and think about how you could answer it better.

Review

Answer the questions about Reading and Use of English Part 1. If you need help, read the Task information on page 10.

1 Is it a good idea to read the whole text before starting to complete the gaps?
2 Do questions have more than one possible answer?
3 Is the task a test of vocabulary?
4 Is it possible to answer some questions by elimination?
5 Will any of the questions test knowledge of phrasal verbs?
6 Will any of the questions test knowledge of key phrases and idioms?

USEFUL LANGUAGE: USING THE CORRECT PHRASAL VERBS

 Complete the sentences below with phrasal verbs from the box. Put the verbs in the correct forms. There are two verbs in the box that you don't need to use.

turn out	brush up	pass by	take off	put forward
take on	cut down	come across	cater for	get over

1 When I was looking for a book in the library, I .... a fascinating study of population changes.

2 Sales of the new car have .... in the last two months.

3 Green's are the latest supermarket chain to announce that they're .... on plastic packaging.

4 Carole decided to .... on her Spanish before she went to Mexico for her holiday.

5 It took me ages to .... my cold and I was off work all week.

6 Ling Mee wants to .... a suggestion about improving the sports facilities in the college.

7 One good thing about the art school is that it has courses which .... all ages.

8 Jane .... a lot of extra work last year, and she ended up working most weekends.

> **TIP** In Part 1 you often need to choose the correct phrasal verb to fill a gap. You might need to choose a whole phrasal verb or just part of one.

USEFUL LANGUAGE: CHOOSING THE RIGHT WORDS IN FIXED PHRASES

 Choose the correct option to complete the sentences.

1 I thought Maisie did really well in the diving competition, bearing in *mind / view / thought* how young she is.

2 I'm not going to tell you how much I earn – it's none of your *affair / business / concern* really.

3 When it *goes / comes* to doing jobs around the house, Terry is really helpful.

4 I would give you a lift, but I don't have a car at my *disposal / benefit / availability* at the moment.

5 Javier always went to great *extents / heights / lengths* to make sure that Anna was included in all the family activities.

6 The construction of the new bridge was completed ahead of *programme / schedule / calendar*, which, for a project that size, was unusual.

> **TIP** In Part 1, you are often tested on your knowledge of phrases. To fill a gap, you might need to choose the whole phrase or part of one.

Read the Action plan on page 12. Then follow the exam instructions, using the advice below to help you.

For questions **1 – 8**, read the text below and decide which answer (**A, B, C,** or **D**) best fits each gap. There is an example at the beginning (**0**).

Mark your answers **on the separate answer sheet**.

Example:

0   **A**   stand   **B**   experience   **C**   support   **D**   bear

When audience members save the day

At a recent performance of the opera *La Bohème*, the singer playing the main male role began to **(0)** .... problems with his voice and was unable to carry on. Fortunately, an audience member, Charles Castronovo, offered to stand in, and the evening's performance was **(1)** ....

In fact, 'audience member' doesn't quite **(2)** .... justice to Castronovo. He is a tenor of some **(3)** .... Castronovo sang from the side of the stage, while the normal singer acted. After the final act, Castronovo joined the cast on stage and received loud **(4)** .... from the audience. In fact, the occasion was so emotional that many tears were **(5)** .... in the audience.

Such a turn of **(6)** .... is rare, but in 2004, the baritone Ian Vayne attended a production of the opera *Carmen* and ended up **(7)** .... the role of Escamillo after the original singer suddenly fell ill in Act 1. More recently, a concert in London was saved by the last-minute substitution of Milly Forrest, the venue's cloakroom attendant. Milly was also, as it **(8)** .... , a trained soprano singer.

1	**A**	preserved	**B**	rescued	**C**	maintained	**D** secured
2	**A**	give	**B**	put	**C**	do	**D** make
3	**A**	renown	**B**	position	**C**	mark	**D** reputation
4	**A**	consent	**B**	regard	**C**	honour	**D** applause
5	**A**	dropped	**B**	shed	**C**	cast	**D** spilt
6	**A**	events	**B**	matters	**C**	incidents	**D** affairs
7	**A**	filling out	**B**	bringing about	**C**	taking over	**D** covering up
8	**A**	goes	**B**	occurs	**C**	appears	**D** happens

Advice

1   Read paragraphs 1 and 2 carefully and ask yourself what Castronovo did at this performance of the opera. This may help you decide what the correct answer is here.

2   The correct verb is part of a fixed phrase: 'to ... justice to someone'.

3   The word needed here has a similar meaning to 'fame'.

4   Think about how the audience would have felt about Castronovo at the end of the performance and how they would have shown their feelings.

5   Only one of these verbs collocates with 'tears'.

6   The sentence containing gap 6 refers to the unexpected things that happened at the performance of the opera. Also, the missing word is part of a fixed phrase: 'a turn of ...'.

7   If you read the text carefully, you find out that Ian Vayne played the part of Escamillo instead of the original singer. Which of the phrasal verbs means 'replacing someone (in a job or role)'?

8   The missing word is part of a fixed phrase.

Review

Answer the questions about Reading and Use of English Part 2. If you need help, read the Task information on page 14.

1 Is Part 2 mainly a test of vocabulary?
2 Will any of the gaps be parts of phrasal verbs or fixed phrases?
3 Can you write more than one word in a gap?
4 Is there more than one possible answer for some gaps?
5 Are contractions such as *we're* or *won't* acceptable answers?
6 Is it necessary to spell the words correctly?

USEFUL LANGUAGE: USING THE CORRECT VERB FORMS

Use the correct words from the box to complete the sentences below. There are more words in the box than you need, and you can use each word more than once. In some sentences, more than one answer is possible.

| having | will | doing | had | might | could | was | would | being | have |

1 The first time Elias heard the song, he knew it .... be a big hit.
2 The markets in ancient Aztec cities are thought to .... been large and sophisticated.
3 I'm not sure where Jeff is, but he .... well be at the gym.
4 After .... his teeth fixed and whitened, Barry looked quite different.
5 The meeting discussed the prospect of Hiri Sako .... given an award for his contribution to physics.
6 After Sofia met Andre nothing .... ever be the same for them again.
7 .... been a teacher for almost 20 years, Fatima was used to dealing with adolescents.
8 The Monarch butterfly migrates from Canada to Mexico and, in .... so, it travels thousands of kilometres.

> **TIP** If you think the gap requires a verb, it is likely to be a common auxiliary verb (*be, has, did,* etc.) or a modal verb (*can, would* etc.) The only time when you might need a 'content' verb is for a fixed phrase or a very strong collocation (e.g. *give* birth, I couldn't *believe* my eyes).

USEFUL LANGUAGE: USING FIXED PHRASES

Complete the gaps in the sentences with the correct word.

1 They arrived at the lecture theatre early in .... to get seats near the front.
2 .... to Dr Akbar, some new medication for epilepsy is likely to be available quite soon.
3 The two men seemed to communicate .... means of gestures and facial expressions.
4 As .... as Schwartz was concerned, the issue had been dealt with in a satisfactory way.
5 Every .... often, a new young athlete emerges who is far better than any of their peers.
6 Opportunities to travel like this are .... and far between.

> **TIP** Some gaps in Part 2 require a word to complete a fixed phrase. Different parts of a phrase could be tested. e.g. ... *common with*; OR *in ... with*.

Exam Practice Test 2 — Reading and Use of English Part 2

Read the Action plan on page 16. Then follow the exam instructions, using the advice to below help you.

For questions **9 – 16**, read the text below and think of the word which best fits each gap. Use only **one** word in each gap. There is an example at the beginning (**0**).

Write your answers **IN CAPITAL LETTERS on the separate answer sheet**.

Example: `0` `B` `E` `E` `N`

A nurse on the night shift

I've **(0)** .... a nurse for almost 30 years and I've pretty much seen everything. **(9)** .... you may be part of the happiest time of someone's life on one day, the next day you're helping patients through very tough experiences. Ups and downs are normal, **(10)** .... is shift work. In a unit **(11)** .... ours, we alternate between day and night shifts. There tend to **(12)** .... fewer managers and office staff around at night, but my job stays the same.

The secret to making it through the night is sleeping well between shifts. There's **(13)** .... worse than being exhausted, but needing to be awake and alert at three in the morning. You can't falter, because you're responsible **(14)** .... the lives of women and their babies. I'm generally a good sleeper, **(15)** .... it be at night or during the day, but if something goes wrong at work, it can be difficult. **(16)** .... long you've done the job, certain things can upset you. The good thing is that babies are generally very robust.

Advice

9   If you look at the whole of the second sentence, you will see that the writer is making a contrast. Which word can be used at the start of a sentence to link two contrasting ideas? There is more than one possible answer.

10   The idea expressed in this sentence is that 'ups and downs are normal and shiftwork is (normal) too'. Can you think of a word to put before 'is' which gives the idea of 'too' here?

11   You need a word that means 'similar to' here.

12   Which verb often follows 'There'?

13   Is the writer talking about something that's really difficult or something's that's not so bad?

14   You're looking for a preposition here.

15   You need a word that introduces two possible times: 'at night or during the day'.

16   The word you need here means 'no matter how (long)'.

Review

Change the following statements about Reading and Use of English Part 3 so that they are true. If you need help, read the Task information on page 17.

1 Part 3 is mainly a test of grammar.
2 You can write either one or two words in each gap.
3 Sometimes the word given in capital letters can be put in the gap without any changes.
4 You need to add a prefix or a suffix, but not both.
5 Only UK spellings are accepted.

USEFUL LANGUAGE: CHOOSING THE CORRECT WORD FOR THE CONTEXT

Choose the correct options to complete the sentences.

1 The *investigation / investigators* into the causes of the economic crisis has been slowed down by personnel changes. (INVESTIGATE)
2 Nancy lives in a rather *fashionable / unfashionable* part of town, which isn't very well known and where nothing much happens. (FASHION)
3 My grandfather grew up in a remote village which had no gas or *electricians / electricity* – they had oil lamps and cooked on open fires. (ELECTRIC)
4 My mother doesn't like it when I spend lots of time playing video games and my father also expresses his *approval / disapproval*. (APPROVE)
5 John Maynard Keynes was one of the most influential *economists / economics* of the 20th century. (ECONOMY)
6 The *explanation / explanations* didn't really convince me, and I spent a good deal of time trying to find out whether there was any truth in it. (EXPLAIN)
7 The students sat quietly writing their history essays and there was very little *action / interaction* between them. (ACT)
8 The film-makers are employing experts to make sure that the film provides an *accurate / inaccurate* picture of what ordinary life was like in the 1890s. (ACCURACY)

> **TIP** Sometimes more than one noun can be formed from the same root word - e.g. CREATE → CREATOR or CREATIVITY or CREATION. Make sure the word you choose fits the meaning of the sentence. Also, check whether the noun you form should be singular or plural.

> **TIP** Many words have positive and negative forms – e.g. *fortunately / unfortunately*. The text before and after the gap will help you choose the right one.

USEFUL LANGUAGE: SPELLING CORRECTLY

Find the spelling errors in these sentences and correct them.

1 My sister has a very sucessful marketing business.
2 The French goverment gave its backing to the initiative.
3 The most expensive restaurants aren't neccesarily the best ones.
4 The negotiacions between the two companies have been long and detailed.
5 The enviromental impact of building a new airport is rather worrying.
6 The town has plenty of excellent student acomodation.
7 To say that the event was a disaster is an exageration.
8 Jake says that lots of people responded to the job advertisment.

> **TIP** There are certain words that students often misspell – make sure you know how to spell those words correctly. Both UK and US spellings are accepted.

Read the Action plan on page 20. Then follow the exam instructions, using the advice below to help you.

For questions **17 – 24**, read the text below. Use the word given in capitals at the end of some of the lines to form a word that fits in the gap **in the same line**. There is an example at the beginning (**0**).

Write your answers **IN CAPITAL LETTERS on the separate answer sheet**.

Example: | **0** | R | E | P | R | E | S | E | N | T | A | T | I | O | N | S | | | |

The wild animals we love most

(0) .... of wild animals, such as elephants, tigers and pandas, are everywhere in movies, books and toy stores. But research suggests that this **(17)** .... may have a problematic effect on public **(18)** .... of how much at risk these animals are in nature. In a survey carried out by French ecologists, people were asked which animals they considered most **(19)** .... The top ten were: lions, elephants, giraffes, leopards, pandas, cheetahs, polar bears, wolves and gorillas. **(20)** .... , the biggest fans of these animals knew very little about their **(21)** .... prospects – the sad truth being that many of them face possible **(22)** .... in the coming decades.

The researchers suggest that the widespread presence of these animals in popular culture makes people think their populations in the wild are strong, and this may lead to **(23)** .... One of the researchers has said that 'companies using giraffes, cheetahs or polar bears for marketing may be contributing **(24)** .... to the false idea that animal populations in the wild are secure and not in need of conservation.'

REPRESENT

POPULAR

PERCEIVE

CHARISMA

IRONY

SURVIVE

EXTINCT

COMPLACENT

INTENTION

Advice

17 The word 'this' before the gap indicates that you need a noun here.

18 'public' here is an adjective. What kind of word normally follows an adjective?

19 'most' is used as part of a superlative form, describing animals. What kind of word should follow it?

20 What kind of word often goes at the start of a sentence and is followed by a comma?

21 What kind of word is likely to be between 'their' and 'prospects'?

22 The word before the gap should help you decide what kind of word is needed here.

23 You need a noun here which refers to an attitude.

24 You need a word that means 'not on purpose'. Your word will need more than one change, including a prefix.

Review

Answer the questions about Reading and Use of English Part 4. If you need help, read the Task information on page 21.

1 How many marks can I get for each question?
2 What is the minimum number of words I can write in the gap?
3 What is the maximum number of words I can write in the gap?
4 What happens if I change or don't include the key word?
5 How many words does a contraction like *don't* count as?

USEFUL LANGUAGE: UNDERSTANDING PHRASAL VERBS

1 **Match the verbs on the left with the phrasal verbs that have the same meaning.**

1	respect	a	chill out
2	become fashionable or popular	b	turn down
3	compensate	c	bump into
4	absorb	d	catch on
5	relax	e	stem from
6	meet someone unexpectedly	f	make up for
7	refuse	g	look up to
8	develop as a result of	h	soak up

> **TIP**
> For part of the answer, you often need to replace a normal verb with a phrasal verb.
> e.g. *The finance manager **cancelled** the meeting because of other commitments.* → *The finance manager **called off** the meeting because of other commitments.*

2 **Use the correct forms of the phrasal verbs from the box above to complete the following sentences.**

1 This game is so complicated to play that I don't think it will .... with children.
2 Paloma .... the offer of a job in London because she wanted to stay in Spain.
3 Many of the company's problems .... not investing enough in new technology.
4 At weekends, Adam mainly likes to stay at home and .... with his brother and sister.
5 We spent the day walking around the historic centre of Naples trying to .... the atmosphere.
6 At the supermarket yesterday, I .... a teacher from primary school who I hadn't seen for years.

USEFUL LANGUAGE: BEING ACCURATE IN THE WAY YOU USE LANGUAGE

 These sentences contain mistakes that students often make. Find and correct the mistake in each sentence.

1 Adam suggested Jane to do a law course.
2 Don't forget to take a small amount of coins with you.
3 Everyone should have equal possibilities in education.
4 I won't let you to make the same mistake again.
5 The bus stopped to allow passengers going to the shops.
6 We could hear some classical music to play in the background.

> **TIP**
> You will lose marks if you make mistakes with grammar, vocabulary and spelling. So check your answers carefully.

Read the Action plan on page 23. Then follow the exam instructions, using the advice below to help you.

For questions **25 – 30**, complete the second sentence so that it has a similar meaning to the first sentence, using the word given. **Do not change the word given.** You must use between three and six words, including the word given. Here is an example (**0**).

Example:

0 'I'm sorry I got to the party so late,' Joanna said to her friend.

    HAVING

    Joanna apologised to her friend .... up so late at the party.

The gap can be filled with the words 'for having turned', so you write:

Example: | **0** | *FOR HAVING TURNED*

Write **only** the missing words **IN CAPITAL LETTERS on the separate answer sheet**.

---

25 Lily has very little chance of getting into the final of the competition this year.

    HIGHLY

    It's .... into the final of the competition this year.

26 I think everyone knows that Ian has decided to retire at the end of this year.

    MADE

    I think it's common .... his mind to retire at the end of this year.

27 I always found the way George spoke on the phone annoying, but I don't any more.

    USED

    The way George spoke on the phone .... nerves, but I don't mind it now.

28 Ten minutes before the end of the game, Silvia realised that she didn't have any energy left at all.

    RUN

    Silvia realised that .... ten minutes before the end of the game,

29 We expected Ed to arrive home by 9 o'clock, but he didn't get there till 10.

    SUPPOSED

    Ed .... arrived home by 9 o'clock, but he didn't get there till 10.

30 We must consider several important things before we can decide whether or not to build a new road.

    ACCOUNT

    Several important things have .... before we can decide whether or not to build a new road.

Advice

25 *The first sentence means that Lily probably won't reach the final. Can you think of a word meaning 'improbable' that goes with 'highly' for the first part of the answer?*

26 *For the first part of the answer, you need a noun after 'common'. In the second part of the answer, think of a phrase including 'made' which means 'has decided'.*

27 *Here you need a phrase including the word 'nerves' which means 'annoy'.*

28 *You need a phrasal verb with 'run' which means 'use all of something so there's nothing left'. Think about the tense of the verb after 'realised'.*

29 *You need a passive structure after 'Ed'. Also, remember that the whole of the first sentence is in the past.*

30 *You need a phrase including the word 'account' which means 'consider'. 'Several important things' is now the subject of the sentence, so do you need an active or a passive structure?*

Review

Decide if these statements about Reading and Use of English Part 5 are True or False. If you need help, read the Task information on page 24.

1 Every question in Part 5 has four options.
2 The texts are usually about subjects to do with science or technology.
3 It's sometimes hard to work out which part of the text each question relates to.
4 Sometimes the answer to a question is not clearly stated and you have to infer the meaning.
5 The whole of an option has to match what's in the text for it to be the correct answer.

UNDERSTANDING ATTITUDES AND FEELINGS

1 Draw a table and categorise the adjectives in the box below as positive or negative. Then underline the words which indicate certainty or lack of certainty.

> proud   doubtful   convinced   resentful   optimistic   dismissive
> confident   enthusiastic   uneasy   delighted   sceptical   frustrated
> cynical   unsure   hesitant   appreciative

2 Use suitable adjectives from the box above to complete the following sentences. Sometimes more than one answer is possible.

1 Jack loves getting to know different places and cultures. So he's very .... about the idea of travelling around south-east Asia, where he's never been before.

2 Tessa always thinks good things are going to happen to her in the future. Basically, she's a very .... person.

3 There's a widespread feeling these days that politicians are only interested in themselves and in holding onto power. In other words, people are quite .... about politicians.

4 My brother can hold a basic conversation in Turkish. He's been trying really hard to improve recently, but he feels he hasn't made any progress. He's quite .... about it.

5 Jenny's parents want her to study law, but she thinks she might not enjoy it. In fact, she's very .... whether she should do it.

6 Everyone in the meeting thought that Jim's proposal would never work. They were all rather .... of it.

7 Kate says we should drive to Paris rather take the train. I'm not sure if it's a good idea, but she's absolutely .... about it.

8 Mark says his manager gives him more work than anyone else in the office. He thinks it's unfair and he's quite .... about it.

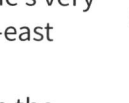

TIP Part 5 questions often test your understanding of opinions, attitudes and feelings expressed in the text.

TIP To practise, read articles and other texts in which opinions, attitudes and feelings are expressed.

TIP When you take the exam, you're allowed to write on the Question Paper. It's a good idea to underline key words in the questions and the text, and make notes on the task itself.

3 For each of the adjectives in the box above, write down any other word forms you can think of.

Example: proud → *pride* (noun)   convinced → *to convince* (verb) → *conviction* (noun)

UNDERSTANDING REFERENCES

1 Look at the phrase in italics in the following paragraph about a footballer. Which underlined part of the text does the phrase in italics refer to?

Bruno Montero is <u>not the most naturally talented of footballers</u>, but when he's on the pitch, <u>Montero gives absolutely everything for the team</u>. Fans say <u>they see him on his bike all around town</u>, which, in an age when footballers are known for <u>wearing the latest fashions and driving expensive sports cars</u>, is *something you wouldn't expect of someone in his profession*. But then Montero has never been a typical footballer.

Why have you chosen that part of the text?

 TIP Part 5 often has a question which tests your understanding of referencing. The words used for referencing (*this, those, ones, something*, etc.) are often not very close to the part of the text which is referred to.

2 Which of the options (A – D) has a similar meaning to the part of the text that *something you wouldn't expect of someone in his profession* refers to?

A his total commitment to his team

B his interest in consumer goods

C his limited ability as a footballer

D his habit of cycling everywhere

3 Read the following paragraphs and answer the questions below them. Underline the key parts of the text to help you.

1

I think Gantner has *certain limitations* as a film-maker. Although his editing is sharp and energetic, and his application of special effects can't be faulted, his story-telling skills are considerably less impressive. The actors he casts tend to make up for his shortcomings in this respect, though.

The words *certain limitations* refer to the way Gantner

A tells a story.

B directs actors.

C includes special effects.

D edits his films.

2

Three years ago, I joined a singing group. It is often said that music is an international language and, despite our age differences – the youngest member is 18 and the oldest nearly 80 – and the fact that we include two nurses, a bus driver, two accountants, a student and a retired judge, we are living proof of *that cliché*. We are from Nigeria, Japan, Mexico, Korea, as well as several European countries, with the diversity of mother tongues, customs and ways of thinking that you would expect, but when we're singing, we're as one.

The words *that cliché* refer to the idea that

A people of all ages enjoy music.

B music appeals to particular professions.

C cultural differences can be explored through music.

D people from different parts of the world can communicate through music.

Read the Action plan on page 26. Then follow the exam instructions, using the advice on page 80 to help you.

You are going to read a review of a book about the psychology of food. For questions **31 – 36**, choose the answer (**A**, **B**, **C** or **D**) which you think fits best according to the text.

Mark your answers **on the separate answer sheet**.

Review of *Gastrophysics: The New Science of Eating* by Charles Spence

As head of a food research laboratory at the University of Oxford and a prolific author on the psychology of food, Spence is ideally placed to reveal recent discoveries such as: heavier cutlery encourages restaurant customers to pay more; ginger biscuits taste spicier when served from a rough plate; and strawberry mousse is perceived as 10% sweeter on a white dish than on a black one. And Spence is not afraid of stirring things up. 'The pleasures of the table reside in the mind, not the mouth,' he writes, no doubt triggering much resentment among cookbook writers the world over. In fact, while his book, *Gastrophysics: The New Science of Eating,* is about how to create the perfect meal, it has almost nothing to do with the everyday practicalities of cuisine. Instead, this is the science of 'everything else', a blending of gastronomy, psychology and physics to probe the numerous factors that influence our perception of flavour, steer our culinary choices and make all the difference between a memorable meal and one to be forgotten.

Top chefs and large food manufacturers alike have been quick to grab a slice of the action. As Spence points out, some restaurateurs have embraced multi-sensory trickery to boost the dining experience by, for example, spraying the scent of saffron over guests to enhance the flavour of lobster, or Googling their guests to tap into the powerful effect of personalisation. On a wider scale, and more worryingly, supermarkets label mass-produced food items with the names of non-existent farms, presumably to exploit consumers' apparent willingness to pay more for a sense of authenticity.

There's another side to the coin. By colouring a drink pink, manufacturers can cut the sugar content, relying on our subconscious association between colour and sweetness to make up the difference. The positive implications for health are not hard to see, although Spence advises against giving this much publicity – if customers were in on the secret, he says, they would then claim to be able to tell the difference. Meanwhile, Spence believes that in years to come, our cuisine could be shaped by his own finding that making the crunch of a crisp louder increases its apparent freshness. 'Playing on the sound of crunch might offer one way in to the popularisation of eating insects,' he writes as he considers how to make insects – a great potential source of protein and a possible solution to future global food shortages – more appetising.

Spence has a way with words and cheerfully leads the reader on a journey through the senses like a magician – an impression backed up by his liking for conjuring up imaginative dining experiences with top chefs and hosting multi-sensory cinema events. He skips from the importance of matching expectations with the taste of a dish to the revelation that people tend to link blob-like shapes to sweet foods – explaining furious accusations, not long ago, that a leading brand of chocolates had changed the recipe of a much-loved chocolate bar when it had, in fact, only rounded off its corners.

Spence's research is regularly dismissed by some chefs, who say that good food 'should speak for itself'. Spence's response to this is that, however much you may believe in the importance of good, simple raw materials, there is always a multi-sensory atmosphere. Even a chef who claims to let food do all the talking will go to the *line 33* trouble of buying good heavy cutlery, he observes, because a plastic fork would mean a spoiled experience. *line 34* Whether we like it or not, we are all affected by these inevitable manipulations. Spence's point is that there is no *line 35* such thing as a neutral context for eating. The flavour in our mouths at dinnertime is affected by the company we *line 36* keep, by the music playing in the room and by where we sit.

But eating is also affected by factors that Spence pays less attention to. He sometimes seems to treat human beings as if they were homogeneous amalgams of sense-organs, unaffected by culture or economic circumstances. Addressing the growing number of people who eat alone, he suggests: 'Next time you get peckish, why not invite someone to eat with you?' For a book on psychology, there is remarkably little here on the multiple ways that eating can become dysfunctional. There are people whose problems with eating go far beyond whether their plate is the right colour. *Gastrophysics* is brilliant when demonstrating how much the environment of the table affects our eating, particularly at high-end restaurants, but it has less to say about what we as humans bring to the table.

31 In the first paragraph, the reviewer suggests that Charles Spence is

   A good at making science accessible.
   B inspirational for other food writers.
   C dismissive of traditional cooking.
   D willing to be provocative.

32 In the second paragraph, the reviewer is expressing

   A disapproval of certain dishonest practices.
   B concern about the use made of technology.
   C surprise at the extent of Spence's influence.
   D admiration for the adaptability of businesses.

33 The reviewer's main point in the third paragraph is that

   A some kinds of information should be withheld from the public.
   B future food resources will depend on people like Spence.
   C developments in gastrophysics can have social value.
   D advances in science often have unlikely origins.

34 The reviewer likens Spence to a magician because of

   A the attention that he pays to detail.
   B the manner in which he communicates.
   C the tendency to keep his methods to himself.
   D the types of places where people often see him.

35 Which words have the opposite meaning to 'a multi-sensory atmosphere' in line 33?

   A a spoiled experience (line 34)
   B inevitable manipulations (line 35)
   C a neutral context (line 36)
   D the company we keep (line 36)

36 What is the reviewer doing in the final paragraph?

   A identifying the type of reader that the book would suit most
   B illustrating a point made in a previous paragraph
   C bringing together the main ideas in the article
   D drawing attention to a weakness in the book

Advice

31 Read the whole of the first paragraph before you answer this question.

32 Each option in this question has two parts: an attitude and what that attitude is about. Both parts must be present in the text for an option to be the correct answer.

33 You will need to read the whole of the third paragraph to answer this question.

34 Find the paragraph in the text where the idea of the magician is mentioned. Then look for words and information in that paragraph which refer to Spence's skills.

35 First, decide what you think 'a multi-sensory atmosphere' means in this paragraph. Then underline the sections of text where the words in the options come from.

36 The first and last sentences of the final paragraph should help you decide on the answer to this question.

Review

Decide if these statements about Reading and Use of English Part 6 are True or False. If you need help, read the Task information on page 29.

1 The four texts are all about the same subject.
2 The texts are usually reviews of books.
3 There are four questions and there will always be one A answer, one B answer, one C answer and one D answer.
4 You need to make sure you know what all four texts say about every question.
5 It's a good idea to read the texts before you look at the questions.

USEFUL LANGUAGE: GIVING OPINIONS

1 The following sentences are taken from different reviews of a book written by an environmentalist called Philip Smith. In each sentence, underline the word or words which show what the reviewer's opinion is. The first sentence is an example of what to do.

1 The <u>strength</u> of Smith's book lies in its organisation.
2 Smith convincingly demonstrates how we have severely damaged many local ecosystems.
3 Some of Smith's solutions are not very feasible.
4 The explanation Smith comes up with for the decline in bird numbers is rather implausible.
5 The main drawback with Smith's book lies in the way he expresses himself.
6 Smith's idea that land should be allowed to go back to being wild is very attractive.
7 Smith's last book quite rightly received some very positive comments.
8 It's impossible to tell whether or not Smith's forecasts are valid.
9 Smith's prose style in this book is its biggest weakness.
10 Smith makes some practical suggestions for dealing with the problems.
11 Smith's evidence for the environmental destruction that humans are causing is compelling.
12 The praise that Smith received for his previous book was well-deserved.
13 Smith offers a very credible theory regarding the falling bird population.
14 As for Smith's predictions about the future, the jury is still out.
15 The structure of Smith's book is a definite plus.
16 Smith puts forward the rather unappealing notion that we should let parts of the country return to a completely natural state.

> **TIP** The writer of a Part 6 text will often refer to other people's opinions. Make sure you know what the writer's opinions are and what the opinions are of the other people the writer is referring to.

2 The reviewers in sentence 1 and sentence 15 express similar views.
- Find four more pairs of sentences expressing similar views.
- Find three pairs of sentences in which the reviewers express opposite views.

Read the Action plan on page 31. Then follow the exam instructions, using the advice on page 83 to help you.

You are going to read four extracts from articles in which experts give their views on using tidal energy. For questions **37 – 40**, choose from the experts **A – D**. The experts may be chosen more than once.

Tidal energy

A

There is currently a wide range of technologies for harnessing the energy potential of the world's seas and oceans. These include a few large barrages built in certain coastal waters, various smaller types of turbine further out to sea capturing wave power, and tidal lagoons where large walls are constructed to trap water at high tide and then release it through turbines at low tide. The challenge of making these technologies work is huge, but so is the prize. Once in operation, they produce no greenhouse gas emissions, and given what we know about the severity of climate change, this is of colossal importance. Any new technology will inevitably affect the environment to some degree. However, the evidence suggests that barrages and underwater turbines have a relatively benign effect. There are also bound to be people who think barrages are an eyesore. These structures, however, are often not easily visible from land and, compared with nuclear power reactors and wind farms, are inoffensive.

B

For the last thirty years, I have lived in a lovely spot next to the sea. From my living room window, I look out over a stunning bay with cliffs and small islands in the distance. I would be the first to resist any change to such a landscape, which is why I have listened carefully to recent objections to a proposal to install tidal energy structures just along the coast from me. All the evidence presented, however, indicates that these installations are minimally intrusive. Everything we know about global warming – its causes and implications for the future – points to the need to expand our ocean power resources without further delay. The technology is already available and is being enhanced all the time. While the initial costs are high, the longer-term benefits are just what we need – clean, renewable, predictable and low-cost energy.

C

Towering concrete barrages situated off coastlines and in river estuaries are clearly unsightly, and even submerged turbines can impinge on an area. The change in the speed and height of tides as a result of these schemes can be dramatic and can detract markedly from the visual appeal of these places. At the same time, things undoubtedly change for all kinds of organisms in the sea. Noise from construction and from turbines, the corrosion of building materials and the way that turbines change water flows can all be very disruptive for flora and fauna. This all sits uncomfortably with tidal power's prime selling point: that it has no toxic by-products of the kind produced by traditional energy sources, which cause temperatures around the world to rise. Also, it would be wrong to forget that other sources of clean, renewable energy cost far less to produce. The sensible choice is to continue to build on the successes of solar, wind and thermal energy until tidal technology has reached a point where it is viable.

D

I've heard plenty of hostile comments regarding the ugliness of tidal energy infrastructure. However, whether it offends aesthetic sensibilities is a trivial matter. The key issues are whether tidal power can deliver energy in a reliable, cost-effective and environmentally friendly way. The uncomfortable truth is that such schemes have a record of being extremely expensive upfront. The sea is a difficult environment for engineers to work in and more traditional energy sources like oil and gas cost less and make more sense to exploit. Once tidal schemes are up and running, they produce relatively little air pollution, but there's a tendency to forget the considerable energy consumption involved in manufacturing materials for them, and constructing and repairing them. This, of course, involves greenhouse gas emissions, which in turn play a role in higher temperatures across the planet. There is also a tendency to overlook how tidal schemes can harm animal and plant life. A major barrage in France, for example, has brought increased levels of silt which favours some plant and animal species, but is disastrous for others.

Which expert

shares C's view on whether developing the use of tidal power should be a priority? **37** [ ]

has a different view from D regarding the impact that tidal power installations have on marine ecosystems? **38** [ ]

has a different view from the others regarding the extent to which the physical appearance of tidal power systems is a concern? **39** [ ]

has a different view from B on the significance of tidal power for global warming? **40** [ ]

Advice

37 *Look at the last two sentences in Text C. Does the writer think there should be a focus now on developing tidal power?*

38 *Look at the last two sentences in Text D. Does the writer think tidal power installations are bad for wildlife that lives in the sea?*

39 *Start by looking at the last two sentences in Text A. Is the writer concerned about the way tidal power installations look?*

40 *Look for the term 'global warming' in Text B. Does the writer think tidal power will help us deal with global warming?*

Review

Read the following statements about dealing with Part 7. Do you agree with each one? Why or why not? If you need help, read the Task information on page 33.

1 It's a good idea to start by quickly reading the main text with the gaps in it.
2 Then you should quickly read through the options A – G.
3 It's useful to underline all the words in the text that you don't know.
4 For an option (A–G) to fit into a gap, there must always be a clear link with the text before and after the gap.
5 The main links to look for are words and phrases like *however*, *in addition* and *as a result*.
6 If you can't find a suitable option for one of the gaps, try completing the other gaps and come back to it later.

USING VOCABULARY TO LINK IDEAS

1 One way to link sentences and paragraphs is through related vocabulary and paraphrasing. Underline the vocabulary links in the following sentences.

The thick frames of fatbikes look rather like those of mountain bikes. Fatbike tyres, though, are wider and have lower air pressure.

These features allow them to grip snow and ice better.

2 Use suitable words from the box to complete the links in the following sentences. Three of the words in the box are not needed.

> misconceptions   reassurances   conclusions   attempts
> conditions   structures   skills   agreements   facilities

1 The resort where I stayed has a comfortable new hostel and a restaurant which offers healthy but affordable meals.

Such .... are likely to attract more visitors, of course.

2 The snow on the higher fatbiking tracks was extremely soft, but then turned icy.

These sorts of .... can be very challenging.

3 When you start riding a fatbike, you need to learn how to lean in a certain way and lift your handlebars as you move forward.

These .... take some time to develop.

4 My instructor told me about an experienced road cyclist he knew who had wrongly assumed that fatbiking was very similar to mountain biking.

Apparently, ... of this type are very common.

5 The second part of the route was very steep and icy. 'You'll find this hard,' my instructor said. 'But give it a go.'

After three unsuccessful ...., I got off my bike and pushed it up the track.

6 'Don't worry,' my instructor said. 'It's normal for beginners like you to fall off.'

These .... made me feel less embarrassed.

Read the Action plan on page 35. Then follow the exam instructions, using the advice on page 86 to help you.

You are going to read an article about beekeeping in Slovenia. Six paragraphs have been removed from the article. Choose from the paragraphs **A – G** the one which fits each gap (**41 – 46**). There is one extra paragraph which you do not need to use.

Mark your answers **on the separate answer sheet**.

The country that loves bees

The door opens and we emerge onto the flat roof. It is a sparse, unfurnished space. To the north-west are mountains, still slightly frosted in the late spring sunshine. Below, bathed in the same glow, is Ljubljana, the capital of Slovenia, with the River Ljubljanica running through its centre. And there, in a corner, is the hotel's current use for its upper level.

41

Going under the title 'President of the Urban Beekeeping Association', Gorazd Trusnovec is particularly proud of these twin outposts of his empire – which stretches to 24 hives, rented to keen beekeepers across the city. He installed them here last year, despite certain doubts he had about the idea.

42

In fact, they've been the basis of a sweet deal. The hotel gets to serve its own honey while Trusnovec has an experimental location for his business. It's not hugely profitable, but he says that 'Working with bees brings me peace of mind. My grandmother had a hive. The smell of honey extraction was incredible. I forgot it for 30 years – then it came back to me, this aroma from my childhood. I started to look at raising bees in the city. And now I couldn't imagine doing anything else.'

43

This national affection flickers at the pretty heart of Ljubljana. It is visible on Medarska Ulica – 'Honeysellers Street'. Admittedly, this thin lane is no longer devoted to the honey business, but the adjacent square of Pogacarjev Trg has stalls selling jars and bottles of gold-amber. The honey theme can be seen in other parts of the capital too: on the early 20th century Mestna Hranilnica bank building, there is a wrought-iron canopy featuring a bee, and at the National Museum, a bee motif floats over the entrance.

44

Less global in ambition, but another great champion of bees, is Blaz Ambrozic. He has turned his farm into a temple to bees, giving tours and advice to would-be beekeepers, as well as to visitors who want to buy his honey. He throws me a net-veil protective hat as soon as I arrive, so that I can stand closer to his main hive – and even encourages me to place tentative fingers inside.

45

The rather pessimistic mood lifts as he starts to tell me about his venture into 'apitherapy'. Across Slovenia, beekeepers have recently been modifying their hives to make them more interactive. In Ambrozic's case, he has expanded his largest hive into an L-shape, with a padded bed in the added corner.

46

Some have taken this concept of the bee as a purveyor of relaxation even further. I later stay in the picture-book town of Mozirje, where a quartet of holiday chalets can be rented. Looking out through the window of one, I see wildflowers swaying in the breeze. It is difficult to say whether bees or tourists will appreciate this panorama more – but both can surely draw inspiration from it.

A 20 kilometres north-east of the capital, in the village of Lukovica, the focus on bees is more scientific than decorative. This is where the headquarters of the Slovenian Beekeepers' Association has its laboratory for testing the quality of independent producers' honey. The association is also an impressive advocate for bees, as an official explains when I visit: in 2017, it managed to persuade the United Nations to launch World Bee Day as a way of raising awareness internationally of the importance of bees for ecosystems.

B Lie down on it, and you can peer through glass and watch the bees as they buzz in and out. Ten minutes gazing at these tireless creatures as they flit in and out of their base has an almost hypnotically calming effect.

C 'I was sceptical about whether you could put hives at this height,' he muses. 'But it didn't take long before it became my best site, in terms of honey. The bees don't actually seem to struggle to reach this elevation.'

D Slovenian beehives look different from the hives I'm familiar with, however. They are smaller, bees enter via narrow grooves at the front, and the frames are removed horizontally and from behind. This, apparently, is less stressful for bees and less likely to result in stings for keepers.

E Its busy residents are unmoved as I do so. 'Every bee has a specific role,' their keeper tells me. 'Some are collectors, others are guard dogs or kindergarten nurses.' Their importance, he stresses, cannot be underestimated. 'Bees are under threat. If bees are not here, then there is less pollination, and less food ... and then starvation. It's that simple.'

F It takes the form of a pair of short beehives. A cloud of bees shakes and shimmers in front of the access slits into the hives. This causes the stocky man next to me to smile.

G Such feelings are not unusual in Slovenia, where there are around 90,000 beekeepers in a population of just two million. Much of the country is forested, and bees thrive there. It even has a distinct strain of the insect – Carniolan bees, which are valued for their non-aggressive nature and team ethic.

Advice

41 In the sentence before gap 41, what might the writer see in the corner of the roof? And in the paragraph after gap 41, what are 'these twin outposts of his empire'? They must refer to something in the missing paragraph, so look for a phrase in an option which relates to 'twin' objects.

42 Look in the options for words or an idea related to the word 'doubts' in the sentence before gap 42.

43 The words 'this national affection' in the sentence after gap 43 must refer back to something in the missing paragraph. Look in the options for evidence of 'national affection'.

44 Look at the words 'another great champion of bees' in the sentence after gap 44. Can you find any reference to the idea of being a champion of bees in one of the options?

45 Look at the words 'the rather pessimistic mood' just after gap 45. Can you find anything suggesting a pessimistic mood in one of the options?

46 Look at the words 'this concept of the bee as a purveyor of relaxation' in the sentence after gap 46. What could these words link back to in one of the options?

Review

Answer the following questions about how to approach Part 8. If you need help, read the Task information on page 38.

Why might it be a good idea to:

1 start by reading all four sections quickly?

2 highlight key words in the questions?

3 read Section A carefully to see which questions it answers rather than start with question 47 and look across the four sections for the answer?

4 highlight the parts of the texts where you find the answers?

5 write the question numbers next to parts of the texts where you find the answers?

6 leave a question and come back to it later?

REPORTING VERBS

 TIP The questions often ask about ideas that are conveyed by one or two sentences, not just a few words.

1 Decide whether the following verbs are 'neutral' or 'convey attitude'.

| describe | highlight | suggest | deny | criticise | acknowledge | express regret |
| mention | confirm | dismiss | explain | claim | question | state | justify |

2 Use suitable verbs from the box above to complete the following sentences.

1 'I'm not obsessed by social media,' Chloe said.

Chloe .... being obsessed by social media.

2 'Is it really necessary to take on extra staff right now?' the finance manager asked.

The finance manager .... the need to take on extra staff.

3 'I'd like to make it clear that going paperless in the job I do is very difficult,' Jeff said.

Jeff .... the difficulty of going paperless in the job he does.

4 'The way the authorities reacted to the problem was totally inadequate,' the local residents said.

The local residents .... the authorities' reaction to the problem for being totally inadequate.

5 'It seems to me that there may be flaws in the methods used by their research team,' Professor Michaels said.

Professor Michaels .... that there were flaws in the methods used by their research team.

6 'I wish I hadn't given up running when I got that injury five years ago,' Sharon said.

Sharon .... about having given up running five years before.

7 'The idea of building a new road in this part of town is just out of the question,' Keith said.

Keith completely .... the idea of building a new road in that part of town.

8 'I completely agree we should all do our best to keep fit,' Marco said.

Marco fully .... the importance of trying to keep fit.

Read the Action plan on page 40. Then follow the exam instructions, using the advice below to help you.

You are going to read an article about yoga. For questions **47 – 56**, choose from the sections of the article (**A – D**). The sections may be chosen more than once.

Mark your answers **on the separate answer sheet**.

In which section does the writer

express unease about the inward-looking nature of yoga? **47** [ ]

describe being surprised by certain behaviour? **48** [ ]

refer to a sense of envy? **49** [ ]

mention suppressing concerns about the commercial exploitation of yoga? **50** [ ]

provide an explanation for giving up yoga? **51** [ ]

mention accepting her own perceived limitations? **52** [ ]

acknowledge the benefits that yoga brought her? **53** [ ]

indicate an aspect of yoga that can be seen as humorous? **54** [ ]

mention being proved wrong? **55** [ ]

offer an explanation for yoga's growing appeal? **56** [ ]

Advice

47 'Unease' is a feeling of being worried about something. Even if you haven't seen the word 'inward-looking' before, you should be able to understand it because it has a literal meaning.

48 The writer refers to people's behaviour in more than one section of the text, but only describes being surprised by it in one section.

49 Look for parts of the text where the writer mentions her attitude towards other people.

50 The writer refers to the commercial side of yoga in more than one text. Where does she mention that she had concerns about it?

51 The writer mentions leaving a class in more than one text. There is only one text where she explains why she gave up yoga.

52 When you 'accept your limitations' you are realistic about what you can and can't do. 'perceived limitations' are limitations that you think you have.

53 The writer mentions doing yoga in more than one text. There is only one text where she describes how it benefited her.

54 Look for words that are related to the idea of 'humour'.

55 Sometimes you need to read two sentences which are quite separate in a section in order to find the answer. Look for a sentence where the writer makes a prediction and then another sentence later where she indicates that her prediction was wrong.

56 The writer refers to the popularity of yoga in more than one text, but there is only one text where she specifically explains why it's growing in popularity.

The rise of yoga

Yoga has become a big business in certain parts of the world. Australian journalist Maggie Curran reports on her own experiences of the ancient discipline.

A

A decade ago, I was commissioned to interview an up-and-coming yoga entrepreneur whose particular brand of yoga involved 26 poses in a humid, heated room with mirrors and carpets. When I visited the man's studio and caught the stench and the robotic instructions from a mic'd-up teacher, I thought: 'This will never take off.' I had been doing a relatively gentle form of yoga for several years, but had never managed to get beyond beginners' level. I had come to assume that was all I was capable of, but somehow had never stopped completely. Halfway through the interview, the yoga businessman looked at me and said: 'You're overweight. You should join my classes. It would transform your life.' 'What?' was all I could splutter in response to this breach in interview etiquette. For years after that interview, I would walk past that man's expanding chain of studios and think: 'How could someone like that become so successful?' At the same time, I wondered if he'd had a point – was it possible to completely change your body shape by doing his yoga? And should this even be an aspiration?

B

These days, yoga has morphed from being an exercise you might do once a week in a gym to a way of life, and a physical and spiritual ideal to aspire to. About 40 million people are estimated to practise yoga in the US and the global yoga market is worth over $80bn. It's not just the studios; yoga mats and clothing have become must-have items in certain places. In my area of Sydney, upmarket yogis have colonised the high street. Most people seem to have stopped wearing proper clothes. Unless you are around the bus stops in time for the morning commute, you see people dressed almost exclusively in exercise gear – yoga pants, vest top and hoodies, flip-flops in the summer, trainers in winter. Rich targets for satirists, these 'devotees' cycle around the neighbourhood, with rolled-up yoga mats on their backs, in search of organic fruit and vegetables. Ludicrous as they are in some ways, though, it would be dishonest not to disclose that I once secretly yearned to be one of them and to have what they had.

C

In many respects, yoga is the perfect pastime for our age – the meditative elements give us the opportunity to find peace and stillness in a time of increasingly hectic and crowded information, the instructional bits give us moral lessons, while the stretchy, bendy, sweaty physical stuff is a great way of countering hours a day spent hunched over a computer. Early last year, putting to the back of my mind any qualms I had about the ethics of how a 5,000-year-old spiritual discipline has been turned into a profit-making machine, I left my old class and joined an intensive programme to become 'a modern yogi'. This meant attending classes six times a week, meditating daily, keeping a journal and taking part in weekly meetings that are part tutorial on mindfulness and part group therapy. I stuck with it and found things started to shift. My body felt looser, more pliable. Physically it was tough, and it took a month to really get my fitness level moving, but gradually I was able to keep up with the most athletic classes and my skin and hair seemed to glow.

D

I then started thinking about what I was doing – about the nature of yoga and how so many people pour energy into their bodies when perhaps they should be trying to pour energy into the people and politics around them. Self-care is great – but what if there's no energy left to care about anyone else? I wrote in my journal, I went to the Monday night tutorials, I meditated, I drank juices, I did all the right things to become a modern yogi. I was on the way to joining the ranks of the chilled-out people I saw every day around me. I was almost there before I started wondering – is this really what I wanted to be? The answer was, of course, no. I kept at it for about two months before the narcissism of the whole enterprise got to me. There were other things, it turned out, that I had to do.

Review

Decide which of the items below are compulsory and which are optional in a Part 1 task. If they are compulsory, explain briefly what the requirement is. If you need help, read the Task information on page 42.

1 the type of task
2 the number of words you write
3 the number of bullet points in the question to write about
4 which bullet points you write about
5 using the opinions included in the question
6 using the same language as in the question
7 giving reasons for your own opinions

TIP Practise writing within the word limit so you know what the essay looks like on the page. Don't waste time in the exam counting words.

ORGANISING YOUR WRITING

1 Read the task below and the sample essay that follows. Then answer these questions about the essay.

1 Which two points did the writer choose to discuss?
2 What examples did the writer give for each point?
3 According to the writer, which of the influences is most powerful and why?

Your class has been following a series of radio programmes about choices young people have to make and the different things that influence them in these choices. You have made the notes below:

Influences on young people's choices

- family and friends
- money
- society

Some opinions expressed in the discussion:

"My friends and family always know what's best for me."

"Money always gives you freedom."

"There are far too many rules about what we should and shouldn't do."

Write an essay discussing **two** of the influences in your notes. You should **explain which influence is the most powerful**, **giving reasons** in support of your answer.

You may, if you wish, make use of the opinions expressed in the discussion, but you should use your own words as far as possible.

Young people have many decisions to make about education, work, travel and home, to name just a few. This can all seem pretty overwhelming at times, so it's no surprise that young people need guidance and support.

This support can come from family members and close friends. They care about the people trying to make the choices and are in the best position to make good suggestions. However, young people should bear in mind that this influence may not always be positive. Are they making choices that are right for them, or are they doing what is expected of them by their family? Are they choosing something that will make them happy, or just copying their friends? Sometimes it's necessary to stand back and check that choices are being made for the right reasons.

Money is also a key factor. Whether we like it or not, everyone – and young people are no exception – needs money to do what they want to do. Otherwise their options are severely limited. Can you travel abroad without money? Maybe, but not easily or quickly. And try finding a suitable place to live with limited funds! It's a struggle. Often a career choice is made because of the salary rather than because it is exactly the right job.

It is clear that both these factors have a huge influence on the choices made by young people. Of the two, the influence of those closest to them is the most powerful, mainly because it's something they may not even be fully aware of.

2 Answer these questions about the sample essay.
   1 What is the topic of each paragraph?
   2 What is the topic sentence in paragraphs 2 and 3? Where does it occur in each paragraph?

TIP The topic sentence announces the topic that is developed in the paragraph. When you move from one point to the next, a topic sentence helps prepare readers for what to expect.

USEFUL LANGUAGE: LINKING EXPRESSIONS AND REFERENCING

 The sentences below are from different essays and all link ideas in a variety of ways. Identify and correct the errors. The first one has been done for you.

1 It's becoming more and more expensive to attend university, as **it** is shown by the fall in the number of people choosing to go there.

2 What is important is to learn from your mistakes so that the same thing it isn't repeated.

3 It was thanks to that experiences that I was offered the job.

4 I noticed an improvement in the facilities as soon as arrived.

5 As a result the new measures, pollution on the streets has decreased significantly.

6 New laws are the only way of guaranteeing that the same thing it won't be repeated.

7 The results is not only unexpected, but also impressive.

8 Teachers should find ways to develop students' learning instead giving homework every day.

Read the Action plan on page 44. Then look at the exam task below and answer these questions.

1 What is the issue that you have to discuss?

2 How could each of the three points relate to the topic?

3 Which two of the three points are you going to focus on?

4 To what extent will you use the opinions expressed in the task in your answer?

5 Which of the two points you've selected will you say is more effective?

6 What reasons will you give in arguing that this point is more effective than the other one?

Now follow the exam instructions, using the advice to help you.

You **must** answer this question. Write your answer in **220 – 260** words in an appropriate style on the separate answer sheet.

---

1 Your class has listened to a radio discussion about ways in which people can be encouraged to have an interest in science. You have made the notes below:

Ways to encourage people to have an interest in science

- science museums
- school lessons
- the internet

Some opinions expressed in the discussion:

"Modern science museums have events and activities, not just displays."

"Lots of people I know found science at school boring."

"You can learn about science by just using your phone."

Advice

1 The question asks about 'people' so be sure to think about different groups of people (not just young people, for instance).

2 What prevents people from attending science museums? What encourages them?

3 Why might science lessons in school be boring? What would make them interesting?

4 How can people use the internet to find out about science?

Write an essay discussing **two** of the ways to encourage people to have an interest in science in your notes. You should **explain which way is more effective**, **giving reasons** to justify your choice.

You may, if you wish, make use of the opinions expressed in the discussion, but you should use your own words as far as possible.

Review

Are the following statements about Part 2 True or False? Correct them if they are false. If you need help, read the Task information on page 46.

1 You can choose which question to answer.
2 There's always the option to write a review.
3 You should write around the same number of words as in Part 1.
4 You have free choice about what to include in your answer.

 TIP For any writing task, consider four key issues.
Purpose: why am I writing?
Audience: who am I writing to?
Content: what do they need to know?
Layout: how will I present the information on the page?

IDENTIFYING CONTENT

Look at the sample Part 2 tasks below and identify the points that need to be included in each answer. There are three points in each task.

1 You have read the following notice on your local council's website.

> As part of our review of recycling in our area, the council is keen to receive letters from the public about what they think of the recycling facilities currently available and why, and their suggestions for improvements. All comments are welcomed, both positive and negative.

You decide to write a letter giving your thoughts and asking to be kept informed about the decisions made.

2 A group of English-speaking students is coming to visit your college for three weeks in May. You have been asked by the college principal to write an email to one of the students, telling them what to expect during those three weeks, at college and in their daily life. You should offer to spend time with them to help them settle in and include information about how they can make the most of their stay.

3 The managers of a tourist attraction are looking for ways to increase its popularity and have asked visitors to send in reviews and suggestions. The best reviews will be included on their new website. Write a review of a tourist attraction that you have visited. Your review should include details about what you enjoyed about the attraction, and you should say who the attraction might appeal to and why. You should also recommend one way in which the attraction could be improved.

USEFUL LANGUAGE: OPENINGS AND CONCLUSIONS

1 Put the following statements into a table with columns labelled 'Reason for writing' and 'Concluding comment'. Decide whether they are suitable for formal (F), informal (I) or neutral (N) texts.

Letters and emails

- Should you require any further information, please do not hesitate to contact me.
- If you've got any questions, drop me a line.
- I would appreciate your immediate attention regarding this matter.
- Can't wait to see you.
- Thank you in advance.
- Thank you for your letter of 1st May concerning ...
- Lovely to hear from you!

Reports and proposals

- As requested, this report/proposal outlines ...
- Based on the information given above, my recommendation is to ...
- This proposal concerns the possibility of ...

Reviews

- I would have no hesitation in recommending ...
- Read on for my thoughts on the recent music festival.

2 ⊙ **Complete the gaps in the additional examples below and add them to the table.**

- I am writing in connection .... your proposed meeting.
- I'm writing .... ask ...
- Sorry for the delay .... getting in touch.
- I look forward to hearing from you in .... course.
- With reference to your letter .... 19th June, ...
- Thank you .... your assistance in this matter.
- So, if you're looking for a new mobile phone, this is .... one!

<table><tr><td>TIP</td><td>Learn closing greetings which are suitable for different styles of letters and emails: 'Yours faithfully/sincerely' for formal letters; '(Best/ Kind) regards' for letters and emails in a range of contexts; 'Love' or 'All the best' for writing to friends.</td></tr></table>

USEFUL LANGUAGE: FUNCTIONAL EXPRESSIONS

1 **Read the quotes from candidates' answers and match them with the functions in the box. Then decide which of the tasks in Exercise 1 each quote relates to.**

give an opinion	make a suggestion	make a request	recommend	make an offer

1 I'd love to give you a tour of the local area.
2 I'd be grateful if you could respond to this letter with details of the plans you make.
3 As far as I'm concerned, there is plenty of room for improvement.
4 Why don't you fine people for not recycling?
5 The best solution to this problem would be to enlarge the gift shop.
6 What I'd do is bring clothes for wet weather, just in case.
7 What about reducing the entrance fees?
8 You might want to think about installing bins at the end of every street.

2 **Complete these sentences with one word in each gap. Then match the sentences with the functions in Exercise 1.**

1 .... you considered increasing the frequency of rubbish collections? (........................)
2 .... my mind, this will be a huge benefit to the organisation. (........................)
3 If I .... you, I'd keep the gallery open later in the evening. (........................)
4 Would it be of any help .... I sent you a few brochures of the area? (........................)
5 .... a doubt, you need a raincoat for this time of year. (........................)
6 I am hoping you .... be able to send me a copy of your report. (........................)
7 The .... I see it, this is one of the biggest issues facing us at the moment. (........................)
8 You .... better check whether any trips have already been organised. (........................)
9 You don't mind bringing me a souvenir of your country, ... you? (........................)
10 It would be a good idea if you .... some research into the size of recycling bins. (........................)

Read the Action plan on page 49. Then look at each of the tasks 2–4 below and answer these questions.

1 Which task do you think would be the best one for you to choose?

2 What factors do you need to consider when choosing a task?

Now follow the exam instructions, using the advice to help you.

Write an answer to **one** of the questions **2 – 4** in this part. Write your answer in **220 – 260** words in an appropriate style on the separate answer sheet. Put the question number in the box at the top of the page.

2 The international college where you study has some funds available for students to take short educational trips. You decide to write a proposal to the college principal proposing a short trip for you and your classmates in connection with your studies. You should describe the trip, explaining how it would benefit you and your classmates. Your proposal should also explain how you could share your experiences with other students in the college.

Write your **proposal**.

3 You have received an email from an English-speaking friend:

> …
>
> I'm really enjoying college! I'm trying my best to be responsible with my money, but it can be hard. What advice could you give me about managing my money? Do you have any tips to help me spend less? What do you think about working part time while studying?
>
> Write back soon!
>
> Suzy

Write your **email**.

4 You work for an international company and recently went on a short training course to develop a skill related to your job. Now your manager would like you to write a report about your training. You should describe the course, evaluating its strengths and weaknesses. You should also explain whether or not you would recommend the course for other employees in the company.

Write your **report**.

Advice

2 *Proposals should be persuasive, with judgements based on objective facts. In this case you are writing to your principal, so the register should be formal or neutral, not informal.*

3 *This email is for a friend, so think about the style you should write in. Also, you are asked for advice, so think about a range of structures you can use for that.*

4 *It is important to write in a style that is appropriate for a report to a person in authority.*

Review

Complete the information about Listening Part 1. In the second paragraph, the first letter of the missing word is given. If you need help, read the Task information on page 51.

In Part 1, candidates listen to **(1)** .... short dialogues. For each dialogue there are **(2)** ....
questions. Each question has **(3)** .... options.

In Part 1, candidates show their understanding of, for example, the main message, **(4)** a d ....,
the speaker's feeling or **(5)** o ...., or whether the speakers **(6)** a .... with each other.

GETTING INFORMATION FROM QUESTIONS

Read the questions (not the options) for the three extracts in the Exam Practice Test on page 97 and answer these questions about them.

Question 1

1 Which speaker must you focus on to get the answer?
2 What feeling do you have to listen out for?
3 What do you think this speaker has recently done?

Question 2

1 How does this question differ in format from question 1 ?
2 Which speaker must you focus on to get the answer?
3 Do you have to listen for this speaker talking about similarities or differences?

Question 3

1 Will you have to listen to one or two speakers to get the answer? Why?
2 What phrases do you know that express agreement?
3 Why do you think architecture students might be talking about trends in shopping?

Question 4

1 From the question, what can you assume about the gender of the speakers?
2 Which speaker must you focus on to get the answer?
3 How many advantages of skyways do you think you will hear this speaker mention and why?

Question 5

1 Which speaker must you focus on to get the answer?
2 To answer this question, do you need to listen to the speaker talking about the past or the future?
3 How could you paraphrase *raise public awareness*?

Question 6

1 Which speaker must you focus on to get the answer?
2 Do you expect the answer to be stated or only implied in the recording? Why?
3 How could you paraphrase *are more likely*?

Read the Action plan on page 52. Then follow the exam instructions, using the advice below to help you.

 You will hear three different extracts. For questions **1 – 6**, choose the answer (**A**, **B** or **C**) which fits best according to what you hear. There are two questions for each extract.

Extract One

You hear Nathalie and her brother David talking about thriller movies.

1 What is Nathalie surprised to read about thriller movies?

  A that very logical people tend to prefer them

  B that families who enjoy watching them together are happiest

  C that when we watch them, our bodies produce a chemical

2 David thinks watching horror movies is similar to going on a short holiday because both activities

  A allow people to escape everyday problems.

  B make people feel emotionally stronger.

  C stimulate people's creativity.

Extract Two

You hear two architecture students discussing covered overhead walkways called 'city skyways'.

3 What do they agree about trends in shopping?

  A Skyways have led to a decline in the number of city-centre shops.

  B Out-of-town shopping malls are less popular nowadays.

  C Increased deliveries from online shopping will cause problems.

4 What does the man think is the greatest advantage of skyways?

  A They are climate-controlled.

  B They are safe areas for pedestrians.

  C They are a solution to overcrowded streets.

Extract Three

You hear a radio discussion in which two educationalists, Sophie Lee and Gary Cole, are talking about sport.

5 Gary would like to raise public awareness of how sport contributes to

  A a child's social development.

  B a child's physical health and growth.

  C a child's understanding of the need for rules.

6 Sophie says that children who do sport are more likely to

  A go on to further education.

  B have a good school attendance record.

  C be motivated to succeed academically.

Advice

1 The speaker's expression of surprise might follow the idea she is talking about, so listen attentively.

2 Listen out for another way of saying 'short holiday' – then you'll know you should focus on question 2.

3 Listen carefully to what the woman says about shops in her first turn and then listen to what the man agrees about.

4 This question asks about 'the greatest advantage'. That means the man will talk about all three advantages in options A, B and C, but will indicate that one of them is 'the greatest'.

5 You will hear similar words to those in all three options in the recording, so make sure you answer the question here.

6 Listen right until the end of the recording because that will help you answer this question.

Review

Answer these questions about Part 2. If you need help, read the Task information on page 54.

1 What task type will you always get in Part 2?
2 Approximately how many words should your answer be for each gap?
3 Do you have to write exactly the same word(s) as you hear on the recording?
4 Will the information and ideas in the recording be in the same order as the information and ideas in the questions?

PREDICTION

1 The context sentence, the title and the questions give information about what you will hear before you start listening. Look at the context sentence on page 99 and answer these questions.

1 The student

   A is a man.   **B** is a woman.   **C** could be a man or woman.

2 The student studies

   A history.   **B** geography.   **C** Egyptian.

3 The student is talking to

   A a class.   **B** a teacher.   **C** a tour group in Egypt.

2 Read the sentences for questions 7–14 on page 99 and decide which type of word goes in each gap (e.g. a verb, a noun, etc.).

3 Read the sentences again. Can you tell if the answer is in the singular or plural form, and do you think the answer is a concrete noun (e.g. *bird*) or an abstract noun (e.g. *freedom*)? Give reasons for your answers.

> **TIP** Try to predict what sort of word can fill each gap so that your answer fits the sentence grammatically. You should not make any changes to the word you hear on the recording.

4 Think through questions 7–14 by considering these questions. Make notes of your answers. After you have completed the task in the Exam practice, go back and see how many answers you predicted.

> **TIP** Try to predict what the answer could be to each question before you start listening. That will help make sure that your answer makes sense in the sentence.

7 Who might have worked for the government in ancient Egypt? They must have been quite important if they were buried in tombs that were decorated.

8 How do you think the animals could be acting in paintings on the walls of tombs?

9 What things might people in ancient Egypt have used to make paint? They must be things that they had to grind.

10 What sort of thing might have been harvested in ancient Egypt?

11 Who might have needed lots of training for fighting in ancient Egypt?

12 What could birds flying symbolise, in your opinion?

13 What types of animals associated with Egypt could be good hunters?

14 What quality might these combined animals show us about Egyptian religious beliefs?

Read the Action plan on page 55. Then follow the exam instructions, using the advice below to help you.

You will hear a history student, called Kylie, giving a presentation to her class about an archaeological site in Egypt called Beni Hassan. For questions **7 – 14**, complete the sentences with a word or short phrase.

TIP You might hear synonyms or paraphrases of the words in the sentences, so before you start listening, think about how words in the sentences could be rephrased.

BENI HASSAN ARCHAEOLOGICAL SITE

The tombs that fascinate Kylie are the ones where **(7)** .... who worked for the government were buried.

The paintings on the walls of many tombs show a good understanding of the **(8)** .... of animals.

Kylie explains that the paint was made by grinding up various **(9)** .... before it was applied to the walls.

The annual harvest, where **(10)** .... was gathered, is found in some of the paintings that Kylie has seen.

Kylie agrees that the wrestling scenes show that **(11)** .... underwent rigorous training.

Kylie has found out that birds that are flying are thought to represent **(12)** .... in the paintings.

Animals such as **(13)** .... were used to help hunters catch other animals.

Kylie explains that creatures made up of two different animals show the **(14)** .... of the ancient people's religious beliefs.

Advice

7 Don't worry if you are not sure about the meaning of a word, e.g. 'tomb', because there will usually be a clue to help you understand its meaning elsewhere in the sentence. Here, 'buried' helps you understand 'tomb'.

8 Both British and American spelling are acceptable, so don't waste time thinking about which one is correct for the sentence.

9 If you think about the past tense of 'grind', that will help you answer this question.

10 Listen carefully to find out what is shown in paintings that Kylie has seen, not ones she has heard about.

11 Who might do wrestling as a form of training?

12 What are some paraphrases of 'find out'?

13 'Such as' always means that the answer will be an example of something.

14 Check your spelling of this answer carefully.

Review

Answer these questions about Listening Part 3. If you need help, read the Task information on page 56.

1 How many people will you hear in Part 3?
2 Approximately how long is the recording?
3 How many options are there for each of the six questions?
4 Why is it important to read the context sentence carefully?

SYNONYMS AND PARAPHRASE

1 Match the verbs on the left with their synonym or paraphrase on the right. These verbs are often used in Part 3 questions.

1	think	a	express disapproval
2	mention	b	propose
3	suggest	c	believe something will happen
4	explain	d	say you will certainly do something
5	admit	e	refer to
6	criticise	f	agree reluctantly that something is true
7	expect	g	make understandable
8	promise	h	believe something or have an idea or opinion

2 Look at the options for questions 15–20 on page 101 and find words that match these synonyms or paraphrases.

Question 15
1 making us feel healthier and more energetic
2 the state of not changing as years go past

Question 16
3 embarrassed

Question 17
4 the action of being worn away by waves and wind
5 causing bad effects

Question 18
6 not easy to find
7 worry
8 need

Question 19
9 the act of providing money for a business

Question 20
10 consider again in order to improve
11 force people to follow

Read the Action plan on page 57. Then follow the exam instructions, using the advice below to help you.

 You will hear a radio interview in which two ecologists, called Jack Benson and Trisha Roberts, are talking about sand. For questions **15 – 20**, choose the answer (**A**, **B**, **C** or **D**) which fits best according to what you hear.

15 Jack thinks the main reason people are attracted to beaches is because

    A we enjoy a feeling of timelessness there.
    B we find breathing the fresh salty air invigorating.
    C the sound of the waves is hypnotic.
    D the quality of the light is special.

16 What was Trisha's reaction when she read an article about 'pop-up' beaches?

    A She was surprised the topic hadn't been explored before.
    B She wanted to research the phenomenon more.
    C She was ashamed at having visited one.
    D She questioned the advice in the article.

17 Jack and Trisha agree that the practice of adding fresh sand to beaches

    A is less effective against coastal erosion than building a seawall.
    B can only be a short-term solution to coastal erosion.
    C interferes with the normal movement of the sea.
    D must be harmful to the wildlife there.

18 Why does Jack mention the fact that more people live in cities nowadays?

    A to criticise people's lack of awareness of environmental issues
    B to illustrate that natural resources are becoming scarce
    C to suggest society's major concern is making money
    D to explain why the demand for sand is so high

19 Trisha is particularly concerned that removing sand from beaches may result in

    A a change in the lifestyles of coastal communities.
    B the creation of new micro climates.
    C fewer visitors going to those areas.
    D the need for considerable financial investment.

20 What does Jack hope will solve the problem of taking sand from beaches?

    A Scientists will develop a new form of sand.
    B Architects will rethink the design of buildings.
    C Governments will impose stricter regulations.
    D The public will become better informed.

Advice

15 Listen carefully for what Jack thinks, not other people or a friend of his.

16 Listen to everything Trisha says about pop-up beaches and don't be distracted if you hear a word on the recording that is in one of the options. That doesn't mean that this option is the answer.

17 Don't forget that you won't always hear a simple phrase to show agreement. Speakers can show they agree by using a wide range of language.

18 Think carefully about the meaning of the verb used at the beginning of each option.

19 The options are sometimes a generalisation of an example given in the recording.

20 Can you think of some specific examples of types of scientist?

Review

Answer these questions about Listening Part 4. If you need help, read the Task information on page 59.

What information is given in the instructions for Part 4 about:

1 the number of short extracts you will hear?
2 the number of questions for each task?
3 the number of options for each task?
4 the number of times you hear the whole series of extracts?

IDEAS AND ATTITUDES EXPRESSED ABOUT THE THEME BY THE SPEAKERS

1 In the Part 4 task on page 103, the theme that links all five short extracts is the future of work. Try to get a feel for who the speakers are by reading these sentences from the recording. What sort of business person do you think each speaker might be?

Speaker 1

I've just got the results of a questionnaire which I sent out to my company's offices in eight countries.

Speaker 2

As I'm still only in my 20s and in my first job ever, I'm aware that by working in a range of different companies, I'll build up useful business experience.

Speaker 3

I've been carrying out interviews with shoppers for a paper I'm writing for a business journal.

Speaker 4

I've been in business for over 40 years and will be retiring soon.

Speaker 5

I give lectures at a business school.

2 Tick the phrases that the speakers could use to express their opinion or attitude.

1 I have no doubt that …
2 Some fears were expressed about …
3 It was clear that people were very keen to …
4 I can't see myself …
5 The trend is …

6 In my view, …
7 It's imperative that …
8 I'm sure …
9 (It) makes sense …
10 if I were to make an educated guess, I'd say …

3 Look at the areas of research in Task One and the predictions about the future of work in Task Two. Think about how they could be expressed using different words and phrases.

Read the Action plan on page 60. Then follow the exam instructions.

🎧 13

You will hear five short extracts in which business people are talking about the future of work.

TASK ONE

For questions **21 – 25**, choose from the list (**A – H**) the focus of each person's research into the future of work.

TASK TWO

For questions **26 – 30**, choose from the list (**A – H**) the prediction each person makes about work.

While you listen you must complete both tasks.

TASK ONE		TASK TWO	
A the social aspect of work		A More jobs will be done by machines.	
B the customers' perspective		B The cost of manufacturing will fall.	
C the standard of living		C Cities will continue to attract workers.	
D communications		D People will retire later than at present.	
E job satisfaction		E More people will work for themselves.	
F globalisation		F Trust in large companies will decrease.	
G business and ecology		G Leadership will be a more democratic process.	
H a historical comparison		H Ongoing learning will become more common.	

Speaker 1 | 21
Speaker 2 | 22
Speaker 3 | 23
Speaker 4 | 24
Speaker 5 | 25

Speaker 1 | 26
Speaker 2 | 27
Speaker 3 | 28
Speaker 4 | 29
Speaker 5 | 30

Review

Are the following statements about Part 1 True or False? Correct them if they are false. If you need help, read the Task information on page 61.

1 In this part of the test, you are encouraged to speak with your partner.
2 Both examiners will ask you questions to help you relax.
3 The questions in this part are on familiar, personal topics.
4 Part 1 lasts about 2 minutes (3 minutes for groups of three candidates).

DEVELOPING YOUR ANSWERS

1 Listen to the two example questions and responses. What do you think about the responses? Think about the range of vocabulary (Lexical Resource) and the extent of the answer (Discourse Management).

14

2 Look at an alternative answer to the first question in the recording for Exercise 1. Can you suggest an improved response to the second question?

> **Interlocutor:** How important is it for you to spend time with your friends?

> **Candidate:** Making sure that I take time away from studying to be with my mates is essential. It's the best way of relaxing.

> **Interlocutor:** What kind of films do you enjoy watching?

> **Candidate:** ....

TIP You should aim to give extended answers and demonstrate a range of vocabulary. One way of doing this is to avoid repeating the exact words used in the questions.

3 Write extended responses to the following Part 1 questions.
- How do you think your life might change over the next five years?
- Which is your favourite room in your home?
- Which sports do you enjoy most?
- Tell me about an amazing place you have visited.
- Is music important in your life?

TIP One way of varying your answers is to use different word types. For example, if the question uses a verb ('What kind of books do you enjoy reading?'), you might answer using a noun phrase ('I get a lot of pleasure from reading crime stories').

Read the Action plan on page 62. Then work with a partner if possible and do the exam task, following the instructions below. Take it in turn to act in the role of the interlocutor.

Part 1
2 minutes (3 minutes for groups of three)

The interlocutor asks you some questions about yourself, your home, work or studies and familiar topics.

Good morning / afternoon / evening. My name is ... and this is my colleague ... .

And your names are?

Can I have your mark sheets, please?

Thank you.

First of all, we'd like to know something about you.

- Where are you from?
- What do you do here / there?
- How long have you been studying English?
- What do you enjoy most about studying English?

The interlocutor then asks you some questions about one or two other topics, for example:

- Do you think you have enough free time during the week? Why? / Why not?
- What's your favourite weekend activity? Why?
- How do you feel about extreme sports?
- Tell me about a special meal you have recently had.

 TIP To give yourself thinking time, use expressions such as 'I haven't thought about that.' / 'That's an interesting question.'

 TIP Remember to extend your answers with at least one or two sentences. For example, in answer to 'Have you travelled anywhere interesting recently?', don't just say: 'Yes, to London'. Add more, for example: 'Last month, I spent a couple of days there and we took in a show and went to a great exhibition. I particularly enjoyed the show, which was ...'.

Review

Complete the task information details below. If you need help, read the Task information on page 63.

If you need help, read the Task information on page 63.

1 You will talk on your own for about .... minute(s).

2 You are given .... photographs. You choose .... to talk about.

3 You have to answer .... question(s) related to the theme represented by the photographs.

4 After your partner has finished talking, you have about .... seconds to answer a question about your partner's pictures.

5 Part 2 lasts approximately .... minutes in total for pairs of candidates (................................ minutes for a group of three candidates).

> **TIP** If you forget the questions the interlocutor asked, they are written at the top of the picture sheet.

USEFUL LANGUAGE: REFERENCING AND SUBSTITUTION

1 Look at the first two pictures on page S6 and answer the questions. Then listen to a candidate answering these questions. What do you notice about her response?

15

- **Why might the people need to listen carefully in these situations?**
- **What might be the consequences of them not listening carefully?**

2 Now listen to another candidate doing the same task and complete the gaps in the audioscript.

16

The first picture shows a girl and a woman in a garden, whereas in **(1)** .... there's just a man on his own. It certainly looks like the woman is listening carefully to what the girl's saying and pointing at, but I wouldn't say **(2)** .... is vital information. **(3)** .... are probably just discussing the plants and **(4)** .... need watering. I suppose if the woman didn't listen carefully, the plants might not do well, particularly if the girl is telling **(5)** .... about some special attention **(6)** .... need. On the other hand, the information in the second picture is pretty important. It looks to me as if the man is standing on a station platform and giving an announcement, probably something about the timetable or a platform change. Announcements **(7)** .... are often very difficult to hear, particularly in noisy, crowded stations – although **(8)** .... appears deserted – so it's essential to listen carefully. Missing the announcement, or not hearing **(9)** .... correctly, could mean you end up missing your train.

> **TIP** Aim to compare the two pictures early on, so you don't forget to include the element of comparison or contrast that is required by the task.

> **TIP** Referencing pronouns (e.g. *the woman > her*) and substitution (e.g. *the plants > ones*) help you organise your ideas effectively and avoid repetition.

3 The questions for the third and fourth pictures on page S6 are the same as in Exercise 1. Practise comparing these pictures and answering the questions, using referencing and substitution where possible.

Read the Action plan on page 64. Then do the exam task, following the instructions below.

Part 2
4 minutes (6 minutes for groups of three)

Work in groups of three if possible. One of you is the interlocutor and the other two are the candidates. The interlocutor should lead the task using the script below. Refer to the pictures on pages S7 and S8.

Interlocutor   In this part of the test, I'm going to give each of you three pictures. I'd like you to talk about **two** of them on your own for about a minute, and also to answer a question briefly about your partner's pictures.

[Candidate A], it's your turn first. Here are your pictures. They show **people preparing for different events**. I'd like you to compare two of the pictures and say **what these people might be preparing for and how you think they're feeling**.

All right?

🕐 *After 1 minute*   Thank you.

[Candidate B], **who do you think will need the longest time to prepare? (Why?)**

🕐 *After 30 seconds* Thank you.

Now, *[Candidate B]*, here are your pictures. They show **people showing things to others.** I'd like you to compare two of the pictures and say **why the people might be showing these things to others and how interested the others might be in what they're being shown**.

🕐 *After 1 minute*   Thank you.

Now, *[Candidate A]*, **who do you think will remember what they're seeing for the longest time? Why?**

🕐 *After 30 seconds* Thank you.

TIP   Remember to use language for speculation when answering the questions (e.g. 'The girls might be preparing for a holiday, but on the other hand they could be going away for just a couple of days. I'd probably say a holiday because of the amount of stuff in the suitcase.').

Review

What can you remember? Make notes on these key points for Parts 3 and 4. Then look at pages 65 and 67 to check your answers.

1 Topics   2 Who speaks   3 Task focus   4 Timing

USEFUL LANGUAGE: RESPONDING TO AND LINKING WITH CONTRIBUTIONS

1 Look at the Part 3 task and then listen to two candidates doing the task. Listen to how they begin, respond to and make links with contributions made by the other speaker(s). How successful are they at doing this?

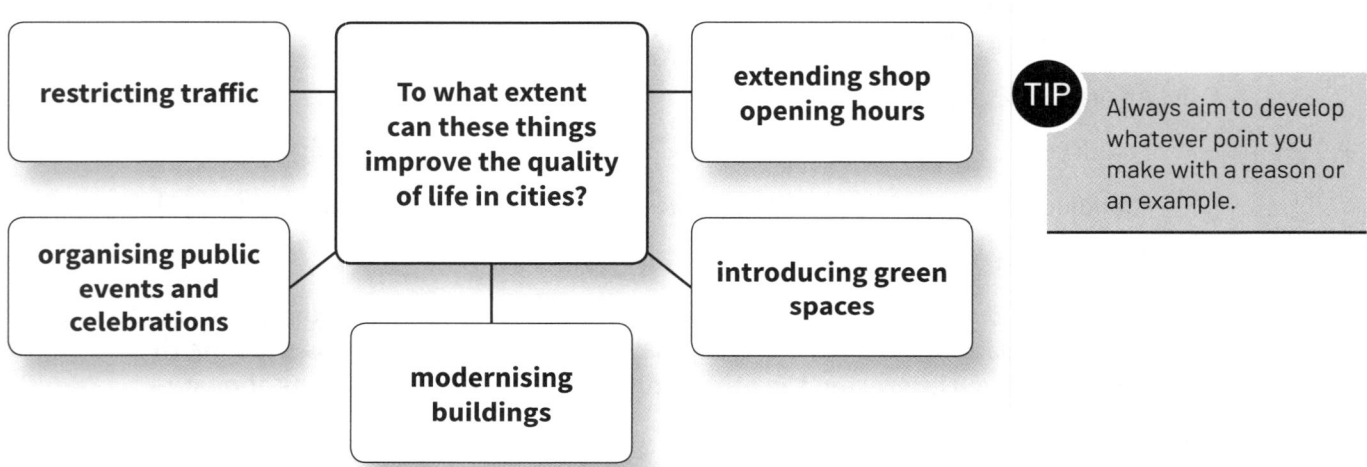

- restricting traffic
- To what extent can these things improve the quality of life in cities?
- extending shop opening hours
- organising public events and celebrations
- modernising buildings
- introducing green spaces

TIP Always aim to develop whatever point you make with a reason or an example.

2 Complete the expressions below with words from the box. Some gaps can be filled by more than one of the words. Then listen to two other candidates doing the task in Exercise 1 and check your answers.

> more   be   point   hadn't   not   so   absolutely   exactly   what   case   about   maybe   yes

1 That's a good ....

2 I see / know .... you mean.

3 I .... thought of that.

4 I couldn't agree ....

5 .... necessarily.

6 That's not always the ....

7 Do you think ....? I'd say ...

8 ....! I was just .... to say the same thing.

9 .... , but ...

10 That may .... true, but ...

TIP One way of making your discussion natural, is to invite responses from your partner. For example, you can use tag questions.

3 Work with a partner to practise your own response to the task in Exercise 1.

TIP Time yourself doing the task. The two minutes may not be as long as you think!

USEFUL LANGUAGE: AGREEMENT AND DISAGREEMENT

1 👁 Natural interaction often involves agreeing or disagreeing with someone. Complete the gaps in these sentences and decide whether they indicate strong or weak agreement / disagreement.

1 I sort of agree with you, but only p_ _ _ _ _ _ _ _ .

2 I agree with you u_ t_ a point, but …

3 I t_ _ _ _ _ _ disagree.

4 I agree with you e_ _ _ _ _ _ _ on that point.

5 No d_ _ _ _ you're right about that.

6 I must take i_ _ _ _ with you on that.

7 Of course, that g_ _ _ without s_ _ _ _ _ .

8 I see where you're c_ _ _ _ _ from on that point.

9 Yes, I'd go a_ _ _ _ with that idea.

10 I t_ _ _ your point, but I'm not sure I agree.

11 I k_ _ _ of agree with you on that.

2 Work with a partner to discuss the sample Part 4 questions below. Use the expressions from the previous exercises to agree, disagree and interact naturally.

- What would you do to improve your own local town or city?
- Who is responsible for making a town or city a good place to live in: the local government or the citizens?
- Would you agree that cities are lonely places to live in?
- Should public transport be free for all people?
- Some people say that you can only get a good quality of life by living in the countryside. What's your view?
- Do you think that going out to do your shopping will soon become a thing of the past?

Read the Action plans on pages 66 and 68. Then do the exam task, following the instructions below.

Part 3

4 minutes (6 minutes for groups of three candidates)

Work in groups of three if possible. One of you is the interlocutor and the other two are the candidates. The interlocutor should lead the task using the script below. Refer to the task sheet on page S9. The candidates should discuss this task sheet together.

Interlocutor Now I'd like you to talk about something together for about two minutes.

Here are some things that people think about when choosing where to live and a question for you to discuss. First you have some time to look at the task.

🕐 *After 15 seconds* Now, talk to each other about **how these things influence people's choices about where to live**.

🕐 *After 2 minutes* Thank you. Now you have about a minute to decide **which of these things you think would have the greatest effect on people's daily lives**.

🕐 *After 1 minute* Thank you.

TIP Share the speaking time with your partner. Don't dominate the conversation or be too shy about speaking.

Advice

Try to consider both living in a city/town and living in the countryside when you discuss the different points, and give examples, e.g. 'Transport is a big consideration if you don't have a car and have to rely on public transport. In a town there will be buses and taxis if you need them – and of course the underground in big cities. In the countryside, however, ...'.

Part 4

5 minutes (8 minutes for groups of three candidates)

The interlocutor asks some general questions which follow on from the topic in Part 3.

Interlocutor
- Do you think people's choices about where they live change as they get older? (Why? / Why not?)
- How can the work environment affect how a person works or studies?
- Many people today live in high-rise buildings. Do you think this is a good or bad thing? (Why?)
- What do you think governments and city councils should do to improve life in big cities? (Why?)
- Some people say that it's much better to live in a modern building than in an old one. What do you think? (Why?)
- Is it true that people can learn about someone's personality from looking at their room? (Why?)

Thank you. That is the end of the test.

TIP

If you and your partner are asked to discuss a question and you both have a lot to say, develop the conversation as long as you can. The interlocutor will always stop you if he/she wants you to move on.

Advice

1   *When thinking about ages, you should consider children, adults and the elderly, and take people you know as examples. Think about the needs of the different age groups.*

2   *You can consider the question from a worker's or a student's point of view. Think about noise, space, physical comfort, etc.*

3   *You could talk about the advantages/disadvantages of high-rise buildings for the residents themselves or for the development of cities in general. Either would be acceptable here.*

4   *Don't think too long about what might be the most important measure that governments could take. Go for the first idea that you think of and develop that idea.*

5   *Try to talk about advantages and disadvantages of both. Think about appearance, cost, efficiency, etc.*

6   *Give an example of your own room and what it says about you, or the room of someone you know. Even a lack of pictures, books or personal items says something.*

For questions **1 – 8**, read the text below and decide which answer (**A, B, C,** or **D**) best fits each gap. There is an example at the beginning (**0**).

Mark your answers **on the separate answer sheet**.

Example:

0   **A** praised   **B** honoured   **C** credited   **D** admired

0	A	B	C	D
	▢	▢	▬	▢

Violins and the human voice

The sixteenth-century instrument-maker Andrea Amati is **(0)** .... with inventing the modern violin. Over a hundred years later, another Italian, Antonio Stradivari, introduced adjustments to Amati's designs, creating violins that are now **(1)** .... considered to be the finest ever made. But why do these violins sound so beautiful? Where does the secret to their brilliance **(2)** ....?

Recent research suggests that it **(3)** .... from the way their sounds **(4)** .... to the human voice. Scientists recorded antique violins and compared them with the sounds of male and female vocalists. Their **(5)** .... focus was on 'formants', harmonic tones characteristic of human voices, and they found that Amati violins produced 'formants' similar to those of bass and baritone singers, while those of Stradivari violins were similar to tenors and altos. 'Stradivari violins clearly possess female singing qualities,' said one researcher, 'and this may well **(6)** .... to their perceived sweetness. '

The **(7)** .... between the violins and human voices is not accidental. 'Early violins accompanied songs and dances,' said the researcher. 'It's conceivable that Amati and Stradivari wanted instruments that could **(8)** .... into the music by imitating human voices.'

1	**A** highly	**B** widely	**C** greatly	**D** strongly
2	**A** stand	**B** rest	**C** sit	**D** lie
3	**A** stems	**B** flows	**C** runs	**D** grows
4	**A** approach	**B** comply	**C** correspond	**D** accord
5	**A** specific	**B** prevalent	**C** eminent	**D** accurate
6	**A** deliver	**B** generate	**C** assist	**D** contribute
7	**A** sympathy	**B** resemblance	**C** coherence	**D** sameness
8	**A** suit	**B** match	**C** blend	**D** mingle

Test 3 Reading and Use of English Part 2

For questions 9 – 16, read the text below and think of the word which best fits each gap. Use only one word in each gap. There is an example at the beginning (0).

Write your answers **IN CAPITAL LETTERS on the separate answer sheet**.

Example: | 0 | I | F | | | | | | | | | | | | | | | | | | | |

Effective learning

At one time, many experts believed that students would become more effective learners **(0)** .... they were made aware of learning styles that suited them. **(9)** .... the 1980s onwards, theorists identified a number of learning styles, some of **(10)** .... were visual, verbal, auditory and kinaesthetic learning. A kinaesthetic learner, for example, would benefit from using their body and sense of touch when learning.

Over time, however, these concepts have fallen out of favour. 'They're **(11)** .... longer up to date,' says educational psychologist Dr Lorna Mulhall. 'Taking a flexible approach **(12)** .... than sticking to one particular learning style makes better sense. In my experience, **(13)** .... an active learner is usually the key to success.'

Research shows that **(14)** .... of the best ways to learn something is to imagine teaching it. 'Think about **(15)** .... you will explain it to someone in a classroom,' says Dr Mulhall. 'To teach something, you need to understand it.' Dr Mulhall also recommends some basic principles. These include 'finding the right environment, efficient note-taking and taking breaks. **(16)** .... comes a point where you can't absorb any more information and you need to do something different.'

For questions **17 – 24**, read the text below. Use the word given in capitals at the end of some of the lines to form a word that fits in the gap **in the same line**. There is an example at the beginning **(0)**.

Write your answers **IN CAPITAL LETTERS on the separate answer sheet**.

Example: `0` `E` `V` `I` `D` `E` `N` `C` `E`

The world's oldest known bread

Archaeologists working at a site in Jordan recently found the oldest reported **(0)** ....   **EVIDENT**

of bread. Identified by means of new **(17)** .... developments involving the   **METHODOLOGY**

magnification of tiny fragments of food, the bread is about 14,400 years old and

(18) .... the advent of agriculture by at least 4,000 years.   **DATE**

The **(19)** .... was made in a location used, over thousands of years, by early hunter-   **DISCOVER**

gatherers. At that time, humans gathered and consumed food for purposes that were

(20) .... nutritional, but archaeologists think the huge effort required to produce   **PRIMARY**

bread meant it was probably reserved for special occasions.

'The **(21)** .... of the ancient remains of burned food in the fireplaces at this site   **PRESENT**

gives us some **(22)** .... useful insights,' said one researcher. 'Bread represents   **EXCEPTION**

a major change in eating practices, away from food as merely a source of energy to the

(23) .... of food for social and cultural reasons. We used to think agriculture led   **CONSUME**

to the development of bread, but now we think bread-making, with wild grain, may have

influenced the **(24)** .... of the practice of growing crops – in other words, the   **EMERGE**

beginning of agriculture.'

Test 3   Reading and Use of English Part 4

For questions **25 – 30**, complete the second sentence so that it has a similar meaning to the first sentence, using the word given. **Do not change the word given.** You must use between **three** and **six** words, including the word given. Here is an example (**0**).

Example:

0   'I'm sorry I got to your party so late,' Joanna said to her friend.

    HAVING

    Joanna apologised to her friend .... up so late at her party.

The gap can be filled with the words 'for having turned', so you write:

Example: **0** | *FOR HAVING TURNED* |

Write **only** the missing words **IN CAPITAL LETTERS on the separate answer sheet**.

---

25   My grandfather can't play any complicated tunes on the piano any more.

    CAPABLE

    My grandfather is no .... any complicated tunes on the piano.

26   Wherever you buy petrol, the price is always the same.

    DIFFERENCE

    It doesn't .... you buy petrol because the price is always the same.

27   'I'm not feeling well, so I won't go to my dance class for once,' Julie said.

    GIVE

    Julie said she wasn't feeling well and that she .... miss for once.

28   Beppe often appears to lack confidence, but he's just shy.

    ACROSS

    Beppe often .... confidence, but he's just shy.

29   The train was cancelled because of a staff shortage.

    RESULTED

    A staff shortage .... cancelled.

30   Sara's father said she shouldn't quit the course, but she still went ahead and did it.

    BEEN

    Sara quit the course in spite .... not to by her father.

You are going to read an article about the sport of indoor climbing. For questions **31 – 36,** choose the answer (**A, B, C** or **D**) which you think fits best according to the text.

Mark your answers **on the separate answer sheet**.

Climbing walls

John Greene visits a climbing centre, called The Crag, to investigate a sport that's becoming increasingly popular.

It's a Saturday morning and I'm just four metres from the ground, clinging to a wall and suddenly remembering that I am terrified of heights. Although my ascent was far from effortless, it was basically fine while I was moving. But now I've reached the top and can't find a foothold to start back down. My heart is hammering and my whole body is cold. I could just let go and drop to the thick, soft safety mats below; but although I know that wouldn't hurt, somehow it seems inconceivable.

I am here to find out why so many people are falling in love with indoor climbing. There were recently estimated to be over 35 million climbers worldwide, and in the UK alone the numbers are growing by 15–20% a year. I tried it once before, two decades ago. It was in a converted warehouse – as with so many climbing centres, enthusiasts had seen the potential in large empty industrial structures. In those days, climbing was a fringe activity, and venues were few and far between. Little had changed since the 1960s, when the first walls were created so that proper mountaineers could get some practice when weather, or lack of time, kept them from their usual haunts. Numbers have exploded since those times and *line* there are now 500 or so walls in different cities around the UK.

Sam Bailey has volunteered to show me around The Crag. Like many indoor climbers, he focuses on 'bouldering' – tackling walls of no more than five metres, free of the usual heavy climbing gear designed to prevent a fall – rather than roped climbing, where lines (to which you're attached with a harness and various metal clips) let you go higher, but with considerably more faff. If that sounds like a soft option, it's not: the hand- and footholds for bouldering can be little more *line* than bumps in the wall, and that wall sometimes tilts back on itself so that it overhangs the floor.

So, what's the attraction? 'I find it really hard not to think about work all the time,' says Katia Lennon, who has been climbing for two years. 'The wall is the one place where I don't even need to try to switch off. You just focus on what you're doing and it's very therapeutic.' 'There's lots of problem-solving, working out where to put your hands and feet,' Sam Bailey says. 'The mental effort distracts you from doing much else. At the same time, all the different muscle groups are working and it's only when you stop that you realise how much you've exerted yourself.' Teresa Ibarra, a climbing instructor, points out – and this is echoed by everyone I talk to – that 'you don't need to be a great athlete to do it. All sorts of body shapes and ages get something out of it.' 'I've never been sporty,' says lab technician Lee Foo. 'But, a year ago, I did bouldering with some friends, and I've been hooked ever since. I now manage things I'd never have imagined possible.'

One thing that intrigues me, is the number of women in The Crag. 'It's non-threatening – super-chilled,' says 24-year-old Yasmine, when I mention this to her, 'unlike most gyms I've been to.' Other women I talk to make the same point. Jasmine has been climbing for three years and relishes the way that flexibility can trump brute force: 'You see muscly gym guys coming in and thinking they're going to do it easily, but it doesn't happen for them.' Another climber, Aleida, says: 'I don't feel at a disadvantage, and I know some other women who come here feel like me. If a tall strong guy does the climb with a one-arm pull-up, I can do it by throwing my leg into a split and balancing on a hold. My years of gymnastics when I was at school have really helped. Although I'm short and look relatively weak compared with others, I've got a leg-up in other ways.'

When I eventually unfreeze and make it back down to earth, I talk to Rebecca Peters, a maths teacher. She's been bringing her nine-year-old daughter Sophie to classes for about two years. 'I'm so impressed by how it develops young people,' she says.

I decide to have another go and share a wall with Sophie and her friend Luke. They are both vastly stronger, more agile and more confident than me. They also seem much more mature in their decision-making and team-working skills than I would normally expect from children their age – though thinking about what I've observed during my visit to The Crag, somehow it doesn't seem that surprising.

31   What does the writer say about his situation in the first paragraph?

   A   The temperature in the centre affects his mobility.
   B   Fear prevents him from climbing any higher.
   C   The idea of jumping to the floor is out of the question.
   D   Tiredness slows down his thoughts and movements.

32   What do the words 'usual haunts' in line 11 refer to?

   A   early climbing walls
   B   outdoor rock climbs
   C   old industrial buildings
   D   urban climbing centres

33   What does the writer mean by the word 'faff' in line 16?

   A   the predictability of some climbing routes
   B   the places where climbers can grip the walls
   C   the technical challenge involved in bouldering
   D   the inconvenience of dealing with safety equipment

34   The climbers mentioned in the fourth paragraph all comment on

   A   the way that climbing appeals to a wide range of people.
   B   the psychological benefits that climbing can bring.
   C   the speed with which new climbers improve.
   D   the impact that climbing has on fitness.

35   Women say they prefer going to the climbing centre than to a gym because of

   A   the welcoming atmosphere.
   B   the way it affects their bodies.
   C   the competitions they can take part in.
   D   the opportunity to meet like-minded people.

36   What is the writer doing in the final paragraph?

   A   drawing attention to an unanticipated perspective
   B   summarising the main ideas addressed in the article
   C   elaborating on a point one of the speakers raised previously
   D   explaining his own feelings about climbing

You are going to read four extracts from articles in which experts give their views on genetically modified crops. For questions **37 – 40**, choose from the experts **A – D**. The experts may be chosen more than once.

Mark your answers **on the separate answer sheet**.

Genetically modified (GM) crops

A

The world has seen very rapid population growth in the last 50 years, and the world's population currently exceeds 7 billion and is forecast to rise beyond 11 billion by 2100. Ensuring an adequate food supply for everyone is a tremendous challenge. Without a massive increase in the quality and deployment of GM crops, unimaginable numbers are likely to go hungry. GM crop farming has taken off in some parts of the world – mainly the USA, Brazil, Argentina, India and Canada – with productivity in those countries improving significantly, generating welcome financial returns for growers. There are other benefits too. The cultivation of insect-resistant and herbicide-tolerant strains of soya beans and maize, for example, means that fewer chemical products are required than for conventional crops. This reduces the exposure of both people and local ecosystems to toxic materials, which has positive long-term consequences for both.

B

A recent study raised concerns about allergen levels in GM crops. Genetic modification often adds or mixes proteins that were not native to the original plant and which might cause new allergic reactions in the human body. In other studies, the introduction of GM crops was found to have decimated a butterfly population dependent on the varieties of plants that had been replaced, and other comparable worrying occurrences have been observed. The conclusion is that much more investigation is needed before such crops should be deregulated. This research is costly, however, and there's a convincing argument that the money would be better invested in improved roads and transportation. The truth is that food supplies have never been more abundant; they just don't get to everyone who needs them. GM technology won't solve this problem. In fact, GM seeds are expensive and growers are increasingly in debt and tied to a handful of large, profit-driven suppliers.

C

Proponents of GM technology will claim it's the only viable way to improve productivity sufficiently to meet the needs of a burgeoning global population. The real problem, however, isn't that there isn't enough food for all, but that what is available isn't distributed efficiently or fairly. GM crop users favour the technology because it simplifies their weed and pest management, bringing savings and improved profit margins. At the same time, certain lines of development are clearly promising. 'Golden rice', for example, is a bio-fortified GM crop which could help thousands of children around the world overcome vitamin A deficiency, and scientists are working on other projects to provide similarly nutritional enhancements. On the other hand, the simplified weed and pest management of GM technology tends to encourage monocultural farming – huge tracts of land are entirely devoted to the cultivation of soya beans, for example – and the elimination of biodiversity like this has adverse consequences.

D

Any major shift in the way we produce food is bound to have certain undesirable results for some people, and opposition to large-scale GM farming is, to a degree, understandable. The evidence for the value of developing herbicide-tolerant and insect-resistant traits in certain key crops is overwhelming, however. They don't require nearly so much spraying of crops or ploughing and tilling of the soil, which, in turn, helps to conserve soil moisture and control erosion. It also means that GM farmers use heavy machinery less than their non-GM counterparts and this lowers their carbon footprint. Higher yields and lower pest management and labour costs mean that GM crop producers gain enhanced revenues. There is also great potential in the engineering of plants with superior levels of protein, essential fats and minerals. They are yet to be commercialised, but will be a valuable addition to our future diets.

Which expert

has a different view from C regarding whether more GM crops are necessary to feed the world? | **37** |

shares B's view on whether GM crops cause environmental damage? | **38** |

expresses a different view from the other three experts about the impact GM crops have on farmers? | **39** |

has a different view from D regarding the effect GM crops may have on human health? | **40** |

You are going to read a magazine article about volunteering at an orangutan research centre in Borneo. Six paragraphs have been removed from the article. Choose from the paragraphs **A – G** the one which fits each gap (**41 – 46**). There is one extra paragraph which you do not need to use.

Mark your answers **on the separate answer sheet**.

Helping out with orangutans – a holiday with a difference

I've got a hammer in my hand when the cry goes up: 'Orangutan in the camp.' Nine people down tools and grab their cameras. This is a chance to snap one of the critically endangered primates that we are here to help at the Pondok Ambung research post run by the Orangutan Foundation in Indonesian Borneo.

41

It's not the first time it's happened since our arrival at the research centre, which is surrounded by towering ironwood trees forming a canopy 50 metres above our heads, blocking out sunshine, but trapping moisture and heat. We had reached it after a long drive and a four-hour boat ride along the Buluh Kecil river in central Borneo.

42

That said, we know we are privileged to be here. The volunteer programme runs every summer, attracting adventurers to spend three weeks sleeping in basic accommodation and building infrastructure for the full-time Indonesian research staff. Over the past 15 years, volunteers have built facilities in Tanjung Puting National Park, further south in Borneo, and the Lamandau Wildlife Reserve to the east.

43

Others have previously given time elsewhere in animal welfare and environmental programmes. We are a part of volunteer tourism, a global business estimated to be worth up to $2bn a year. It's also highly controversial: many volunteer placements are not much more than

'expensive holidays', providing healthy returns to travel companies while doing little for the causes they are meant to benefit.

44

The rebuilding of the main building housing the laboratory and offices is an example of this. Our work enables researchers to study the wildlife of this protected area and to educate people about the risk of extinction faced by the apes and other animals. It's a delicate mission: the palm oil industry is destroying animal habitats; on the other hand, it has dramatically raised the standard of living in the region.

45

It may not be too long before they start coming to the site we are working on. It's certainly popular with orangutans. In the three weeks I am there, we get several visits from the fascinating animals as they forage for food and good nesting sites. Proboscis monkeys and macaques also regularly hang around in the trees opposite our jetty.

46

What we don't get used to is the mosquitoes, the one thing I am glad to escape when my stay ends. On the final day, the centre director tells us we have surpassed his expectations for this year's programme. We know we haven't solved the socio-economic problems that are driving orangutans to extinction, but we have made a difference to people who are working to save them.

A Given that most of the work is done by people like me who know little about construction, these are impressive achievements. The main motivation is to do something positive for the beleaguered orangutans, although, naturally, we all want to actually see some. Two people in my group are so committed that they have come back for a second year.

B The centre staff make sure we are aware of the difficult issue. They also take us on trips upriver to a long-established primatology site. Daily feeding time there draws a crowd of orangutans. It also attracts day-tripping eco-tourists on boats from the regional capital Pangkalan Bun.

C A fellow participant has personal experience of such dubious schemes elsewhere. He says it's hard to find programmes with the high standards of the Orangutan Foundation: 'Finding eco-trips where you can make a real difference isn't simple. But with this one, you've got a clear, physical outcome at the end of it.'

D Apparently, every volunteer group is different. Ours ranges from 18 to 60 years old, with eight women and four men when we begin. Despite the supportive atmosphere, the basic conditions are hard to cope with: one volunteer takes a boat back to civilisation within a day of arrival, and two more return home after a week.

E And that's just in the daytime. At night we go on walks to spot tarantulas, civets and tiny huge-eyed tarsier primates, and we take boat rides at dusk to look for saltwater crocodiles. We become accustomed to the low-riding, wobbly motorised canoes that ferry everything along the rivers.

F It's Rimba, a 17-year-old male, and he doesn't disappoint. He circles the camp, going from tree to tree just a few metres above our heads for almost 30 minutes. The spectacle is a well-earned reward after a week of hard physical work in the 32°C heat and extreme humidity of the jungle.

G So remote is it that there's no mobile signal. Our luxuries are rationed biscuits, sliced watermelon and oranges, and the conditions are so draining that by the end of the first week we feel as though we've sweated out more toxins than in a year of hot yoga.

You are going to read an article in which four people who study psychology at university talk about their course. For questions **47 – 56**, choose from the students (**A – D**). The students may be chosen more than once.

Mark your answers **on the separate answer sheet**.

Which student mentions feeling

concerned about the breadth of the subject?   **47** ☐

unsure about how useful the skills developed on the course would be?   **48** ☐

surprised by how scientific the course was?   **49** ☐

frustrated by a lack of definite answers?   **50** ☐

amused by certain perceptions of the subject?   **51** ☐

inspired by the opportunity to work independently?   **52** ☐

proud to have made a difficult decision?   **53** ☐

appreciative of the support available?   **54** ☐

impressed by the popularity of the course?   **55** ☐

fascinated by a particular topic area within psychology?   **56** ☐

Studying psychology

A

When I was at school and still considering whether to apply to do psychology, a teacher warned me that it involved a great deal of science. I didn't realise at the time, though, the extent to which it does relate to science. Given the rather superficial understanding of psychology that most non-specialists have, however, perhaps it's to be expected that people have little idea of the amount of science that it involves. But whatever area of psychology you're talking about – and there are many of them – I soon discovered that there are always numbers, statistics, trials and evidence to get to grips with, and in the process of doing so, you develop a repertoire of competencies. When I first walked into a psychology lecture and saw that every seat in the auditorium was taken, I was stunned. I've got used to that over the three years of my degree and it's reassuring in a way to think that there are many other people my age who recognise both the practical and sheer interest value to be gained from the subject.

B

When I tell people I'm studying psychology, they often say things like 'Can you read my mind, then?' or 'Can you give me some advice about a problem?' This used to get on my nerves. How could anyone be so ignorant, particularly given the large numbers of people that study psychology? I tend to see the humorous side of it these days, though. One plus is the wide ground that psychology covers – more than most would imagine – from genetics to the psychology of organisations. The latter might not sound very glamorous, but it's something that intrigues me greatly and, hopefully, is an area I can find employment in at some point. Whatever aspect of psychology you look at, however, it's important to take a critical approach. That's drummed into us from the word go. We're also always encouraged to work with other students, as well as on our own, and to seek advice from our tutors whenever we're faced with anything we feel we can't deal with by ourselves. This has been tremendous for me personally.

C

At school, the idea of being a doctor had always appealed to me. A few months into my first year studying medicine, however, I began to feel that I wasn't suited to it after all, and I managed to switch to psychology. It was quite traumatic, giving up the prospect of a great career and disappointing my parents. They had very little idea about what my new subject involved and whether I'd learn anything from it that could set me up for a good job. To be honest, I was far from convinced myself initially. With hindsight, however, I know I did the right thing, and I derive a certain satisfaction from having gone ahead with the move. Frankly, it puzzles me why more people don't end up doing the same. There's so much to psychology, including a scientific emphasis, which, given my background, I'm comfortable with. It can take you down all sorts of exciting career paths.

D

It would be wrong to say that I had a clear idea about what a psychology degree entailed when I applied to do one, but I think I made the right choice. At school, I loved science and I was advised that, although people often don't think of psychology as a science, it would suit me – and that proved to be the case. One thing about my degree is that it's incredibly diverse. The terms *neuro-*, *educational*, *forensic*, *clinical* and *sports*, for example, all precede *psychology* to describe well-established fields, and I must admit that, initially, I found this somewhat overwhelming. I also struggled with the notion that any idea or 'fact' has to be endlessly cross-examined and debated, to the extent that you doubt whether you know anything for certain. This still irritates me sometimes, but I can live with it. I'm in my third year now, and doing a project which involves some research and then delivering a presentation and submitting a written report. It's complex, but doing it on my own is exciting and has made me think about a career in which research plays a part.

You **must** answer this question. Write your answer in **220 – 260** words in an appropriate style on the separate answer sheet.

---

1 Your class has listened to a panel discussion about different ways of learning about another culture. You have made the notes below:

Ways of learning about another culture

- taking a course about the culture
- visiting the place in person
- reading about the culture

Some opinions expressed in the discussion:

"A good teacher can make sure you understand a culture."

"If you see something yourself, you never forget it."

"Reading material about cultures is very accessible because of the internet."

Write an essay for your tutor discussing **two** of the ways of learning about another culture in your notes. You should **explain which way you think is most effective**, **giving reasons** in support of your answer.

You may, if you wish, make use of the opinions expressed in the discussion, but you should use your own words as far as possible.

Write an answer to **one** of the questions **2 – 4** in this part. Write your answer in **220 – 260** words in an appropriate style on the separate answer sheet. Put the question number in the box at the top of the page.

2 There has been a decrease in the number of people shopping in the town centre and now the town council has asked for proposals on how to improve this situation. In your proposal, you should briefly state what you think are the reasons for this decrease, explain what impact this has had on the town centre and suggest what can be done to encourage more people to shop there.

Write your **proposal**.

3 You see the following announcement on an English-language website:

Have you recently seen a movie based on a person's life?
If so, send us a review!

You should tell us briefly about the person the film was based on, explain which aspects of the person's life the film highlighted and say how accurate you think the film was.

The best reviews will be published online next month!

Write your **review**.

4 You recently organised some activities for a student on a short visit to the international college where you study. Now the college principal has asked you for a report. You should explain what you organised and evaluate how successful you think your contribution to the visit was. You should also make recommendations for future visits to the college.

Write your **report**.

19

You will hear three different extracts. For questions **1 – 6**, choose the answer (**A**, **B** or **C**) which fits best according to what you hear. There are two questions for each extract.

Extract One

You hear two scientists, Peter Cameron and Lisa Mackie, discussing generating electricity from the energy in the oceans.

1 What does Peter believe is the greatest advantage of generating electricity from the oceans?

   A The seas provide a reliable energy source.

   B It will be cost-effective in the long run.

   C Many countries will be able to create their own energy.

2 What is Lisa doing?

   A correcting the information that Peter gives

   B suggesting an alternative opinion

   C predicting future developments

Extract Two

You hear two friends discussing the practice of urban foraging, which is picking nuts and fruit from around a city.

3 Why does the woman think urban foraging is popular?

   A People seek a strong connection with nature.

   B Wild food is guaranteed to be organic.

   C It can save money on grocery bills.

4 How do they both feel about urban foraging becoming possible in their local park?

   A worried that many plants will be destroyed

   B hopeful that plant identification courses will be held

   C surprised that local residents weren't consulted about it

You hear a husband and wife talking about planning a holiday.

5   The woman mentions last year's holiday in an attempt to

    A   justify increasing their holiday budget this year.

    B   avoid a similar situation occurring this year.

    C   influence their choice of holiday this year.

6   What approach to packing for their holiday do they agree on?

    A   It's essential to make a detailed list.

    B   It's a good idea to do it well in advance.

    C   It's better to pack too many items than too few.

You will hear part of a podcast by a biologist, called Dr Larry Clark, on the subject of butterflies. For questions **7 – 14**, complete the sentences with a word or short phrase.

BUTTERFLIES

Larry explains that butterflies are less effective than **(7)** .... at

pollinating plants.

Larry has done research into plants that have a strong **(8)** .... and how

they attract butterflies.

Larry points out that butterflies are a vital link in the **(9)** .... , both as a

prey and predators.

Butterflies can be a good form of **(10)** .... , which means they can be a

benefit to farmers.

Butterflies are known by scientists to be good indicators of **(11)** ....

A type of butterfly called the Checkerspot now populates areas at **(12)** ....

than in the past.

Butterflies can attract **(13)** .... to an area and boost the local economy.

The European Meadow Brown butterfly produces a natural **(14)** ....

which may be of use to humans.

You will hear an interview in which two students, a girl called Tamsin and a boy called Farid, are talking about whether to go to university or not. For questions **15 – 20**, choose the answer (**A**, **B**, **C** or **D**) which fits best according to what you hear.

15 What alternative to going to university has Farid's sister suggested to him?

    A travelling for a year

    B setting up his own business

    C doing charity work

    D working for a large organisation

16 Tamsin worries that many students go to university because

    A they are attracted by the social life.

    B it's expected of them by their school teachers.

    C they believe they'll be able to find a better job afterwards.

    D certain courses are fashionable.

17 What do both Tamsin and Farid say about working while at university?

    A It's a good way to get practical experience.

    B It can reduce the time available for studying.

    C It enables more students to afford to go to university.

    D It may result in poor health.

18 Why does Tamsin think going to university is the right choice for her?

    A She excelled at academic subjects at school.

    B She believes university will broaden her mind.

    C She needs more time before deciding on a career path.

    D She thinks the contacts she'll make there will be invaluable.

19 How did Farid feel about a university Open Day he went to?

    A confident he would fit in with other students at the university

    B pleased that the university's facilities were so modern

    C surprised that he could talk to so many of the staff

    D reassured that his questions were answered

20 Farid suggests Tamsin's letter of application to a university should include more about

    A her commitment to the subject.

    B her positive attitude to learning.

    C her ability to express herself in writing.

    D her clear long-term aims.

You will hear five short extracts in which film critics are each reviewing a film.

TASK ONE

For questions **21 – 25**, choose from the list (**A – H**) what each critic believes is the main message of the film they are reviewing.

TASK TWO

For questions **26 – 30**, choose from the list (**A – H**) the weakness each critic identifies in their chosen film.

While you listen you must complete both tasks.

A	what it means to be successful	
B	the value of strong family relationships	Speaker 1 **21**
C	the importance of telling the truth	Speaker 2 **22**
D	how humour can ease tense situations	Speaker 3 **23**
E	the difficulties of living in a small community	Speaker 4 **24**
F	the challenge of working with relatives	Speaker 5 **25**
G	how happiness can be found in everyday things	
H	how unpredictable life is	

A	the inappropriate soundtrack	Speaker 1 **26**
B	the lack of character development	Speaker 2 **27**
C	the skilled photography	
D	the confusing plot	Speaker 3 **28**
E	the lack of attention to detail	Speaker 4 **29**
F	the predictable ending	
G	the lack of originality in the dialogue	Speaker 5 **30**
H	the performance of the lead actor	

Speaking Part 1

Work with a partner if possible, taking it in turn to act in the role of the interlocutor.

Part 1
2 minutes (3 minutes for groups of three)

The interlocutor asks you some questions about yourself, your home, work or studies and familiar topics.

Good morning / afternoon / evening. My name is ... and this is my colleague ... .

And your names are?

Can I have your mark sheets, please?

Thank you.

First of all, we'd like to know something about you.

- Where are you from?
- What do you do here / there?
- How long have you been studying English?
- What do you enjoy most about studying English?

The interlocutor then asks you some questions about one or two other topics, for example:

- If you could visit any country in the world, where would it be? (Why?)
- Have you read an interesting book or article recently?
- What hobby or interest do you remember enjoying as a child?
- Do you prefer to make plans about weekends and holidays, or not to plan ahead?

Part 2

4 minutes (6 minutes for groups of three)

Work in groups of three if possible. One of you is the interlocutor and the other two are the candidates. The interlocutor should lead the task using the script below. Refer to the pictures on pages S10 and S11.

Interlocutor	In this part of the test, I'm going to give each of you three pictures. I'd like you to talk about **two** of them on your own for about a minute, and also to answer a question briefly about your partner's pictures.
	[Candidate A], it's your turn first. Here are your pictures. They show **people feeling tired for different reasons**. I'd like you to compare two of the pictures and say **why the people might be feeling tired and how long you think this tiredness might last**.
	All right?
⏱ After 1 minute	Thank you.
	[Candidate B], **who do you think will be the first to feel tired again? (Why?)**
⏱ After 30 seconds	Thank you.
	Now, [Candidate B], here are your pictures. They show **people celebrating different events**. I'd like you to compare two of the pictures and say **how long the people might have taken to prepare for these events and how they might be feeling**.
⏱ After 1 minute	Thank you.
	Now, [Candidate A], **who do you think will remember the celebration the longest? (Why?)**
⏱ After 30 seconds	Thank you.

Part 3 4 minutes (6 minutes for groups of three)

Part 4 5 minutes (8 minutes for groups of three)

Part 3

Work in groups of three if possible. One of you is the interlocutor and the other two are the candidates. The interlocutor should lead the task using the script below. Refer to the task sheet on page S12.

Interlocutor   Now I'd like you to talk about something together for about two minutes.

Here are some skills that young people sometimes learn in addition to traditional subjects at school and a question for you to discuss. First you have some time to look at the task.

🕐 *After 15 seconds*   Now, talk to each other about **how important it is for young people to learn these skills at school**.

🕐 *After 2 minutes*   Thank you. Now you have about a minute to decide **which of these things you think would be most useful for students' future lives**.

🕐 *After 1 minute*   Thank you.

Part 4

The interlocutor asks some general questions which follow on from the topic in Part 3.

Interlocutor
- Do you think all secondary schools should include teaching other skills, such as life skills, in their timetables? (Why? / Why not?)
- Some people think that it's the parents' responsibility and not the schools' to teach young people how to deal with financial matters. What's your opinion? (Why?)
- Do you think that arts subjects are as important as other subjects for students to study at school? (Why? / Why not?)
- How do you think studying at college or university is different from studying at school?
- Is it better to study something you're good at or something you're interested in? (Why?)
- Which subjects do you think will become more important for students to learn at school in the future? (Why?)

Thank you. That is the end of the test.

For questions **1 – 8**, read the text below and decide which answer (**A**, **B**, **C**, or **D**) best fits each gap. There is an example at the beginning (**0**).

Mark your answers **on the separate answer sheet**.

Example:

0 A hand   **B** favour   **C** support   **D** benefit

	A	B	C	D
0	☐	▅	☐	☐

Saying 'Thank you'

If you do someone a **(0)** .... , you might assume they would normally say 'Thank you'. However, recordings of more than a thousand casual conversations between friends and family around the world **(1)** .... that this is not necessarily the **(2)** ....

A study of how often people **(3)** .... gratitude for a relatively trivial act found that 'Thank you', or words with the same meaning, occurred only once in every 20 interactions. There were some differences between the eight languages recorded, but even in the language which featured 'Thank you' most, it was only observed in 14% of exchanges. The researchers say 'Thank you' is **(4)** .... for unusual requests, and they also point to its standard use in more formal **(5)** ....

Experts believe the global reluctance to **(6)** .... helpful acts does not indicate rudeness. Rather, it demonstrates that close-knit groups take co-operation for **(7)** .... 'Social life **(8)** .... because it is in our nature to ask for help and pay back in kind, rather than just words,' said a researcher. 'There is an unspoken agreement that people will co-operate.'

1	**A** display	**B** uncover	**C** expose	**D** reveal
2	**A** point	**B** matter	**C** case	**D** event
3	**A** assert	**B** express	**C** utter	**D** announce
4	**A** reserved	**B** devoted	**C** engaged	**D** maintained
5	**A** backgrounds	**B** settings	**C** sites	**D** frames
6	**A** admit	**B** realise	**C** perceive	**D** acknowledge
7	**A** given	**B** agreed	**C** granted	**D** established
8	**A** thrives	**B** grows	**C** booms	**D** shines

For questions **9 – 16**, read the text below and think of the word which best fits each gap. Use only one word in each gap. There is an example at the beginning (**0**).

Write your answers **IN CAPITAL LETTERS on the separate answer sheet**.

Example: **0** | A | F | T | E | R |

Manuka honey

Manuka honey, produced in New Zealand by bees that pollinate the manuka tree, has become highly sought **(0)** .... as an alternative medicine. It is claimed to be effective in treating allergies, colds, flu, sore throats, infections and wounds. With a jar of genuine, undiluted manuka costing **(9)** .... to £100 in the UK, for example, it's **(10)** .... wonder that the food industry calls it 'liquid gold'.

But **(11)** .... beneficial is manuka in reality? The evidence is limited on **(12)** .... or not it helps with high cholesterol, diabetes and gastrointestinal problems – all conditions for **(13)** .... it has been marketed as an answer. But reputable studies have concluded that it can protect **(14)** .... damage caused by bacteria.

However, scientists are generally sceptical. '**(15)** .... benefits it may have in theory, or may be shown in laboratory trials, you need to think about volume,' says one. 'To obtain a significant antibacterial effect, you would need to consume huge quantities of high-grade manuka. And it's not as **(16)** .... the health benefits of manuka aren't available in other much cheaper foods and supplements.'

For questions **17 – 24**, read the text below. Use the word given in capitals at the end of some of the lines to form a word that fits in the gap **in the same line**. There is an example at the beginning **(0)**.

Write your answers **IN CAPITAL LETTERS on the separate answer sheet**.

Example: | 0 | L | E | N | G | T | H | | | | | | | | | | |

The songs of the bowhead whales

Bowhead whales are the second largest whale species after blue whales, and can grow up

to 20 metres in **(0)** .... About 10,000 bowheads are estimated to live in the   **LONG**

Arctic region, but because they spend most of their time under the polar ice, their lives

remain an **(17)** .... quantity. Recently, however, oceanographers managed to   **KNOW**

record a group of bowheads producing 184 different musical **(18)** .... during a   **COMPOSE**

three-year study off the coast of Greenland. Such was the **(19)** .... of the songs   **DIVERSE**

that the researchers felt inspired to **(20)** .... the whales to jazz musicians.   **LIKE**

Whale songs are not simple mating calls; they are complex musical phrases that are not

(21) .... hard-wired, but have to be learned over a period of time. Only a   **GENE**

(22) .... of mammals – including some bats and apes – are able to vocalise in   **HAND**

ways that are **(23)** .... to birdsong. Bowheads are particularly impressive in that   **COMPARE**

their songs are never repeated from one year to the next and they appear able to improvise

(24) .... Researchers are now keen to explore why bowheads change their   **CONTINUE**

songs so frequently.

For questions **25 – 30**, complete the second sentence so that it has a similar meaning to the first sentence, using the word given. **Do not change the word given.** You must use between **three** and **six** words, including the word given. Here is an example (**0**).

Example:

0 'I'm sorry I got to the party so late,' Joanna said to her friend.

    HAVING

    Joanna apologised to her friend .... up so late at the party.

The gap can be filled with the words 'for having turned', so you write:

Example: | **0** | *FOR HAVING TURNED*

Write **only** the missing words **IN CAPITAL LETTERS on the separate answer sheet**.

---

25 I regret not discussing things with Fiona before she went away on holiday.

    WISH

    I .... things over with Fiona before she went away on holiday.

26 People can promise anything they like, but my dad will never agree to sell his business.

    MATTER

    My dad will never agree to sell his business .... people make.

27 It definitely won't rain this afternoon.

    CHANCE

    There's absolutely .... raining this afternoon.

28 The party didn't really start to get going until Sam arrived.

    ONLY

    It .... up that the party really started to get going.

29 Someone stole Kazuo's wallet when he was on a crowded train.

    HAD

    Kazuo .... when he was on a crowded train.

30 Piotr thought the two cars looked exactly the same.

    TELL

    Piotr .... the two cars.

You are going to read an article about teenagers. For questions **31 – 36**, choose the answer (**A, B, C** or **D**) which you think fits best according to the text.

Mark your answers **on the separate answer sheet**.

Teenage brains

Journalist Martin Baines talks to neuroscientist Professor Sarah-Jayne Blakemore about the development of the brain during adolescence.

Until I read *Inventing Ourselves* by Professor Sarah-Jayne Blakemore, I'd always assumed that what we   *line 1* think of as teenage behaviour is largely an invention of contemporary western society. I hadn't imagined, for example, that 15-year-olds in the Kalahari Desert also complain about having to get up early – but they do. It was for people like me – there are lots of us – that Blakemore wrote her book explaining the science of everything from why teenagers can't get out of bed in the morning to why they sometimes appear to be irresponsible narcissists. 'We demonise teenagers more than any other section of society,' she told me. 'And it's not right. They're going through an essential stage of their development. Most adults don't realise this.'

This is arguably inevitable. Blakemore says that until 20 years ago, it was assumed that teenage behaviour was largely down to hormonal changes in puberty and that children's brains were more or less fully developed. The findings of brain scans and psychological experiments have now revealed that the reality is very different, however. In fact, the brain continues to change all through the teenage years and well into adulthood, and important neurodevelopmental processes enable it to be moulded by the environment. So adolescence is a critical period of neurological change, much of which is responsible for adolescent behaviour.

Blakemore quotes from a teenager's diary dated 20 July 1969: 'I went to arts centre (by myself!) in yellow cords and blouse. Ian was there but didn't speak to me. Got a rhyme put in my handbag from someone who's apparently got a crush on me. It's Nicholas, I think. UGH. Man landed on the moon.' This may look like amazing – even jaw-dropping – self-absorption. But Blakemore says it's essential neurological development, because the biological function of adolescence, today and in the past, is the creation of a sense of self. Teens achieve this through creating new allegiances, independent of their parents – which is why their friendships suddenly become extremely important. What is known on social media as FOMO – fear of missing out – may look like an irrational sense of priorities if it means skipping revision to attend a run-of-the-mill get-together, but at that age, nothing matters more than peer approval.

Blakemore designed an experiment to explore this. Adolescents were asked to play an online ball game, with what they believed to be two other players of their own age. In fact, the game was with a computer programmed to ignore the human participants; these found themselves watching the ball being passed between two players on the screen who chose not to include them. She repeated the experiment with adults, and found that, while the game lowered the mood and increased the anxiety levels of all participants, the effect was dramatically greater for the teenagers.

In her book, Blakemore also discusses how the neurologically driven preoccupation with peer approval underlies adolescent risk-taking and acute self-consciousness, and how it determines adolescent sleep patterns. It's fascinating, and I'm curious about the implications. What could be done to accommodate the changes adolescents go through?

Blakemore suggests we might harness the power of peer pressure by getting adolescents to run educational campaigns – for example, on healthy eating. She also mentions schools which have altered their start times to fit in with teenage sleep patterns, though she points out there may be practical issues about implementing this on a wider scale. But generally, she's wary about putting forward concrete solutions. This seems regrettable, but she insists she's a scientist rather than a consultant. She doesn't even like to be asked for parenting advice, although she admits her work does inform her own parenting. When she recently visited her teenage son's school, he asked her to pretend not to know him. 'I could've been so offended by that. But I thought: "That's absolutely normal."'

One thing that makes Blakemore's empathy and affection for teenagers so striking is its rarity. 'Yes, I'm a champion of them,' she agrees. But why does she think so many other adults feel differently? She often thinks about why we find it hilarious to 'take the mickey out of teenagers'. She points out that there are whole comedy *line 44* shows mocking their behaviour. She wonders if adults do it to cope with their rejection; small children obey adults *line 45* and want to be with them, but teenagers, through necessity, look for independence, and the older generations feel *line 46* hurt about this. They resent adolescents' desire to rebel and their sense of embarrassment when they're with *line 47* parents. 'Our way of dealing with these changes is to sneer at them.' *line 48*

31 What is the writer doing in the first paragraph?

   A outlining how he feels about the way teenagers are generally perceived

   B giving his reasons for writing a profile of Professor Blakemore

   C pointing out international variations in teenage behaviour

   D acknowledging his relative ignorance about teenagers

32 The writer suggests that the way teenage behaviour is commonly regarded is unsurprising because

   A behavioural development is a complex subject.

   B significant progress in relevant areas of study is relatively recent.

   C people's outlook on life is partly determined by neurological factors.

   D differences between generations will always cause misunderstanding.

33 What does the writer suggest is 'jaw-dropping' about the teenager's diary entry?

   A the strong desire for independence that comes across

   B the similarity with what young people talk about today

   C the negative comments about two acquaintances

   D the focus on personal rather than wider events

34 The experiment described in the fourth paragraph was designed to provide evidence of

   A how competitive teenagers tend to be.

   B how easily teenagers can be deceived.

   C how sensitive teenagers are to social exclusion.

   D how immersed teenagers can become in video games.

35 In the sixth paragraph, the writer expresses

   A disappointment at Blakemore's reluctance to advocate specific policies.

   B enthusiasm for the idea of giving teenagers more responsibility.

   C amusement at Blakemore's difficulties with her own children.

   D doubt regarding the feasibility of changing school hours.

36 Which words in the final paragraph echo the phrase 'take the mickey out of' in line 44?

   A cope with (line 45)

   B feel hurt about (lines 46 – 47)

   C resent (line 47)

   D sneer at (line 48)

You are going to read four extracts from reviews of a book called *Happy City* by Charles Montgomery. For questions 37 – 40, choose from the reviews **A – D**. The reviews may be chosen more than once.

Mark your answers **on the separate answer sheet**.

Four reviews of *Happy City* by Charles Montgomery

A

The last twenty years have seen a significant growth in the field of happiness studies and a revival of interest in urban design. Using insights from both fields, Charles Montgomery develops fresh perspectives on a number of key issues and does so in an accessible, engaging manner. Pre-eminent among his notions is the view that people are happier if they lead a connected life, and that connectedness is best secured through regular relationships with people met through simple residential proximity. Montgomery finds that suburban sprawl, in which cars and roads dominate, mitigates against connectedness; it's hard to argue with the proposition that spending a large proportion of your life in a car is more isolating than walking among fellow citizens or travelling on a bus. Montgomery provides detailed descriptions of such developments as the pedestrianisation of Copenhagen and the enhanced cycle lanes and public transport of Bogotá to illustrate his themes very effectively.

B

My first challenge in reading *Happy City* by Charles Montgomery was to get past the title – it suggests something sentimental, insubstantial and illusory. Then I had to get past the occasionally over-the-top prose about figures like the former mayor of Bogotá, Enrique Peñalosa, who radically reversed policies favouring motor traffic and instead promoted cycling and buses and invested in public buildings and spaces. Montgomery also gushes about Vancouver, a thriving, partly high-rise city in which people of different levels of income live close together, with its streets animated by multiple activities. Having said that, Bogotá and Vancouver both demonstrate admirably what Montgomery points out can be done to truly enhance urban life. The bottom line with this book, however, is that it says forcefully what can't be said too much: that the growth of low-density, car-dependent development on the outer edges of cities is, for the most part, no recipe for happiness.

C

'The most important psychological effect of the city is the way it moderates our relationships with other people,' says Charles Montgomery in a typically lucid, thought-provoking fashion. Densely populated cities, which encourage people to travel on foot or by public transport, and offer mixtures of housing types, create more opportunities for interaction – which leads to happiness. The opposite is true of the dispersed urban landscape, in which the car is king. All this seems self-evident, although there's no harm pointing it out. It's unlikely that you'll never have come across these notions before, however. They've been debated over the past half-century. It should also be said that Montgomery doesn't strive for impartiality. He chooses the worst case of suburban sprawl he can find – a town whose residents spend four hours a day commuting – and at the other extreme, the ultra-civilised setting of Copenhagen as an unrealistic benchmark for what cities elsewhere can achieve.

D

I admit that I indulged in some wishful thinking when I picked up *Happy City* by Charles Montgomery. I was hoping for unexpected, acute insights into modern life. Instead, it's more of the standard urbanist message that we have long been fed. Montgomery thinks that living in the city – and here city means a dense, probably high-rise urban village where everyone knows your name – is the answer to all our problems with unhappiness, loneliness, ill-health and lack of spiritual fulfilment. He gives short shrift to all the legitimate reasons why people might choose 'suburban sprawl' over 'urban jungle'. Fear of crime and desire for privacy and space – justifiable feelings of many who choose the suburbs – get passing mentions, but Montgomery seems to think these are silly prejudices. The insulting implication is that people don't know what's best for them. Laden with starry-eyed, but empty, turns of phrase, the book is repetitive and, at nearly 400 pages, too long.

Which reviewer

shares C's view about Montgomery's writing style?

| 37 | |

has a different view from B regarding the examples of cities that Montgomery uses to support his arguments?

| 38 | |

expresses a different view from the other reviewers regarding Montgomery's thinking about suburbs?

| 39 | |

has a different view from C on the extent to which Montgomery's ideas are new?

| 40 | |

You are going to read an article about a rafting trip along the Colorado River in the USA. Six paragraphs have been removed from the article. Choose from the paragraphs **A – G** the one which fits each gap (**41 – 46**). There is one extra paragraph which you do not need to use.

Mark your answers **on the separate answer sheet**.

Rafting through the Grand Canyon and beyond

The fierce sun had little effect on the freezing-cold water of the Colorado river as it splashed over the sides of our raft. Ahead lay a rapid called Bedrock. The four of us on our inflatable raft had already conquered numerous cascades in the Grand Canyon, but I was very nervous about this one. 'Go right,' we shouted at Rick, our pilot for the day, who was desperately trying to steer against the powerful current.

41

'Go for the channel!' I yelled, pointing towards a narrow opening. Our guides had said this way was 'un-runnable' and we were about to find out. I felt the boat twisting into a whirlpool and knew we were about to flip.

42

Bearing in mind our inexperience, I'm not sure how we did. As we had prepared to leave from Lees Ferry on the banks of the Colorado in Arizona, our lead guide had asked: 'How many of you have done anything like this before?' Two of the group raised their hands. Our guide explained that ahead of us lay 450km of white water through one of the most formidable environments on earth – and no phone signal for 17 days.

43

For the next two and a half weeks, we'd see few other humans; the Canyon may be one of the world's biggest attractions, but it's also one of the most inaccessible places in the US and is usually only seen from above. We negotiated nearly 90 major rapids in all, and only

flipped once, although several of us ended up in the water on different occasions.

44

Humans hadn't been there as long, of course, but well before tourists came, it was the land of the Navajo and Hualapai American Indians. Their ancestors left buildings carved into the cliff faces, and prehistoric stone engravings in the warren of caves and gorges accessible only from the river. Some of these were filled with luscious palms and others were so narrow you could touch both sides.

45

As a result, we had no idea what was going on in the rest of the world, not that we cared. There, on the river, we were completely focused on the here and now and extra vigilant every time we encountered a significant rapid. Even the guides were nervous as we approached the infamous Lava Falls, which has a terrifying 9/10 difficulty rating. Before attempting Lava, we stopped and scrambled up a nearby cliff. From the top, we looked down anxiously at the crashing roar of white water and tried to work out our route.

46

Then, as soon as it had begun, it was over. There were whoops of joy and relieved high fives. We were soaked – but we'd all got through it safely. There were still a couple more days to go, but after Lava nothing could defeat us. We were a team, united by a river and a great sense of accomplishment.

A We'd been made aware of this when we booked the trip. But 16 of us had eagerly signed up for the adventure of a lifetime, renting four rafts, with all the necessary provisions included.

B Fierce winds threatening to blow our rafts backwards and vicious sandstorms driving grit into our eyes, nostrils and cameras were two of the worst. Our hands, feet and lips were soon cracked from the constant exposure to water and the dry desert air.

C It was no use. We were quickly drawn towards a rock the size of a bus. Then the raft was sucked around the wrong side of the boulder and into an eddy. Our paddles were now being bashed against the rock.

D Eventually, we just had to go for it. Nervously, we let the waters pull us towards the boiling foam, and one by one the four rafts entered the fray. Our raft rocked and creaked and smashed through waves the size of a car; at one point it was almost vertical. There were 20 seconds of sheer terror.

E In the quieter stretches of this magical setting, we'd fish off the rafts, and at night on the river bank, there were jokes and storytelling before we fell asleep under the stars. The internet became a distant memory as the Canyon closed in and the signal disappeared. It was a digital detox to the extreme.

F I wondered if I could hold my breath long enough to survive underwater, and then saw my friend John being hurled off the raft and into the crashing waves. Suddenly, I too was flung headfirst into the freezing water. Bad thoughts filled my mind. But somehow we all survived.

G As we progressed, the Canyon grew grander in scale, cutting a deep gorge, over a kilometre deep in places. It's a geologist's dream, with layers of rock dating back almost two billion years and ancient lava fields that are some of the oldest exposed rock on earth.

You are going to read an article about being a film and television drama extra. For questions **47 – 56**, choose from the sections (**A – D**). The sections may be chosen more than once.

Mark your answers **on the separate answer sheet**.

In which section does the writer

describe how one advantage of the job didn't go according to plan?	**47**
mention experiencing a sense of guilt?	**48**
point out the possible consequences of breaking rules?	**49**
offer advice to people thinking of applying to work as an extra?	**50**
refer to times when the gap between actors and extras appears to narrow?	**51**
acknowledge how appropriate certain terms are?	**52**
explain a common motivation for taking on work as an extra?	**53**
mention gaining insights into hardships that actors experience?	**54**
explain the purpose of an anecdote?	**55**
refer to an incident when he was disappointed by people's behaviour?	**56**

The life of an extra

Most films and TV dramas require extras, those people we glimpse in the background behind the main actors. Mike Jones describes what it's like to be an extra.

A

During a break in the filming of a TV drama, I gravitated towards the table laden with hot coffee and biscuits. As I reached it, however, I was duly informed that it was reserved for the 'talent' – the real actors – and was directed towards a rickety table, on which sat an urn of hot water, some sugar packets, and nothing else. I tell this tale, not just to grumble, but because it sums up the stark divide between the cast and the little people in the background. Referring to us on set by our technical name of 'supporting artistes' is meant to make us feel more important, I suppose. 'Walking background' and 'human props' are common, faintly humorous labels for us, but they're fitting. Extras aren't supposed to say anything during a take; we aren't paid to talk. Nor are we allowed to talk between takes when everything is being reset. A gentle murmur of conversation will inevitably well up among some groups, at which point one of the assistant directors will immediately bellow for silence.

B

There are other non-negotiables, and failing to obey them could result in you being fired and blacklisted from the industry. Your contract specifically orders you not to talk to any of the actors. On one production, I was introduced to the lead actor and told what my role would be in that particular scene. I smiled at him in a mild attempt at camaraderie and he stared right through me. Then, the expression on the face of the lead actress made it clear she had decided not to make an effort with me. I knew I was only an extra, but they might have at least feigned some interest. So why go through this? Well, when I first signed up, I, like many others I know, saw it as an interesting way of earning a second income. The far from generous fees, however, soon meant I regarded it as little more than a hobby, and had I had a family, I probably wouldn't have been able to do it.

C

Occasionally, you're picked out to play a more substantial part in one scene, and you feel as if maybe the professional / supporting artist divide isn't so insurmountable after all. Then, when you're finally released to go home at 2 a.m., after walking up and down some stretch of pavement 50 times, and you realise that the actors still have hours more to go, their job no longer seems quite so glamorous or privileged. Actually, night shoots tend to be the worst, although the extra money you receive almost makes up for it. Once on the set of a blockbuster, a mix-up in the costume department resulted in me spending two nights in an aircraft hangar, drinking terrible coffee and reading books – and getting paid for it. Meanwhile, the other extras all ran around outside in the freezing drizzle for an action scene. Every time they trudged back in from a take, their very visible fatigue and discomfort made me feel somewhat fraudulent, aware as I was that we were all being remunerated at the same rate for our efforts.

D

One of the bonuses of being an extra is the free catering. Getting up at 4 a.m. isn't so bad when you can go straight in for a large breakfast, and a filling lunch is always provided, though you obviously aren't allowed to eat anything before the 'talent' and the crew. For period dramas, you will also get a free haircut, although this can sometimes make things awkward. On one shoot, I had to phone in 'sick' to my day job, and then had trouble explaining to my boss the next morning why I now had a 1950s-style haircut. Another plus may be seeing yourself on screen, usually as a blurry outline to one side or a tiny figure in the distance. That's what extras do: blend into the background and not divert attention from the main characters. Would I encourage anyone to sample this life? Hardly, if the aim is to make money or get into the industry. If, however, you like the idea of dressing up, with the possibility of glimpsing yourself on the big screen for a few seconds, well, maybe.

You **must** answer this question. Write your answer in **220 – 260** words in an appropriate style on the separate answer sheet.

---

1 Your class has watched an online discussion about the factors that should be considered when choosing a college course. You have made the notes below:

> **Factors that should be considered when choosing a college course**
>
> - cost
> - career prospects
> - reputation of the course

> Some opinions expressed in the discussion:
>
> "There are lots of grants to help with the cost of college."
>
> "You should only study a subject that is likely to get you a good career."
>
> "It's best to study a well-known course."

Write an essay for your tutor discussing **two** of the factors in your notes that should be considered when choosing a college course. You should **explain which factor is more important, giving reasons** in support of your answer.

You may, if you wish, make use of the opinions expressed in the discussion, but you should use your own words as far as possible.

Write an answer to **one** of the questions **2 – 4** in this part. Write your answer in **220 – 260** words in an appropriate style on the separate answer sheet. Put the question number in the box at the top of the page.

---

2 The manager at the organisation where you work has invited staff to apply for the opportunity to do a short placement in another city. You have decided to apply. Write an email to your manager, describing your current role in the organisation, explaining why you are a suitable candidate for a placement and saying how the experience will be beneficial for both you and your organisation.

Write your **email**.

3 You have seen the following announcement on an English-language website:

Shopping online or in-person?

Which is better?

Write us a review comparing one online and one in-person shopping experience. Evaluate which experience was preferable in terms of choice, convenience and service.

The best reviews will be featured on our website.

Write your **review**.

4 You study at an international college and help to run a club that received some funding from the college. Now the college principal would like a report. You should describe how the funding you received supported the club's activities, and explain how these activities have contributed to the life of the college. You should also explain why the club deserves to receive funding again this year.

Write your **report**.

23

You will hear three different extracts. For questions **1 – 6**, choose the answer (**A**, **B** or **C**) which fits best according to what you hear. There are two questions for each extract.

Extract One

You hear two sociologists, Nina Havers and Dan Herńandez, discussing praising children.

1 Nina compares praising children to rock climbing because in both activities

   A time is needed to get it right.

   B trust plays an important role.

   C mistakes can have unwanted consequences.

2 What advice does Dan give parents about praising children?

   A Focus on praising effort rather than results.

   B Explain the reason for giving praise.

   C Include praising personal qualities.

Extract Two

You hear two friends, Martha and Robert, discussing golf.

3 Robert had been put off taking up golf until now because he believed

   A it was practised only by a privileged few.

   B it provided relatively little exercise.

   C it was perceived as old-fashioned.

4 What do they agree they should do next?

   A take up an opportunity to find out about a venue

   B get more information about golf from a colleague

   C look into the expense involved in playing golf

Extract Three

You hear two friends talking about a summer music festival they have just been to.

5 According to the man, what element do music festival organisers often overlook?

    A having good communication between sound engineers and bands

    B designing the grounds so that the sound is enhanced

    C ensuring all the equipment is of the highest quality

6 How did the woman first find out that a local band was good?

    A Other musicians were recommending them.

    B Everyone was talking about them in one of the cafés.

    C The number of people listening to them was increasing.

24

You will hear a woman, called Estelle Tinios, giving a talk to students about her job as a pharmacist. For questions **7 – 14**, complete the sentences with a word or short phrase.

WORKING AS A PHARMACIST

Estelle chose to study **(7)** .... for her undergraduate degree.

She recommends working part time as a **(8)** .... in order to make contacts.

She explains that she learnt a great deal from the **(9)** .... she did during

her postgraduate studies.

She was surprised to find out how important **(10)** ....

skills are for a pharmacist.

She suggests that pharmacists who have some **(11)** .... in their

schedule are more likely to find a job.

She worked in research and development, where she was involved in the

(12) .... of medications.

She describes how making sure **(13)** .... are accurate is an important

part of a pharmacist's job.

She explains that there is a growing demand for pharmacists because the

(14) .... is increasing.

25

You will hear an interview in which two entrepreneurs, called Charles and Betty, are talking about their experience of setting up a business when they were young. For questions **15 – 20**, choose the answer (**A**, **B**, **C** or **D**) which fits best according to what you hear.

---

15 What does Charles say about the failure of his first company?

    A   He learnt some valuable lessons from the experience.

    B   He was glad this happened when he was young.

    C   It could have been avoided if he had acted earlier.

    D   It resulted from taking poor advice.

16 Betty and Charles both say that the key to being a successful young entrepreneur is

    A   to be a creative thinker.

    B   to have clear long-term aims.

    C   to have a positive attitude to risk.

    D   to be willing to dedicate enough time to business.

17 In the first year of her business, what did Betty find most difficult?

    A   raising money

    B   hiring employees

    C   getting enough sales

    D   dealing with the paperwork

18 It surprised Charles that his competitors were willing to

    A   recommend professional specialists.

    B   discuss their company structure.

    C   share industry-related data.

    D   refer customers to him.

19 How did Betty feel after she won a Young Businessperson of the Year award?

    A   curious to find out why her business had been selected

    B   determined to live up to the standard of the other contenders

    C   uncertain about the attention her winning attracted

    D   inspired to expand her business

20 According to Charles, technology has made it easier to become an entrepreneur because

    A   websites can reach potential customers.

    B   networking can be done on the internet.

    C   video conferencing makes meetings effective.

    D   online training is outstanding.

You will hear five short extracts in which young people are talking about travelling alone.

TASK ONE

For questions **21 – 25**, choose from the list (**A – H**) the reason each person gives for choosing to travel alone.

TASK TWO

For questions **26 – 30**, choose from the list (**A – H**) what each speaker says was the unexpected consequence of travelling alone.

While you listen you must complete both tasks.

A to keep costs down

B to have time to consider an important decision

C to travel in an eco-friendly way

D to get inspiration for a hobby

E to look for job opportunities

F to become independent

G to be able to act spontaneously

H to be able to achieve fitness aims

Speaker 1	21
Speaker 2	22
Speaker 3	23
Speaker 4	24
Speaker 5	25

A becoming a good problem solver

B feeling calm

C becoming more tolerant

D making new acquaintances

E learning to recognise risk

F developing language skills

G enjoying different foods

H covering a greater distance

Speaker 1	26
Speaker 2	27
Speaker 3	28
Speaker 4	29
Speaker 5	30

Work with a partner if possible, taking it in turn to act in the role of the interlocutor.

Part 1
2 minutes (3 minutes for groups of three)

The interlocutor asks you some questions about yourself, your home, work or studies and familiar topics.

Good morning / afternoon / evening. My name is ... and this is my colleague ... .

And your names are?

Can I have your mark sheets please?

Thank you.

First of all, we'd like to know something about you.

- Where are you from?
- What do you do here / there?
- How long have you been studying English?
- What do you enjoy most about studying English?

The interlocutor then asks you some questions about one or two other topics, for example:

- How has the internet changed the way we communicate?
- What negative effects has the internet had on our social lives?
- Do you like talking on the phone? (Why? / Why not?)
- If you could learn another language, what would it be? (Why?)

Work in groups of three if possible. One of you is the interlocutor and the other two are the candidates.
The interlocutor should lead the task using the script below. Refer to the pictures on pages S13 and S14.

Part 2
4 minutes (6 minutes for groups of three)

Interlocutor	In this part of the test, I'm going to give each of you three pictures. I'd like you to talk about **two** of them on your own for about a minute, and also to answer a question briefly about your partner's pictures.
	[Candidate A], it's your turn first. Here are your pictures. They show **people using screens in different situations**. I'd like you to compare two of the pictures and say **why the people might be using the screens in these situations and what problems they might experience using them**.
	All right?
⏱ *After 1 minute*	Thank you.
	[Candidate B], **who do you think depends on their screen the most? (Why?)**
⏱ *After 30 seconds*	Thank you.
	Now, *[Candidate B]*, here are your pictures. They show **people in situations that require good weather**. I'd like you to compare two of the pictures and say **why good weather is important in these situations and what the people might do if the weather changed**.
⏱ *After 1 minute*	Thank you.
	Now, *[Candidate A]*, **who do you think would be most disappointed by a change in the weather? (Why?)**
⏱ *After 30 seconds*	Thank you.

Part 3 4 minutes (6 minutes for groups of three)

Part 4 5 minutes (8 minutes for groups of three)

Part 3

Work in groups of three if possible. One of you is the interlocutor and the other two are the candidates. The interlocutor should lead the task using the script below. Refer to the task sheet on page S15.

Interlocutor   Now I'd like you to talk about something together for about two minutes.

Here are some places where rules about what people must wear are sometimes important and a question for you to discuss. First you have some time to look at the task.

🕐 *After 15 seconds*   Now, talk to each other about **how important is it to have a dress code in these situations**.

🕐 *After 2 minutes*   Thank you. Now you have about a minute to decide **which of these places should have the strictest dress code**.

🕐 *After 1 minute*   Thank you.

Part 4

The interlocutor asks some general questions which follow on from the topic in Part 3.

Interlocutor
- How far do you think clothes reflect the personality of the person wearing them? (Why?)
- Given a choice, would you prefer to dress comfortably or smartly? (Why?)
- Do you think it's true that wearing different types of clothes can change our moods or the way we feel? (Why? / Why not?)
- Some people prefer to dress similarly to their friends. Why do you think this is?
- Do you think that fashion designers have too much influence over the way we dress? (Why?)
- In your opinion, is it important to spend a lot of money on clothes, in order to look good? (Why? / Why not?)

Thank you. That is the end of the test.

For questions **1 – 8**, read the text below and decide which answer (**A**, **B**, **C**, or **D**) best fits each gap. There is an example at the beginning (**0**).

Mark your answers **on the separate answer sheet**.

Example:

0   **A** feature   **B** matter   **C** point   **D** character

0	A	B	C	D
	▬	▭	▭	▭

Goals

An obsession with achieving goals is a common **(0)** .... of life in many parts of the world today. From childhood, people are encouraged to **(1)** .... goals, and then strive to achieve them. This means people accomplish things they wouldn't otherwise have managed, but such a narrow focus can **(2)** .... to problems.

One problem is that after reaching a goal, the **(3)** .... of achievement is often brief, and you're left unsure where to direct the energy you've been using to **(4)** .... your goals. Another issue is that you're so used to pushing, often well beyond your **(5)** ...., that you don't recognise the need for recovery time. Also, while you're so focused on one thing, other demands in life inevitably **(6)** .... up, and it's easy to lose **(7)** .... of those aspects of life which replenish you – relationships, exercise and hobbies.

What can be done? Besides allowing time to recover and **(8)** .... neglected needs, it helps if you divide the process of achieving a goal into small steps and reward yourself each time you reach one. It's the process that brings happiness, not the endpoint.

1	**A** lay	**B** fit	**C** set	**D** mark
2	**A** result	**B** lead	**C** trigger	**D** cause
3	**A** flavour	**B** mood	**C** taste	**D** sense
4	**A** pursuing	**B** searching	**C** persisting	**D** aspiring
5	**A** margins	**B** limits	**C** borders	**D** restrictions
6	**A** pile	**B** climb	**C** grow	**D** rise
7	**A** touch	**B** vision	**C** sight	**D** mind
8	**A** respond	**B** attend	**C** engage	**D** address

For questions **9 – 16**, read the text below and think of the word which best fits each gap. Use only one word in each gap. There is an example at the beginning (**0**).

Write your answers **IN CAPITAL LETTERS on the separate answer sheet**.

Example: `0` `O` `N` `E`

The 'walk' button at pedestrian crossings

Waiting for the green signal to cross the road can be (**0**) .... of the most frustrating experiences of urban life. (**9**) .... pedestrian crossing buttons are installed at most traffic lights, many people ignore them, believing that pressing them (**10**) .... no difference. Are they right?

Traffic lights are controlled by computerised systems and vary considerably. (**11**) .... a rule, however, at a stand-alone pedestrian crossing away from a junction, pressing the button will turn the traffic lights red. How long you wait is a function of how long (**12**) .... the crossing light was last activated and the volume of traffic. On the other hand, at most junctions and intersections, the system is set so the 'walk' button only functions between midnight and 7a.m. In (**13**) .... words, for most of the day, the timing of the lights is fixed.

At all crossings, however, (**14**) .... the time of day or night, the button (**15**) .... ever needs to be pressed once. Pressing it multiple times will not cause the 'walk' signal to appear any sooner – (**16**) .... if you think it might.

For questions **17 – 24**, read the text below. Use the word given in capitals at the end of some of the lines to form a word that fits in the gap **in the same line**. There is an example at the beginning (**0**).

Write your answers **IN CAPITAL LETTERS on the separate answer sheet.**

Example: | 0 | L | I | K | I | N | G | | | | | | | | | | | | |

Does taste in music reflect personality?

If you have a strong **(0)** .... for uncomplicated, relaxing and acoustic music, the   **LIKE**

chances are you will be an extrovert. At least, this is what the **(17)** .... of research   **FIND**

into the links between musical taste and personality suggest.

Psychologists conducted worldwide online surveys with over 20,000 voluntary

(18) .... of different ages and backgrounds. Each volunteer completed a   **PARTICIPATE**

standard test that rates the five main components of personality – openness, extroversion,

agreeableness, neuroticism and conscientiousness – and was asked to state their

(19) .... from a selection of 25 pre-categorised musical excerpts.   **PREFER**

The surveys showed that open personalities liked dynamic music, but were relatively

(20) .... by slow, mellow music. They also revealed that extroverts, who are very   **IMPRESS**

(21) .... and energetic, tended to like unpretentious music. Perhaps   **TALK**

(22) .... , agreeable people usually rated most music they listened to highly,   **PREDICT**

(23) .... of genre, while neurotics did the reverse. Conscientiousness was the   **REGARD**

only trait which revealed no **(24)** .... with musical type.   **CORRELATE**

So the researchers concluded that if you know someone's musical taste, you can have a good

guess at their personality – and vice-versa.

For questions **25 – 30**, complete the second sentence so that it has a similar meaning to the first sentence, using the word given. **Do not change the word given.** You must use between **three** and **six** words, including the word given. Here is an example (**0**).

Example:

0 'I'm sorry I got to the party so late,' Joanna said to her friend.

HAVING

Joanna apologised to her friend .... up so late at the party.

The gap can be filled with the words 'for having turned', so you write:

Example: | **0** | *FOR HAVING TURNED*

Write **only** the missing words **IN CAPITAL LETTERS on the separate answer sheet**.

---

25 I knew nothing at all about who was to blame for the mistake in the report.

WHOSE

I had absolutely .... the mistake in the report was.

26 Jack couldn't solve the problem because he didn't have enough time.

ABLE

Jack would .... out the problem if he'd had enough time.

27 Gabi soon learned how to communicate in Romanian every day.

LONG

It .... Gabi to learn to communicate in Romanian every day.

28 I found Catherine's commitment to her job impressive.

HOW

I was .... Catherine was to her job.

29 Frank doesn't dream of being a professional footballer any more.

GIVEN

Frank .... being a professional footballer.

30 Moussa doesn't think that ironing his T-shirts every time he washes them is important.

BOTHERED

Moussa .... iron his T-shirts every time he washes them.

You are going to read an article about bilingualism. For questions **31 – 36**, choose the answer (**A, B, C** or **D**) which you think fits best according to the text.

Mark your answers **on the separate answer sheet**.

Bilingualism

What do we know about the impact that speaking more than one language has on people?
Journalist Jane Morgan investigates.

In a café in south London, two construction workers are engaged in cheerful banter. Their cutlery dances during more emphatic gesticulations and they occasionally break off into loud laughter. They are discussing a friend, that much is clear, but the details are lost on me. It's a shame, because it sounds intriguing, especially to a nosy person like me. I can't help but interrupt to ask what language they are speaking. They both switch easily to English, explaining that they are South Africans and had been speaking Xhosa. In Johannesburg, where they are from, most people speak at least five languages. One of them speaks seven. Was it easy to learn so many languages? 'Yes, it's normal,' he laughs.

A week later, I am sitting in a laboratory, headphones on, looking at pictures of snowflakes on a computer. It's part of a seemingly simple experiment – though there's a catch – run by Panos Athanasopoulos, a leading *line 9* researcher of the bilingual mind. As each pair of snowflakes appears, I hear a description of one of them through the headphones. There's nothing else to look at. All I have to do is decide which snowflake is being described. The descriptions, however, are in an invented language called Syntaflake, bearing no similarity to languages I know. The task is strange and incredibly difficult, and by the end, I have to admit defeat.

I join Athanasopoulos and glumly recount my struggle to learn the language, despite my best efforts. But it appears that was where I went wrong: 'The people who perform best on this task are the ones who don't care at all and just want to get it over with. Interested people like yourself try to find a pattern and they always do worst,' he says. 'It's impossible, in the time given, to decipher the rules of the language and make sense of what's being said to you. But your brain is primed to work it out subconsciously. That's why if you don't think about it, you'll do OK. Children do the best.'

What lies behind Athanasopoulos' invention of a new language for the snowflake test is a desire to look at the connections between language and culture. Part of his research is about teasing out the language from the culture it is threaded within.

Ask me in English what my favourite food is and I will picture myself in London choosing from the options I enjoy there. But ask me in French and I transport myself to Paris, where the options I'll choose from are different. So the same deeply personal question gets a different answer depending on the language in which you're asking me. This idea that you gain a new personality with every language you speak is a profound one.

The interest of Athanasopoulos and his colleagues in the capacity of language to change people's world views builds on earlier research. In the 1960s, Susan Ervin-Tripp, a linguist based at the University of California, asked Japanese-English bilingual women to finish sentences in each language. She found that the women ended the sentences very differently, depending on which language was used. For example, 'When my wishes conflict with my family ...' was completed in Japanese as 'it is a time of great unhappiness'; in English, as 'I do what I want'. Ervin-Tripp concluded that human thought takes place within language mindsets and that bilinguals have different mindsets for each language. It's an extraordinary idea, but one that has been borne out in subsequent studies; and many bilinguals say they feel like a different person when they speak their other language.

To assess the effect that trying to understand the Syntaflake language had on my brain, I took another test before and after the snowflake task. This test involved matching patterns of arrows and required great concentration. It's not a task where practice improves performance, but when I did the same test again after the snowflake task, I was significantly better at it. The arrow task involved blocking out impulses and heeding rules. The part of the brain that manages this is the anterior cingulate cortex (ACC). Part of the brain's 'executive system', the ACC enables the brain to concentrate on one task while blocking out competing information and to switch focus between different tasks. The snowflake test primed my ACC for the second arrow task, just as bilingual activity seems to train the executive system more generally. In fact, a steady stream of studies has shown that bilinguals outperform monolinguals in a range of cognitive and social tasks and suggests that the executive systems of bilinguals are different from, and in some ways superior to, those of monolinguals.

31 What feeling does the writer express about the two construction workers she comes across in a café?

    A envy about the skills they possess

    B irritation over the disturbance they are causing

    C frustration at her limited ability to understand them

    D embarrassment at the extent of her interest in them

32 When the writer describes the 'snowflake experiment', what is the 'catch' referred to in line 9?

    A the artificiality of the situation

    B the difficulty of the audio task

    C the uniformity of the onscreen images

    D the poor level of her own performance

33 What point is made about the snowflake experiment in the third paragraph?

    A It required a degree of commitment that many people are unwilling to give.

    B The researcher was unsurprised by the writer's lack of success in it.

    C It was designed with specific personality types in mind.

    D The writer misunderstood the point of it.

34 In the fifth paragraph, the writer is

    A explaining her own views.

    B introducing a new subject.

    C illustrating a point made previously.

    D exploring the implications of a theory.

35 The writer says that Susan Ervin-Tripp's research findings

    A are particularly convincing because of how distinct the two languages are

    B are in line with the intuitions that lots of people have.

    C are based on a limited amount of evidence.

    D have been disputed by other researchers.

36 What point does the writer make about the three tests that she did?

    A They reflect the impact that speaking more than one language can have on the brain.

    B They highlight how switching from one language to another can cause difficulties.

    C Doing them provides insights into how best to learn multiple languages.

    D Their usefulness depends on having a repetitive structure.

You are going to read four extracts from reviews of a book about sport and philosophy by David Papineau. For questions **37 – 40**, choose from reviews **A – D**. The reviews may be chosen more than once.

Mark your answers **on the separate answer sheet**.

Reviews of *Knowing the Score* by David Papineau

A

In *Knowing the Score*, David Papineau, an eminent philosopher and a passionate lover of sport, applies his philosopher's brain to various sporting questions that interest him. The anecdotal delivery is more in keeping with a dinner table discussion than an exposition in a lecture theatre, but, given the intended general readership, that's no bad thing. Topics addressed include rule-breaking, decision-making, co-operation, and the extent to which genes and/or the environment determine sporting ability. Papineau points out that when sporting success runs in a family, it tends to be in certain sports with very specific environments. Formula 1, where access to fast cars enhances your chances of being good at driving them, is an obvious example. This idea makes good sense, though it's not particularly groundbreaking. Papineau may have been able to take it further, had he looked at more empirical research on the subject. In fact, the limited statistical data that Papineau offers is a frustratingly recurrent feature of the book. That said, *Knowing the Score* is enjoyable and thought-provoking.

B

David Papineau is a professional philosopher whose thoughts on sport are cogent and fluently expressed in everyday English, with specialist references that might deter the non-philosopher rarely intruding. The fairly infrequent citation of scientific research might be a weakness in a scholarly text, but it's an asset in a book of this type. Papineau examines an array of sporting questions – from the disputed question of what actually constitutes a sport to why people 'choke' in highly pressurised situations. At times he strays too far from sport – his chapter on questions of ethnicity being a case in point – but on many questions he is very enlightening. For example, he shows why sporting dynasties are more common in some sports than others. In ice hockey, access to ice and specialist equipment confers advantages on those growing up with ice-hockey-playing parents, while in equipment-light sports, such as football or basketball, genetic disposition will be a more significant factor.

C

Knowing the Score is not a book on the philosophy of sport as much as a collection of meditations by a philosopher who happens to be a sports fan. At a time when data analysis dominates 'serious' discussion of sport, Papineau's faith in pure reasoning is particularly refreshing, as he explores an extensive list of sporting issues in informal, enthusiastic, charming prose. Among the sections I relished, was his explanation of the moral case for accepting authority while retaining the right to transgress against it, as demonstrated by the professional foul in football. On the debit side, the book could do with an examination of gender in the context of sport, and the relevance of his chapter on race was not particularly convincing. But overall, a book which is highly recommended.

D

Knowing the Score is written by a philosopher who applies his skills to a subject he loves, but it's a series of essays rather than a scholarly work. The bibliography is sparse and there are very few references. What's more, Papineau's reflections are mixed. His discussions of the nature–nurture distinction are as logical, sensible and instructive as anything I have read on the subject, but his chapter on amateurism consists almost entirely of the tired old cliché that amateurism is elitism in disguise – Papineau clearly hasn't looked at other recent studies on the subject. In fact, he rarely backs up any of his claims by quoting from serious research findings, which, to my mind, is a flaw. I have no argument with the issues that Papineau has decided to look at. However, his eye seems to be on a mass readership, including people who don't know much about either sport or philosophy and, consequently, the book has a popularising, somewhat condescending tone.

Which expert

shares B's view regarding how appropriate Papineau's choice of topics is? **37** ☐

shares A's view regarding Papineau's use of evidence to support his ideas? **38** ☐

expresses a different view from the others on Papineau's writing style in this book? **39** ☐

has a different view from B regarding Papineau's treatment of the issue of nature versus nurture? **40** ☐

You are going to read an article about an architect, called Victor Gruen, who designed one of the first shopping malls in the USA. Six paragraphs have been removed from the article. Choose from the paragraphs **A – G** the one which fits each gap (**41 – 46**). There is one extra paragraph which you do not need to use.

Mark your answers **on the separate answer sheet**.

Victor Gruen and the Southdale shopping mall

According to its critics, the shopping mall is central to the mindless, car-bound consumerism of suburban USA. Yet Southdale Center, the first fully enclosed, climate-controlled mall from which so many other malls descend, came from the mind of an anti-car European idealist. In 1938, Victor Gruen arrived in America from Vienna in Austria with high architectural aims. He soon launched a career designing storefronts in New York City, but in 1952 he was commissioned to design something else entirely: a shopping centre 15 kilometres outside the city of Minneapolis.

41

A somewhat extreme view, perhaps, but it's important to understand the historical background. When Gruen first came up with the concept of the shopping mall, it seemed very radical. He first publicly submitted such a design in 1943 to a competition run by an architectural magazine, which had called upon architects to imagine the city of the future.

42

The next decade saw a shift in thinking. The 1952 commission that brought the Southdale Center into the world came from the Dayton family, a name synonymous with department stores in 1950s Minneapolis. They wanted a shopping centre to house a new store planned for the growing suburb of Edina. When it opened in 1956, Southdale contained that new branch of Dayton's, another large department store, and space for more than 70 smaller shops in between.

43

But where the open-air design of those projects left them exposed to the elements, Southdale sealed off the outside environment in order to better create its own world within. Southdale's vast, blank walls turned their backs to the street, enclosing stores, cafés, pedestrian boulevards and a courtyard, through whose skylight the sun shone on a fishpond, foliage and a centrepiece cage filled with songbirds.

44

But the utter controllability of the enclosed shopping mall had to do with much more than the climate. It both appealed to Gruen's design philosophy and played straight into the fears of many Americans. They didn't just want protection from the heat, rain, snow and traffic encountered downtown; they also wanted protection from the people encountered there.

45

To this end, he designed Southdale as one element of a masterplan, including hundreds of hectares of residential, commercial, medical, office and mixed-use projects around a lake and public park. The developers, however, ignored most of this wider vision and, instead, set the precedent for all the huge, unimaginative-looking malls surrounded by enormous car parks – 1,500 of which appeared across America in the half-century after Southdale's unveiling.

46

Hence the nostalgia that often accompanies the 21st century's desertions, or even demolitions, of some of the United States' enclosed malls. But suburban Americans now have a host of revitalised genuine downtowns to choose from, as well as a new wave of high-design, urban-flavoured, outward-looking shopping malls. Time has moved on for the mall.

A By then, the concept had some precedents around America. These included the Northgate Mall in Seattle, which opened in 1950, Valley Fair Mall in Appleton, Wisconsin, which opened in 1954, and Gruen's own Northland Mall outside Detroit.

B Despite this, when the renowned architect Frank Lloyd Wright visited Southdale, he was sceptical. He believed that Gruen's notion of moving 'downtown' to the suburbs was unrealistic. Victor Gruen's real aim, however, was to build a new kind of city, not just a shopping centre, and he later claimed that his conception of the shopping mall never came into being.

C Those social concerns were somewhat at odds with Gruen's own. He was interested in creating not just a 'gigantic shopping machine', but a community centre where, free from 'the terror of the automobile', people could stroll, congregate, debate and enjoy the human experience.

D Unfortunately, Gruen's entry, with its full enclosure and lack of a central square, struck even the most forward-thinking judges as a bit much. So Gruen went back to the drawing board.

E Gruen would eventually criticise, even disown, this form that the US shopping mall took. Local residents, however, loved Southdale, and across the country, subsequent generations growing up far from a genuine city centre turned to places like Southdale for the closest thing to an urban experience they could find.

F The writer James Lileks says of that early Southdale aesthetic: 'You have no idea what an innovation it was in the 1950s; there wasn't any place where you could sit "outside" in your shirt-sleeves in the middle of winter' – least of all in a place where it gets as cold as it does in Minneapolis.

G This was Gruen's opportunity to realise his long-imagined vision of an indoor city centre that would import the urbanity of his native Vienna into his fast-growing adopted homeland. Southdale itself was constructed. Nothing else went as he'd envisaged, however, and by the 1970s, Gruen had returned to Austria, having concluded that he'd created a monster.

You are going to read an article about ultramarathons. For questions **47 – 56**, choose from the sections of the article (**A – D**). The sections may be chosen more than once.

Mark your answers **on the separate answer sheet**.

In which section does the writer mention

a sense of nostalgia for what ultramarathons used to be like?	**47**
a view that there's a misconception about how most runners approach ultramarathons?	**48**
a method for dealing with excessive numbers of race applicants?	**49**
a belief that an increased demand for ultramarathons to take part in is inevitable?	**50**
an issue that many ultramarathon runners deliberately ignore?	**51**
an individual's initial motive for running an ultramarathon?	**52**
a contrast between everyday life and the ultramarathon experience?	**53**
a state of mind that ultramarathon runners seek?	**54**
a general shift in perceptions about what constitutes a genuine challenge?	**55**
a theory explaining the rapid rise in the popularity of ultramarathons?	**56**

Ultramarathons

At 80 kilometres or more in length, ultramarathon races are at least double the length of the traditional marathon. Yet the number of people running ultramarathons is rising fast. Long-distance runner Louis Adu investigates.

A

About a year ago, I was standing at the office tea point when a colleague, who had heard I was a runner, asked me if I did ultramarathons. He looked put out when I told him I didn't. 'Triathlons?' he asked. I shook my head. 'Oh, just marathons?' In terms of impressing colleagues, family and friends, it seems marathons no longer cut it. We are in the post-marathon age, when everybody knows somebody who has run a marathon. Now, it seems, for a feat to impress, it's better if you can reel off numbers in the hundreds, and preferably over an insanely steep mountain range or a desert. The last decade has seen an explosion in the number of races. 'In previous years,' one ultramarathon race organiser, Karl Lang said, 'you could just turn up on the day and enter, but now the most popular races sell out in minutes.' Many of the world's most oversubscribed events, such as the Ultra-Trail de Mont-Blanc in France, have had to implement lottery systems to manage the hordes wanting to take part.

B

I myself have now completed five ultramarathons. I had run six marathons, when someone suggested I run the six-day, 165km Oman Desert Race. In strict running terms, the race held little appeal, but the notion of crossing a vast stretch of barely charted land, with only myself and a backpack of energy bars to keep me going, lured me in. While adventure has always appealed to the human spirit, Lang puts the almost overnight boom down to the growth of social media, which spreads the word and fires imaginations: 'People see their friends' pictures and go, "Wow, I want to do that."' Some in the ultramarathon world, however, are disdainful of this, saying it has given rise to people looking for kudos by calling themselves ultra-runners, and that the sport has lost its edge as a result. 'Once all ultras had a sense of danger,' one race director told me wistfully. 'Now so many races make it easy for runners to achieve this 'status' with 'everyone-that-enters-is-a-winner' and finisher-hand-holding events.'

C

Experienced ultra-runner Josefina Gomez sees things somewhat differently. 'So many people have done a marathon, that now if someone tells you they're running one, you ask if they're doing it in a panda outfit or something,' she says. 'It's not that the marathon is no longer a stiff test because it is. It's just, over time, that there's a kind of natural race inflation. The human spirit will always want more. It will always crave that feeling of pushing itself to the edge.' I often hear ultra-runners talking about pain. As the world becomes ever more sanitised and automated, there's a deep stirring to get out of our comfort zone. At one event, I met a Swiss couple in their late 60s. They looked completely shattered after three days pushing themselves through scorching heat. This was their 15th ultra. 'Why do we do this?' Melanie asked rhetorically. 'We have such a nice home.' Her husband, Ralf, looked at her and said simply: 'Because we have such a nice home.'

D

After completing his first ultra, Omar Nasri blogged that 'the race pounded me almost into submission before somehow I was lifted on a wave of euphoria.' Veteran ultra Keiko Sato recognises the experience. 'You move from agony to a place where the beauty and timelessness of the present moment come into sharp focus – you actively chase that.' A number of recent studies, however, including a widely publicised one led by James O'Malley, suggest that the obvious health benefits of running begin to tail off, and even reverse, if you run 'excessively'. An irreversible hardening of the tissue around the heart is the main concern. Physiologist and ultra-runner Greg Smith says 'the evidence is there, and we – the ultra community – often bury our heads in the sand over things like this.' But researchers like O'Malley tend to conflate intensity and duration of exercise to define 'extreme'. Ultra-running may, on the surface, seem extreme, but, in practice, it is usually undertaken at a low intensity – with walking forming a large chunk of most ultra races for the majority of competitors. 'Anyway,' says one runner, 'it's difficult to do enough to put you at greater risk than couch potatoes.'

You **must** answer this question. Write your answer in **220 – 260** words in an appropriate style on the separate answer sheet.

1 Your class has watched a television discussion about the qualities that contribute to people having a successful life. You have made the notes below:

Qualities that contribute to a successful life

- ambition
- honesty
- flexibility

Some opinions expressed in the discussion:

"It's so important to have goals."

"If you're not honest, people can't trust you."

"These days, the skills you need change so fast."

Write an essay for your tutor discussing **two** of the qualities in your notes that contribute to a successful life. You should **identify which quality is more important, giving reasons** to support your opinion.

You may, if you wish, make use of the opinions expressed in the discussion, but you should use your own words as far as possible.

Write an answer to **one** of the questions **2 – 4** in this part. Write your answer in **220 – 260** words in an appropriate style on the separate answer sheet. Put the question number in the box at the top of the page.

---

2   You are a student at an international college. The course you are following does not currently have a work experience element to it. Write a proposal for your college principal in which you describe the course you are on, and explain why you think a period of work experience would be beneficial. You should also suggest how work experience could best be included on the course.

Write your **proposal**.

3   You work for an international organisation which is located outside a major city. Your manager has asked you to write a report on the impact of commuting to this location. You should briefly say how your colleagues get to and from work, and evaluate the impact of the daily commute on them. Also, you should make suggestions about suitable ways to deal with the issues related to commuting.

Write your **report**.

4   An international website that you enjoy has asked readers to contribute reviews of places of natural beauty. You have decided to write a review for the website. You should briefly describe a place of natural beauty that you know and evaluate its significance. You should also say how this place could improve its accessibility without damaging its beauty.

Write your **review**.

27

You will hear three different extracts. For questions **1 – 6**, choose the answer (**A, B** or **C**) which fits best according to what you hear. There are two questions for each extract.

Extract One

You hear two friends, Jeanette and David, talking about playing the guitar.

1 What does Jeanette say about being motivated to practise playing the guitar?

   A Not wanting to practise sometimes is normal.

   B Studying how to increase motivation is a waste of time.

   C There is no link between feeling motivated and musical ability.

2 Why did David take up playing the guitar as a hobby?

   A to improve his maths skills

   B to feel less stressed about his college course

   C to be able to concentrate for longer

Extract Two

You hear two engineers who work in the same company talking on the radio about new technology and roads.

3 At the moment, the man is working on new technology for

   A road markings.

   B electric lights on roads.

   C a special type of road surface.

4 What is the woman doing when she talks about roads made of glass?

   A reassuring listeners that these roads are safe

   B clarifying what the man said about these roads

   C outlining a potential problem with these roads

Extract Three

You hear two sociologists talking about disagreeing.

5 Why does the woman think disagreeing is a complex topic?

   A People can feel a range of emotions when others disagree with them.

   B People express disagreement differently depending on their age.

   C People's reactions to disagreeing depend on their culture.

6 What did the man do when a colleague disagreed with him?

   A asked questions to try to understand the reasons

   B repeated his opinion politely

   C attempted to change the subject

You will hear a fabric designer, called Pedro Carwin, talking about sources of inspiration for the design of fabrics used in fashion. For questions **7 – 14**, complete the sentences with a word or short phrase.

28

INSPIRATION FOR FABRIC DESIGN

Pedro believes that some types of film are better sources of inspiration than others, especially

(7) .... films.

Pedro recommends that designers should look carefully at the **(8)** ....

of the food when they eat out.

Pedro gets ideas by listening to music and visualising what he calls a

(9) .... of the music.

Pedro is often stimulated by the different **(10)** ....

of objects in the natural world.

What surprised Pedro most was when a colleague used a **(11)** ....

for inspiration.

Pedro says that studying the **(12)** ....

of colours in photos can be helpful.

Pedro uses the word **(13)** ....

to describe the Art Deco style of architecture, which he particularly appreciates.

According to Pedro, fabric which has been influenced by **(14)** ....

can look stunning for jackets.

29

You will hear a discussion in which two food technology students, called Bill and Kelly, are talking with their tutor about the Mediterranean diet. For questions **15–20**, choose the answer (**A**, **B**, **C** or **D**) which fits best according to what you hear.

15 What difficulty has Bill had with the term 'Mediterranean diet'?

   A There's little evidence of it in Mediterranean countries.
   B It's used incorrectly by anti-ageing adverts.
   C It means different things in different countries.
   D Globalisation has influenced the original concept.

16 Why does the tutor mention bread and pasta?

   A to remind the students that lifestyles have changed
   B to point out that these are common foods in most cultures
   C to question the health claims for the Mediterranean diet
   D to suggest that healthy food is usually simple

17 What point does Kelly make about olive oil?

   A Many people find it unappetising.
   B It's too expensive for most people.
   C It's said to be good for the heart.
   D How it's manufactured is important.

18 Bill and Kelly agree that the Mediterranean diet is hard to follow because

   A many people have less time now to cook from scratch.
   B many people prefer to have snacks rather than eating meals.
   C advertising of processed food is prevalent.
   D people have a natural love of sugar.

19 Bill thinks that people are happier when

   A they eat outdoors.
   B they eat with others.
   C they eat a balanced diet.
   D they eat and then have a nap.

20 Kelly would like to do some research into

   A traditional recipes based on the Mediterranean diet.
   B how the Mediterranean diet alters according to the season.
   C the connection between the Mediterranean diet and memory.
   D how the Mediterranean diet has been widely adopted in other countries.

🎧 30

You will hear five short extracts in which people are talking about sports.

TASK ONE

For questions **21 – 25**, choose from the list (**A – H**) the reason each person gives for the decline in traditional sports.

While you listen you must complete both tasks.

A the length of games

B the rigid rules

C the shortage of sportsgrounds

D the expense of equipment

E the lack of interest in physical fitness

F the acceptance of a wider definition of sport

G the change in TV viewing habits

H the shift away from group activities

Speaker 1 [   ] 21

Speaker 2 [   ] 22

Speaker 3 [   ] 23

Speaker 4 [   ] 24

Speaker 5 [   ] 25

TASK TWO

For questions **26 – 30**, choose from the list (**A – H**) what each person predicts about the future of sports.

A Sports will become more dangerous.

B Different sports will combine with each other.

C Technology will replace referees.

D Sports fans and players will be younger.

E Sports video games will replace traditional sports.

F Sports will be much more fun.

G Fans will access more data about performance.

H Sportspeople will be paid less.

Speaker 1 [   ] 26

Speaker 2 [   ] 27

Speaker 3 [   ] 28

Speaker 4 [   ] 29

Speaker 5 [   ] 30

Work with a partner if possible, taking it in turn to act in the role of the interlocutor.

Part 1
2 minutes (3 minutes for groups of three)

The interlocutor asks you some questions about yourself, your home, work or studies and familiar topics.

Good morning / afternoon / evening. My name is ... and this is my colleague ... .

And your names are?

Can I have your mark sheets please?

Thank you.

First of all, we'd like to know something about you.

- Where are you from?
- What do you do here / there?
- How long have you been studying English?
- What do you enjoy most about studying English?

The interlocutor then asks you some questions about one or two other topics, for example:

- What are the benefits of having a fixed routine?
- Would you say that you lead a healthy lifestyle? (Why? / Why not?)
- Have you learned a new skill over the last year?
- Is there something that you hope to have done by this time next week?

Work in groups of three if possible. One of you is the interlocutor and the other two are the candidates. The interlocutor should lead the task using the script below. Refer to the pictures on pages S16 and S17.

Part 2
4 minutes (6 minutes for groups of three)

Interlocutor	In this part of the test, I'm going to give each of you three pictures. I'd like you to talk about **two** of them on your own for about a minute, and also to answer a question briefly about your partner's pictures.
	[Candidate A], it's your turn first. Here are your pictures. They show **people painting in different situations**. I'd like you to compare two of the pictures and say **what might have inspired the people to paint in these different situations and how they might feel when they have finished painting**.
	All right?
⏱ *After 1 minute*	Thank you.
	[Candidate B], **who do you think is enjoying painting the most? (Why?)**
⏱ *After 30 seconds*	Thank you.
	Now, *[Candidate B]*, here are your pictures. They show **people sharing different experiences**. I'd like you to compare two of the pictures and say **how the people might benefit from sharing these experiences and how long they might remember them**.
⏱ *After 1 minute*	Thank you.
	Now, *[Candidate A]*, **who do you think is likely to repeat the experience the soonest? (Why?)**
⏱ *After 30 seconds*	Thank you.

Part 3 4 minutes (6 minutes for groups of three)

Part 4 5 minutes (8 minutes for groups of three)

Part 3

Work in groups of three if possible. One of you is the interlocutor and the other two are the candidates. The interlocutor should lead the task using the script below. Refer to the task sheet on page S18.

Interlocutor	Now I'd like you to talk about something together for about two minutes.
	Here are some things that can influence our future careers and a question for you to discuss. First you have some time to look at the task.
🕐 *After 15 seconds*	Now, talk to each other about **how these things can influence a person's future career**.
🕐 *After 2 minutes*	Thank you. Now you have about a minute to decide **which of these things has least influence on our choice of career**.
🕐 *After 1 minute*	Thank you.

Part 4

The interlocutor asks some general questions which follow on from the topic in Part 3.

Interlocutor
- Do you think it's a good idea to listen to advice from friends or family when choosing a future career? (Why? / Why not?)
- Some students have a period of work experience while they are still studying. How valuable do you think this is? (Why?)
- Some people say that good qualifications are the most important thing to have when looking for a job. Do you agree? (Why? / Why not?)
- Would you say that it's better to make a career choice at an early age, or to keep your options open as long as possible? (Why?)
- How far do you think celebrities and popular culture influence people's career ambitions? (Why?)
- What sort of jobs do you think will not be done by robots in the future? (Why?)

Thank you. That is the end of the test.

For questions **1 – 8**, read the text below and decide which answer (**A**, **B**, **C**, or **D**) best fits each gap. There is an example at the beginning (**0**).

Mark your answers **on the separate answer sheet**.

Example:

| 0 | A informed | B announced | C reported | D notified |

```
    A   B   C   D
0  □   □   ▣   □
```

A lost Amazonian civilisation

In the early years of the 16th century, the first Europeans to travel to the Amazon region **(0)** .... seeing widespread settlements, including cities and roads. These accounts were subsequently **(1)** .... as fantasies, however, and for centuries the region was considered a largely untouched wilderness.

In recent decades, however, deforestation has helped reveal evidence, mainly in the **(2)** .... of large earthworks, of extensive ancient settlements. In one recent study of a **(3)** .... remote part of the Amazon, researchers **(4)** .... satellite images and identified 81 ancient sites, **(5)** .... from single hamlets to large fortified villages. The team also visited many sites and came **(6)** .... fragments of ceramics and other traces of human presence.

These discoveries have added **(7)** .... to the idea that populations in the Amazon were much greater than once thought, and it is now estimated that as many as 10 million people lived there. What happened to them all? According to one expert, 'Diseases travelled faster than people, and populations were weakened by European diseases, like smallpox, even before Europeans ever **(8)** .... foot in the area.'

1	A declined	B dismissed	C denied	D dispelled
2	A form	B model	C pattern	D feature
3	A virtually	B roughly	C practically	D relatively
4	A sought	B probed	C scoured	D peered
5	A ranging	B lining	C covering	D grading
6	A over	B about	C across	D through
7	A size	B force	C charge	D weight
8	A left	B set	C put	D stepped

For questions **9 – 16**, read the text below and think of the word which best fits each gap. Use only one word in each gap. There is an example at the beginning (**0**).

Write your answers **IN CAPITAL LETTERS on the separate answer sheet**.

Example: **0** | W | H | I | L | E | | | | | | | | | | | | | | |

Birds as 'language' learners

Birds gain life skills in various ways. **(0)** .... some of what they know is innate, some is acquired by direct experience. Scientists in Australia have been exploring a third way: a type of social learning, in **(9)** .... individual birds learn from others **(10)** .... than through direct experience.

Like many wild animals, birds listen to the alarm calls of other species, **(11)** .... it possible for them to take advantage of many eyes looking out **(12)** .... danger. The Australian scientists have found that the fairy wren, a small songbird, can learn those unfamiliar calls, **(13)** .... the bird that made the call even being visible.

The researchers trained fairy wrens, **(14)** .... the absence of any predator, by broadcasting unfamiliar sounds together with the alarm calls of other fairy wrens and other bird species. Initially, the fairy wrens didn't flee from the unfamiliar sounds. But after training, they usually **(15)** .... so. The results show the rapid way learning can occur. One researcher says: 'It's something that can come in handy, given **(16)** .... hard it can be to see predators and callers in many environments.'

For questions **17 – 24**, read the text below. Use the word given in capitals at the end of some of the lines to form a word that fits in the gap **in the same line**. There is an example at the beginning (**0**).

Write your answers **IN CAPITAL LETTERS on the separate answer sheet**.

Example: | 0 | E | X | C | E | S | S | I | V | E | | | | | | | | | |

Too much exercise?

How do you stop yourself from doing an **(0)** .... amount of exercise?   **EXCEED**

(17) .... , this is a question that doesn't worry too many of us. Health experts are   **ADMIT**

often mocked for changing their advice **(18)** .... from one day to the next, but on   **DRAMA**

one thing the message has been constant: the more exercise you do, the better.

A major recent study, however, found that while those who exercised regularly felt better

than those for whom the norm was **(19)** .... , people who regularly exercised for   **ACTIVE**

more than 90 minutes at a time reported a **(20)** .... of their mental health.   **WORSE**

Personal trainer Liam Shelby believes that exercise is just as important for our mental

(21) .... as for our physical fitness. But he acknowledges there are people who   **BEING**

'don't know their limits and **(22)** .... it. Some people I've met, for example, confuse   **DO**

(23) .... with lacking strength or motivation – and it's not the same thing.'   **TIRED**

Liam agrees that people can have an unhealthy **(24)** .... to exercise. 'Still, for the   **ADDICT**

majority of people, the compelling issue is how to do more exercise, not less.'

For questions **25 – 30**, complete the second sentence so that it has a similar meaning to the first sentence, using the word given. **Do not change the word given.** You must use between **three** and **six** words, including the word given. Here is an example (**0**).

Example:

0 'I'm sorry I got to the party so late,' Joanna said to her friend.

HAVING

Joanna apologised to her friend .... up so late at the party.

The gap can be filled with the words 'for having turned', so you write:

Example: | **0** | *FOR HAVING TURNED*

Write **only** the missing words **IN CAPITAL LETTERS on the separate answer sheet**.

---

25 The police didn't allow the visiting team's fans to leave the stadium until an hour after the match.

PREVENTED

The visiting team's fans .... the stadium by the police until an hour after the match.

26 I don't get the impression that Gareth is particularly disorganised.

STRIKE

Gareth .... particularly disorganised.

27 Alexis and John are trying to spend less money on fast food.

EFFORT

Alexis and John are .... on the amount of money they spend on fast food.

28 We must remember that the organising group is planning to make changes to next year's festival.

BEING

We must bear .... planned by the organising group for next year's festival.

29 What the charity most wants to do is make teenagers more aware of the importance of regular exercise.

RAISE

The charity's main aim is .... of the importance of regular exercise.

30 No one else apart from Keith complained when he had to work late.

OBJECTED

It was only Keith .... late.

You are going to read an article about opera. For questions **31 – 36**, choose the answer (**A, B, C** or **D**) which you think fits best according to the text.

Mark your answers **on the separate answer sheet**.

Opera today

Journalist Laura James meets three young composers of operatic works.

We're crammed in along one wall of a studio in London as two singers rehearse a short scene from a new opera. From a piano jammed between members of the assembled team, a pianist plays simple harmonies soon to be played by an orchestra. The singers sound lyrical, but hesitantly so, fixating on just a handful of notes: they are playing a mother and son struggling to communicate. It's moving to watch, even in this raw form – but it's also constantly evolving. Frustrated with the pacing, the conductor stops the singers mid-phrase. 'We've lost some reality now because it's become "opera",' she says. There are nods all round. Hang on a minute. We're in a rehearsal for a new operatic work and the conductor is worried it's sounding like opera?

Then I understand. She wants to avoid the age-old model of European opera as over-the-top melodrama full of improbable plot twists – the stuff that has long fed the genre's reputation for elitism, prejudice and all-round silliness.

When I arrive at the rehearsal, the performers are just speaking their lines, searching for an unaffected-sounding *lin*
delivery, feeling their way through the human drama. The piece is by the composer Jane Peel. Peel leaves no space for *lin*
timeworn clichés, and this seems to fit in with an emerging trend, which includes some repertory-ready works already *lin*
playing at some of the great opera houses.

'I only found out about opera as an adult,' says Peel, who holds a special studentship – Doctoral Composer-in-Residence – at the Royal Opera House in London. 'I came to it from contemporary music and then sort of went backwards.' I wonder whether being a relative newcomer has meant that Peel has partly sidestepped the pressures exerted by opera's long history – both its masterpieces and its elitist reputation. 'Working in an amazing building like the Royal Opera House, full of photos of great singers and productions from the past, it feels nice to be part of that history – but I don't feel terrified by it,' she explains. 'I have no fixed ideas about what a good subject for an opera is. I'm more driven by intuition.'

Her opera is set in Montreal in Canada. It's one of the first operas to feature Inuit throat music, an ancient singing form of the Inuit people of northern Canada. It's a breathy, rhythmic sound, as far from classical European opera as you get. The cast includes an Inuit singer, Eva Kattuk. But Peel is keen for this to be more than a compositional gimmick arousing attention, to ensure that the throat singing doesn't stand out like a 'decoration or oddity'. It should be integral and, to help her achieve this, she carried out extensive background research and preparation.

The Liverpool-based composer Julie Williams has 'nothing against classical opera'. 'I just don't think it should be a historic genre,' she says. 'I like to look forward.' Her opera *Satellite* is based on a science-fiction story by Edward Hanwell in which a person has been sentenced to indefinite solitary confinement on a space station for the crime of 'unwillingness to engage with other people'. 'The main character in my *Satellite* has both a male and female voice,' she says. 'They have this amazing duet sound. I've got a male singer with a deep bass voice but who can also sing high notes, and a wonderful female singer with an amazing range. Together they produce this unworldly, haunting sound.' It's a striking reminder that opera's weirdness needn't be an obstacle. *Satellite* uses opera's vocal extremity as an expressive device, a means of marking out a character's difference from everyone else.

For Pippa Miles, opera is all about the power of the voice: 'There's a magnetism to it – there's something about people singing on a stage that I find irresistible.' One of her works, *Forest*, contains just two vocal roles – for a male tenor classical singer and a female singer who improvises. 'I love the energy that comes when you put those together,' she says. *Forest* is 'a story about a man who makes a journey of self-discovery. He ends up in a remote forest.' Miles is fascinated by forests. 'They're alive, yet timeless, and I try to get at this in my music.' She is keen for people listening to feel immersed in the soundscape, and admits to a sense of panic because opera tends to be performed on a big stage and it can feel distant: 'Artists have got to reach people, to open hearts and open minds,' she says. 'Opera has to change.'

31 What does the writer find strange about the scene in the studio?

   A   the extent to which the singers push themselves
   B   the reason for a sense of dissatisfaction
   C   the limited amount of space available
   D   the number of mistakes being made

32 Which words in the third paragraph echo the way opera is characterised in the second paragraph?

   A   unaffected-sounding delivery (lines 10–11)
   B   human drama (line 11)
   C   timeworn clichés (line 12)
   D   repertory-ready works (line 12)

33 In the fourth paragraph, the writer suggests it is fortunate for Jane Peel that

   A   she has been appointed to a prestigious post.
   B   she has only recently moved into the field of opera.
   C   she has had exposure to diverse musical influences.
   D   she has come to an ideal place to learn about opera.

34 In using Inuit throat singing, Jane Peel aims to

   A   make it feel like a natural part of her composition.
   B   show how it differs from more mainstream genres.
   C   stay faithful to the traditions that it comes from.
   D   ensure there is greater public awareness of it.

35 What particularly impresses the writer about Julie Williams' approach to opera?

   A   her determination to find singers who share her understanding of it
   B   the respect she shows for its technical sophistication
   C   her interest in combining it with literary ideas
   D   the way she exploits its unusual qualities

36 What problem does Pippa Miles think opera has?

   A   It often lacks genuine emotion.
   B   Audiences find it difficult to relate to.
   C   The themes it tackles are too limited.
   D   There's a reluctance to use its strengths.

You are going to read four extracts from articles in which experts give their views on whether e-sports (competitive video gaming) should be included in the Olympic Games. For questions **37 – 40**, choose from **A – D**. The experts may be chosen more than once.

Mark your answers **on the separate answer sheet**.

Should e-sports be included in the Olympic Games?

A

As a keen amateur video games player, I am well aware that e-sports professionals have intensive training programmes and highly developed eye–hand coordination. However, I have never shared the desire of many fellow gamers to have their hobby recognised in the same bracket as such activities as sprinting, gymnastics or weight-lifting. They are simply not comparable. I also fully acknowledge that whatever other gamers might say, the most popular e-sports involve eliminating some sort of enemy through use of violence. I'm a big fan of the *Street Fighter* series, which hasn't made me want to assassinate random citizens, but I fail to see how it conforms to the Olympic principles of peace and co-operation. I also have serious reservations about the effect that e-sports would have on the ethos and atmosphere of the Olympics. They might well provide a financial boost – which is why, ultimately, they will probably be admitted – but the cost in other ways could be monumental.

B

What exactly is a sport? Most definitions focus on competition and physical exertion. Many of today's most popular e-sports are team-based competitions, demanding lightning-quick reflexes and intense concentration. So if rifle shooting deserves to be described as a sport, why not gaming? Those who argue that video games promote violence in a manner that is not in keeping with the Olympic spirit betray a lack of familiarity with video games today. By continuing to exclude e-sports, the Olympic movement forgoes the opportunity to tap into a huge international community and the considerable economic power that comes with it. What's more, the Olympics have always had to adapt with the times. For example, women were gradually allowed to compete in more and more sports, while mountain-biking became an Olympic discipline in 1996. Hasn't the time come to change the status of e-sports?

C

Competitive e-sports constitute a huge and still growing industry. It's also true to say that e-sports' reputation for being all about violence is unfair, and their appeal to the Olympic authorities is obvious – it's the millions of young fans who play the games. But I would argue that the Olympics are already over-sized and too commercial, and any further expansion could be a recipe for disaster. There's little doubt that pro gamers train for many hours a day – like real elite athletes – and have impressive manual dexterity, but should the Olympics really be favouring a sedentary activity which, in physical terms, does the opposite to what genuine sports do? There are plenty of perfectly good sports which have failed to gain inclusion in the Olympics. Why should a sport which has only been in existence for about 20 years be given priority? Thankfully, the odds against it happening seem very high.

D

E-sports are an international phenomenon. Audiences pack stadiums to watch teams compete against each other, and the global audience for broadcast e-sports is over 500 million. Even a small fraction of this fan base and associated revenue would be of immense benefit to the Olympic Games, and because of this it appears inevitable that we will see video gaming in the Games in the not too distant future. The objection that e-sports were not part of the Olympic charter, as established in 1894, is spurious. Volleyball and basketball, now major Olympic sports, had not even been invented in 1894. Moreover, the claim that video games are all about fighting and explosions, and that this contravenes Olympic principles, is based on false premises. Many e-sports are violence-free, while some long-standing Olympic sports – boxing, for example – are quite the opposite. As for the assertion that the 'sports' part of the name is misleading, there are plenty of activities requiring far less speed and stamina – archery comes to mind – which have long been classed as Olympic sports.

Which expert

shares B's view on whether e-sports can be regarded as true sports? **37** [ ]

has a different view from D on how likely it is that e-sports will be included in the Olympic Games? **38** [ ]

has a different view from the others about whether violence in e-sports should disqualify them from the Olympics? **39** [ ]

shares C's view regarding the potential impact on the Olympics that inclusion of e-sports would have? **40** [ ]

You are going to read an article about smiling. Six paragraphs have been removed from the article. Choose from the paragraphs **A – G** the one which fits each gap (**41 – 46**). There is one extra paragraph which you do not need to use.

Mark your answers **on the separate answer sheet**.

What does a smile mean?

'The curve that sets everything straight' was how the comedian Phyllis Diller once described the smile. And it's true that there's something charming, trustworthy and disarming about a smile – but this can be misleading. Dig a little deeper and you will find a less wholesome side, because the smile is actually one of the biggest fakes going.

41

Psychologists, in fact, have given it a name: the Duchenne smile, in honour of the French neurologist Guillaume-Benjamin-Amand Duchenne. This smile utilises the muscles around the eyes to lift the cheeks, producing wrinkles around the eyes, and has long been held as an inimitable sign of true human emotion. Or at least it was until 2013, when psychologists from Boston, USA, destroyed that myth.

42

These findings indicate that even the supposedly genuine Duchenne smile can be convincingly simulated. So much for smiling being an inimitable sign of true human emotion. But why are some people so good at this kind of simulation? The answer isn't necessarily sinister. In fact, some research has demonstrated that you can actually smile yourself into a better mood.

43

This indicates that smiling can actually improve your mood; as opposed to the usual idea of it being an outward sign of what you are already feeling. Taking this one step further, researchers from University of Kansas asked volunteers to bite on a pair of chopsticks: either biting one end, with the lips closed to produce no smile; or the same but with lips apart in a standard

smile; or biting along the length of the chopstick, to produce a Duchenne smile. The volunteers were then made to feel stressed by having them submerge one hand in ice-water for one minute.

44

But though there may be times when it is advantageous for us to smile when we don't feel particularly cheerful, there is a flipside. Researchers in California wondered whether professional fighters' smiles during the face-off before a bout might predict who the victor would be. They obtained face-off photographs of 152 Ultimate Fighting Championships competitors and rated them for smile intensity. Interestingly, winning fighters displayed less intensive smiles in pre-fight face-offs than losers did, and fighters winning by a knock-out displayed the least intensive smiles of all.

45

What seems to have happened, is that the fighters who smiled were unintentionally leaking information about their own sense of weakness, so passing a psychological advantage to their opponent. The message from this is that taking control of your emotional state, avoiding smiling, and showing that you have the upper hand, even where that is not felt, is a good strategy in competitive environments.

46

But, as the saying goes, if you can't beat them, join them. Next time you're having your photograph taken, don't say 'cheese'; say 'cheeks'. Saying 'cheeks' will not only shape your mouth nicely, but will also remind you to squeeze your cheeks upwards into a visually satisfying, genuine-looking Duchenne smile.

A The main point of interest was how smiling would affect their ability to cope with the discomfort. The full, Duchenne smile was shown to be superior to the other facial expressions in this respect. So, fake or not, putting on a Duchenne smile may be just the tonic to combat physical and psychological difficulties.

B In a straightforward study, one group of volunteers was asked to reproduce smiles shown in photographs, and another group to evaluate whether the first group's smiles were authentic. Some of the photographs depicted mouth-only smiles, but others showed smiles using both mouth and eye muscles. Two-thirds of individuals turned out to be able to fake a supposedly authentic smile, and they were also able to do this well in their everyday lives.

C Culturally, smiling resonates across human history, from the grinning Greek kouros sculptures of 2,500 years ago to modern-day emojis. The most popular emoji of all is the face with tears of joy. Just as this emoji expresses more than mere happiness – tears adding an ironic twist – smiles themselves convey so much more.

D The smile, then, can be a false friend. People smile – or not – for all kinds of reasons beyond simply how happy they are feeling.

E I know what you're thinking: we all put on a smile now and again to placate our fellow humans and avoid unnecessary conflict. We all suppose, however, that a genuine smile of true enjoyment is something very different.

F What does this tell us? It suggests that in a context where physical dominance is important, smiling can be a sign of appeasement – possibly some kind of peace offering – and subordinate status.

G Participants were asked to hold a pen in the mouth by its tip. Some held it with the teeth, creating a smile without the person concerned realising it, while others held the pen with the lips producing a pout rather than a smile. Pens in mouths, the participants then rated the humour in some cartoons. Intriguingly, the cartoons were rated as funnier when the pen was held with the teeth than when held with the lips.

You are going to read an article about art forgery. For questions **47 – 56**, choose from the sections of the article (**A – D**). The sections may be chosen more than once.

Mark your answers **on the separate answer sheet**.

In which section are the following mentioned?

the belief that forgery will continue to be a problem in the future	**47**
the diverse nature of skills required in forgery detection	**48**
a sense of pride in an achievement	**49**
a reluctance to reveal how something is done	**50**
a reason underlying a belief that certain types of forgery were unlikely	**51**
a technical process which is difficult to control	**52**
details that can reveal whether or not a painting is authentic	**53**
forgers' familiarity with detection techniques	**54**
distinctive features of a particular work of art	**55**
how forgery can cause serious financial problems	**56**

Detecting forgery in the art world

A

The suggestion of a smile about the lips; the translucent headscarf over the forehead; the barely visible eyebrows; the muted colours blended in the *sfumato* style. It took John Myatt four months to complete his latest task: a replica of the world's most famous painting, Leonardo da Vinci's *Mona Lisa*. Myatt, who spent time in prison in 1999 for forging works by, among others, the great 20th century artists, Alberto Giacometti and Ben Nicholson, has no intention of trying to pass off his work as the real thing; he produced it for a film about the theft of the *Mona Lisa* in 1911. 'I'm delighted with it,' says Myatt. 'I even got the cracking right,' referring to the tiny lines that emerge over time on the surface of old oil paintings. He reproduces the effect by carefully applying two sets of varnishes — one quick-drying, one slow, to open up the cracks. Even though he has done it before, he says, 'it's a heart-stopping moment because the results largely come down to the atmosphere in the room, and so forth.'

B

Artistic deception has fallen under the spotlight in recent years. First came the shock that a well-known gallery in the US had been unknowingly selling forged works for millions of dollars – and as a result, went bankrupt. Next came the news that Sotheby's, the renowned international auction house, had been caught out when it auctioned a work supposedly by the 17th century Dutch painter Frans Hals for £8.4m. When doubts emerged, Sotheby's arranged for it to be sent for scientific analysis, revealing the forgery and prompting the auction house to reimburse the buyer. That a forger could create lookalikes of such high quality caused great concern among dealers, collectors and art lovers, who had previously assumed that the technical difficulty of reproducing historical masterpieces acted as a natural defence against fakes. 'Good forgeries of old masterpieces were thought to be virtually impossible,' says art expert Frank Crossland. He adds that the recent scandals are in some ways positive. 'They've made us realise we need to be much more careful about authenticity.'

C

One of the core tasks of an art analyst is to ensure that the materials present in a painting or sculpture were available at the time the work is said to have been made. The German forger Wolfgang Beltracchi was unmasked when he inadvertently used titanium white, a material first created in 1916, for a forgery dated two years earlier. Then there is an inappropriate frame or canvas: Myatt says the forger's 'standard procedure' is to obtain an inferior painting from the right period and remove the paint, leaving a suitably aged, but clean, canvas still stretched with pieces of wood from the correct era. But even if the individual materials in a work check out as historically appropriate, alarm bells may be set off by the way they are assembled. 'The best analysts need to know about the chemical characteristics of different types of paint, so they need to be scientists,' says Crossland. 'But they also need to know how particular artists went about their work, the subjects they were interested in, and so on. So they need to be historians and art lovers too.'

D

Part of the problem is the mass of published literature, essential for academic scholarship but accessible to forgers, setting out exactly how artists throughout history have worked. Forgers also keep up to date with the testing instruments. While galleries and auction houses now use digital microscopes and handheld XRF spectrometers that identify works' constituent elements, some forgers are creating works in anticipation of such close inspection. 'This seems to be more or less the current standard,' says one art analyst. Careful to avoid giving the criminals any tips, he declines to talk about specific cases. Myatt, however, is more open: he is convinced the latest successful forger of historical paintings is someone trained in art restoration who has seen great works pass through their hands over many years. He says it takes years before 'you can look at the way the paint leaves the brush, the "handwriting" of an artist, and really understand it.' Such insights lead him to take the view that any hopes that the cat and mouse game between the art establishment and the forgers is about to end are based more on wishful thinking than hard facts.

You **must** answer this question. Write your answer in **220 – 260** words in an appropriate style on the separate answer sheet.

1 Your class has listened to a podcast about the factors that motivate people to take part in sport. You have made the notes below:

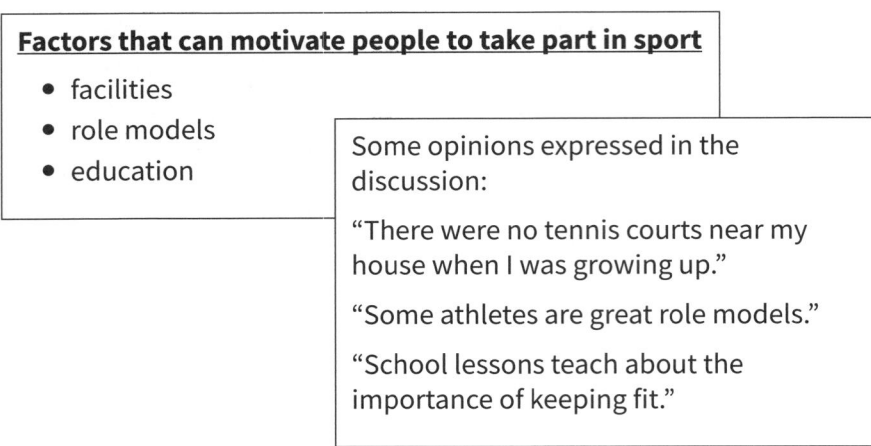

Factors that can motivate people to take part in sport

- facilities
- role models
- education

Some opinions expressed in the discussion:

"There were no tennis courts near my house when I was growing up."

"Some athletes are great role models."

"School lessons teach about the importance of keeping fit."

Write an essay for your tutor discussing **two** of the factors in your notes. You should **explain which factor is more significant in motivating people to take part in sport, giving reasons** to support your answer.

You may, if you wish, make use of the opinions expressed in the podcast, but you should use your own words as far as possible.

Write an answer to **one** of the questions **2 – 4** in this part. Write your answer in **220 – 260** words in an appropriate style on the separate answer sheet. Put the question number in the box at the top of the page.

---

2 You study at an international college and are active on the student council. Now the principal, Ms Harper, has asked you to write a report about the college's official social media accounts. The principal would like to know about the main ways that the social media accounts have been used. She would also like you to make recommendations about how they could be used more effectively, for the benefit of the college and its students.

Write your **report**.

3 You recently read an article on the website of a popular newspaper which made several criticisms of young people in today's society. You have decided to write an email to the editor of the website in response to the article. In your email, you should say what the criticisms were and what you think about them, and persuade the editor to publish your email on the website.

Write your **email**.

4 A lifestyle website you enjoy has asked readers to share their opinions of a paid streaming service they use, either for music, films, or TV programmes. Reviews should include a brief description of the service, evaluating its strengths and weaknesses and whether it is worth the cost involved.

Write your **review**.

31

You will hear three different extracts. For questions **1 – 6**, choose the answer (**A, B** or **C**) which fits best according to what you hear. There are two questions for each extract.

Extract One

You hear two friends, Lizzie and Raphael, talking about playing the keyboard and the drums.

1 Raphael is thinking of learning the keyboard instead of the drums because

    A finding somewhere to practise the keyboard is less problematic.

    B it's easier to control the volume on a keyboard.

    C keyboards are much more portable.

2 What's Lizzie doing?

    A trying to persuade Raphael to make up his mind

    B questioning whether he has made the right decision

    C suggesting he takes more time to choose which instrument to play

Extract Two

You hear two colleagues talking about first impressions.

3 What does the woman say about meeting clients for the first time?

    A She doesn't feel comfortable wearing formal clothes.

    B She isn't as open as she usually is.

    C She tries not to be influenced by the surroundings.

4 What do they agree about long-term business relationships?

    A First impressions can turn out to be right.

    B Friendships can develop over time.

    C Promotion can change the way a person behaves.

Extract Three

You hear a chef, called Nick, talking to his sister about his work.

5 How did Nick feel when he made a dish he used to love as a child?

    A disappointed that it was less sweet than he remembered

    B frustrated that it took a long time to make

    C embarrassed that it tasted so unpleasant

6 What aspect of Nick's job is his sister interested in?

    A how competitive it is

    B how unpredictable it is

    C how technical it is

32

You will hear a woman, called Diana, giving a talk about her experience as a volunteer at a riding school in Costa Rica in Central America. For questions **7 – 14**, complete the sentences with a word or short phrase.

RIDING SCHOOL VOLUNTEER

In addition to working on her horse-riding skills, learning **(7)** .... was

another reason Diana wanted to volunteer.

Diana was especially impressed with the **(8)** .... of the area where the

riding school is located.

Diana loved the fact that the **(9)** .... in the accommodation had been

handmade nearby.

In the mornings, Diana's first job was to carry out what are known as

(10) .... , which were supervised by an experienced employee.

Diana explains that the owner of the riding school had studied **(11)** ....

at college.

When Diana was giving children riding lessons, she advised them to

(12) .... if they felt nervous.

As a result of riding every day, Diana's **(13)** .... improved.

The most thrilling ride for Diana was when she jumped over a

(14) .... on her favourite horse.

You will hear an interview in which two journalism students, called Matthew and Tracy, are talking about fact and opinion in the news. For questions **15 – 20**, choose the answer (**A**, **B**, **C** or **D**) which fits best according to what you hear.

---

15 Matthew believes it is difficult to differentiate fact from opinion because

  A the news is delivered in short segments.

  B people fail to give their full attention to the news.

  C there is a wide range of sources for news.

  D people may be unfamiliar with the background to a news story.

16 What change did Tracy make to the questionnaire they prepared?

  A She reduced the number of options.

  B She added more open questions.

  C She reworded some questions.

  D She defined some terms.

17 Matthew and Tracy were both impressed by an article they read about

  A education.

  B pollution.

  C transport.

  D sport.

18 Matthew feels worried about writing factual articles

  A in case he misleads readers.

  B in case he includes inaccuracies.

  C because he has little experience of it.

  D because his first one was criticised by his classmates.

19 What does Tracy point out about using photos or video when reporting news?

  A Images have a stronger impact than the written word.

  B Photos make the news seem more factual.

  C The public expect visual support for news.

  D The public prefer video to photos.

20 Matthew's style of writing when expressing his opinion

  A is inspired by a contemporary novelist.

  B is based on authentic dialogue.

  C varies according to the topic.

  D reflects his personality.

34

You will hear five short extracts in which people are talking about boredom.

TASK ONE

For questions **21 – 25**, choose from the list (**A – H**) the situation in which each person felt bored.

TASK TWO

For questions **26 – 30**, choose from the list (**A – H**) the positive result each person experienced after having felt bored.

While you listen you must complete both tasks.

A	waiting in a queue	Speaker 1	21
B	during journeys		
C	after finalising a project early	Speaker 2	22
D	in an imposed period of inactivity		
E	during sports training	Speaker 3	23
F	doing a task repeatedly	Speaker 4	24
G	attending a talk		
H	on a shopping trip	Speaker 5	25

A	being more creative	Speaker 1	26
B	finding solutions to problems more easily	Speaker 2	27
C	completing tasks faster		
D	planning a career change	Speaker 3	28
E	being able to prioritise better	Speaker 4	29
F	getting things into perspective		
G	paying more attention to detail	Speaker 5	30
H	having better social skills		

Work with a partner if possible, taking it in turn to act in the role of the interlocutor.

Part 1
2 minutes (3 minutes for groups of three)

The interlocutor asks you some questions about yourself, your home, work or studies and familiar topics.

Good morning / afternoon / evening. My name is ... and this is my colleague ... .
And your names are?
Can I have your mark sheets please?
Thank you.

First of all, we'd like to know something about you.

- Where are you from?
- What do you do here / there?
- How long have you been studying English?
- What do you enjoy most about studying English?

The interlocutor then asks you some questions about one or two other topics, for example:
- What do you spend most of your time online doing?
- Have your tastes in music changed over the last few years? (How?)
- Have you been to an enjoyable celebration recently?
- What are your main ambitions for this coming year?

Work in groups of three if possible. One of you is the interlocutor and the other two are the candidates. The interlocutor should lead the task using the script below. Refer to the pictures on pages S19 and S20.

Part 2
4 minutes (6 minutes for groups of three)

Interlocutor	In this part of the test, I'm going to give each of you three pictures. I'd like you to talk about **two** of them on your own for about a minute, and also to answer a question briefly about your partner's pictures.
	[Candidate A], it's your turn first. Here are your pictures. They show **people in situations that require confidence**. I'd like you to compare two of the pictures and say **why confidence is needed in these situations and how they might feel when the event is over**.
	All right?
⏱ After 1 minute	Thank you.
	[Candidate B], **who do you think is feeling the most nervous? (Why?)**
⏱ After 30 seconds	Thank you.
	Now, [Candidate B], here are your pictures. They show **people dealing with customers**. I'd like you to compare two of the pictures and say **what skills are important for these people when they deal with customers and how rewarding the jobs might be**.
⏱ After 1 minute	Thank you.
	Now, [Candidate A], **who do you think will be the most tired after their work? (Why?)**
⏱ After 30 seconds	Thank you.

Part 3 4 minutes (6 minutes for groups of three)

Part 4 5 minutes (8 minutes for groups of three)

Part 3

Work in groups of three if possible. One of you is the interlocutor and the other two are the candidates. The interlocutor should lead the task using the script below. Refer to the task sheet on page S21.

Interlocutor	Now I'd like you to talk about something together for about two minutes.
	Here are some things that can help form a good friendship and a question for you to discuss. First you have some time to look at the task.
🕐 *After 15 seconds*	Now, talk to each other about **how important these things are when forming a strong friendship**.
🕐 *After 2 minutes*	Thank you. Now you have about a minute to decide **which of these things is most important for a long-lasting friendship**.
🕐 *After 1 minute*	Thank you.

Part 4

The interlocutor asks some general questions which follow on from the topic in Part 3.

Interlocutor	• Some people say that the friends we've had for the longest time are our best friends. Do you agree? (Why? / Why not?)
	• Do you think it's important to have more than just a few very good friends? Why do you think they say that?
	• What's the best way to maintain a close friendship if you live a long way apart? (Why?)
	• Should parents have some influence over their child's choice of friends? (Why? / Why not?)
	• Why is the number of 'friends' some people have on social media important to them?
	• Do you think friends can give better advice on important things than family? (Why? / Why not?)
	Thank you. That is the end of the test.

Audioscripts

Test 1

TRAINING

 Listening Part 1

01 *David:* Could you help me prepare for the job interview I've got next week, Tessa? It's really important because the job seems ideal for me, so I'm going to go all out to get it.

Tessa: Of course – although I must admit I didn't do too well in my last job interview because nerves got the better of me. But anyway, if I were you, I'd first find out everything you can about the company.

David: Thanks, but I've already done that. What's vital to get right is the actual interview. Perhaps we could roleplay it? Look, here's the ad for the job.

Tessa: Wow! This is great, gives me lots to go on – it even states the salary! But why in dollars? Well, I suppose it's to attract international applicants. Anyway, why don't I come up with a list of questions to ask you?

David: That'd be perfect.

EXAM PRACTICE

 Listening Part 1

02

Extract One

Juliet: Hi, Adam. How are you finding living in Montreal?

Adam: Hi, Juliet. It's a great city and I've got some good buddies now, guys who live on our street and work colleagues. Are you going to the street party to celebrate Canada Day?

Juliet: You bet. It's a real important thing for me and my family; celebrating it is an annual ritual for us.

Adam: I'll see you there then; it's going to be a beautiful day. That sudden shift from biting cold gales to beautifully balmy evenings when you can sit outside in a T-shirt until midnight is what drew me to Montreal. It's awesome!

Juliet: I know what you mean. So are you staying on in your apartment? I think you said you only leased it for a year?

Adam: Yeah. It makes sense to rent in Montreal – you don't have to fork out a fortune for a place downtown.

Juliet: You can get a deal because there's so much on the market.

Adam: And getting a place of my own is, well, financially out of the question. But quite a few people on our street are moving out, right?

Juliet: Yeah, like my sister's moving again. She wants to be more in the centre.

Adam: Oh, OK.

Extract Two

Halim: Hi, Soraya, how are you getting on with your essay on plastic?

Soraya: Hi, Halim. Well, the background reading's fascinating. OK, there's been a complete U-turn in the views expressed in journals and even in the popular press in recent years. But actually, when I read about the 1950s, I get that at that time plastic was seen as revolutionary. You could make anything from it, from bottles to roofs; it was so strong and durable. What was not to like? Whereas now, it's seen as a real threat to the planet.

Halim: Yeah. I've read a couple of really thought-provoking articles and I watched the documentary our tutor recommended, you know the one called *Plastic Madness*.

Soraya: Oh yeah, any good?

Halim: Wildly over-dramatic at the end, in my view. To be fair, it did go into the pros and cons of the uses of plastic, and it covered the main ideas we'd discussed in class, but to close with statements like *Most species of fish will be extinct within ten years* was way over the top.

Soraya: And did it go into issues like plastic causing air pollution?

Halim: It did, yeah.

Extract Three

Ed: So, Jane, I'm the parent of a sixteen-year-old, Max, and my wife and I are constantly wondering if we're doing the right thing.

Jane: The teenage years are critical in human development, Ed. Parents are programmed to care for their child, but in evolutionary terms, the infant must develop, mature and eventually separate from them. And although the majority of parents cope admirably with their child becoming a monosyllabic and at times difficult teenager, few know when to let go. At the same time, parents do generally adapt well to having to provide more emotional support than physical support.

Ed: With Max, we're going through things like, he seems reluctant to wake up before ten.

Jane: Some schools have changed their timetable to take into account the fact that teenagers perform better later in the day.

Ed: Not his, unfortunately. The good thing is Max and I are both seriously into gaming and I'm fascinated by how so many games promote universal values like hard work pays off, collaboration works better than confrontation and thinking things through is to be admired. I encourage Max to invite his mates round to our house because I want him to build up a circle of good friends who share common interests.

TRAINING

 Listening Part 2

03 *Meg:* And before I knew it, I'd graduated and was working alongside my parents full time. They helped me understand when to water the flowers using our automatic irrigation system and they frequently congratulated me on how well I could grade flowers before they were taken to the shops we supplied. I was always excited when my parents asked me to deliver our flowers to shops. I was happy to talk to the florists and find out about their customers, and when our flowers were displayed I was proud of what I'd achieved.

 EXAM PRACTICE

04 **Listening Part 2**

Ben: Hi, I'd like to tell you a bit about myself and my work as a citrus fruit farmer. My name's Ben Tyrell and my family's been growing oranges, lemons and grapefruit for several generations. As an organic grower, I don't use synthetic pesticides on our farm, so to ensure all the trees are healthy, observation becomes that much more important; even more important than, for example, the protection of young trees. If a tree needs fertiliser, there'll be discoloration of the leaves rather than the bark. When a tree's off-colour, it might be because it's running low on potassium or nitrogen. Deciding *when* to start putting some organic fertiliser on the trees has to be carefully calculated. It'll depend partly on the deadlines for delivering the fruit to the packing house, but mainly on the weather. Do it at the wrong time and its efficiency is greatly reduced.

In springtime, my day will also include checking the fungus situation on the fruit on the trees. At this time of year, we're mainly concerned with the fungi Alternaria and Melanose. While harmless, if the fruit has either of these fungi, it'll have blemishes and that'd put our fruit into a lower grade at the packing house. So, if we find any fungi, I use bacteria to attack and control the fungi as an organic solution to the problem. Some growers use a type of soap made from organic fats, but not me.

During the summer, weeds start growing up around the trees. We're completely against using any sort of chemicals as a weed killer and I guess our neighbours might think our farm looks a bit messy, but I don't get hung up about weeds. The only time we do something about them is when they start appearing right next to the irrigation setup. Then we might use small grass mowers that we keep in a shed to control the weeds.

In late fall, harvest time, I begin to check if the fruit's ready to pick. In the US, there are state regulations for when to pick fruit. We have to check that the fruit contains certain levels of sugar and juice. After meeting these requirements, finally, we'll look at size because there are regulations for that as well. So, when we're sure the fruit is ready, we call in the pickers. All the fruit's picked by hand – our workers use scissors so that we don't damage the fruit. We don't use ladders or metal baskets for the same reason.

I love growing organically and knowing that the fruit we produce is as healthy as it can be. We do tours of the farm for school kids because I'm keen that future generations can 'touch the earth', if you know what I mean. They can make what we call 'intelligent food choices', based on the knowledge of how a food was grown, how it was processed and how it was stored.

Now, any questions …

TRAINING

 Listening Part 3

05 *Interviewer:* And Clare, what do you think you're getting out of being at university?
Clare: Well, the school I went to was really good in the sense that we did lots of group work, so I was already used to collaborating with others and good at being able to get my opinion across. But now I'm so much better at finding answers to quite tricky issues. I'm studying politics and we're sometimes given scenarios and we have to analyse them. I'm even giving a talk to the rest of my tutorial group on the last scenario we looked at.

 EXAM PRACTICE

06 **Listening Part 3**

Interviewer: I'd like to hear your views on students using smartphones at school, a topic that's been in the press a great deal recently. Amy, what's your opinion?
Amy: Yes, there's a really interesting debate going on about it. In one school where I worked as a trainee teacher, teachers were concerned that students weren't paying enough attention to the lessons, as they were thinking about when they could next take a look at their phones. In my view, the role of education should be to enable students to assess a situation and then decide if using a smartphone is appropriate – polite – and how long to use it for. In another school, I saw a lesson where students had to actually look for pop-up messages selling products aimed at young people on their phones and then there was a class discussion about the ethics of that.
Interviewer: And John, what do you think?
John: But what about the role of parents in this? Don't you think most parents talk about how, where and when to use

phones a lot with their children before they allow them to have one, especially if the child's still young?

Amy: You mean they say, you can only use it to talk to friends for one hour a day and not after 7 pm, that sort of thing?

John: Exactly, or …

Amy: But how do they monitor that? And anyway, lots of parents say things like 'Don't use your phone during dinner' and then they actually do that themselves!

John: Or they're always doing internet shopping. They can't expect their child not to do what they themselves are doing, I guess. But in my experience, parents do monitor their kids' use of smartphones.

Interviewer: Coming back to smartphone use at school, John, do you think students should be able to use phones in class time?

John: For some things yes, but with limits. I think using the camera should be a no-no, even if students say they want to show a painting they've done or something to their parents. That'd lead to inappropriate use of phones, I'm sure. Like the record function – as a teacher I wouldn't like students recording me in class. But if they wanted to check a spelling or find out what the capital of Norway is, for instance, that's fine in my book. Some teachers let students use phones in maths lessons for difficult calculations and things, but I'd rather students understood how to work it out for themselves.

Interviewer: And Amy, didn't you work in a school where smartphones were banned?

Amy: Yes, when I was doing teaching practice last term as part of my course to become a teacher, the school had just introduced the ban. It didn't go down well with some mums and dads who wanted their child to have a phone in case there was an emergency. There'd just been a police report in the local newspaper about crime near the school, and parents felt young people might need to contact them or the police at any time.

John: I bet the students weren't very happy about the ban either.

Amy: Strangely enough, after the first week, they seemed almost to forget about it! And some even said they enjoyed their teachers' lessons more.

John: Interesting. And actually, in most workplaces you can only use your smartphone during your official breaks; it's part of your terms and conditions when you accept the job. So perhaps it'd be a good idea if more schools looked again at their policy regarding smartphones, so that children get used to the fact that restriction is the norm and not a rule that they think can be easily broken. Of course, there are offices where smartphones are totally forbidden, like where they deal with confidential information, or they're banned when a worker's operating machinery because being distracted by their phone might result in an accident.

Interviewer: So, Amy, any final words on this topic?

Amy: Well, there'll always be heated discussions about this sort of thing in education. And sometimes the debate may seem trivial, but schools have to always make sure they're doing the best for students. With new gadgets coming out at such a rate, schools are just keeping pace with what's going on in the wider community. And, let's face it, new technology has a huge effect on our lives.

John: And soon, we'll all have forgotten about smartphones because some other piece of technology will be all the rage!

Interviewer: Thank you both.

 EXAM PRACTICE

07 **Listening Part 4**

Speaker 1

I was thrilled when I heard I'd won first prize – a substantial amount of money! I'd had a sneaky look at all the novels that had been entered and I must admit every single one was a gripping read and well written. The ironic thing about winning the money was that I needed it less after I'd won. I'd spent a couple of years earning enough to live on, but not exactly living the high life. Then, once news was out about me winning, bookshops were overwhelmed with readers suddenly wanting anything and everything I'd ever written! Thankfully, my agent dealt with the emails that flooded in from fans and she also managed my social media presence.

Speaker 2

I live in Australia and I was on a flight back from Europe when the news broke, so I'd no idea I'd won the competition until the next day. Sure, I remember the publicity that surrounded winning, but what marked the event for me was the mental switch I made from writing novels based on historical facts to more descriptive, character-driven stories. I also recall, when I'd just sent off the entry form, thinking whatever the result, win or lose, it'd give me the chance to get feedback on my work and I'd take it on board. The judges were all highly respected writers and publishers, and even if they'd poured scorn on my work, it'd still have been useful.

Speaker 3

Well, to be honest, winning the prize has been a double-edged sword. Yeah, it was great to be headline news, but after that all died down, I spent hours staring at a blank screen thinking – what now? Obviously, I knew I was a good writer, I wouldn't have won otherwise, but it was hard for about a year. It's weird, because when I went in for the competition I had numerous sleepless nights thinking: what'll happen if I don't win? Would I go into some sort of decline and not want to face my friends and colleagues? Fortunately, I did win, so those anxieties never had to be faced.

Speaker 4

The minute I'd completed the form to enter the competition, the only thing I could think about was: what would I say when I accepted the prize? At that stage I had no idea whether I'd even win or not. I knew there'd be a big formal dinner and the winner would have to get up and come out with words of wisdom and the thought made me feel numb with fear! Anyway, I managed to mumble thanks to all my readers and the usual stuff when the time came. In contrast, afterwards there was no time to think at all – I was being asked to write a follow-up novel by companies in countries I knew little about!

Speaker 5

I was so hacked off by all the criteria I had to meet for the competition that by the time I'd checked this, that and the other, sent endless confirmations of my ID, and read the competition style guide for the tenth time, I hoped I'd have nothing more to do with it all. Of course, having won, I can now see the funny side of all that. Winning has also made me a more assertive person, sure enough of myself to say, 'No thank you, I won't be doing that interview or attending that party.' The same's happened as far as writing goes – I know what works for me!

TRAINING

Speaking Part 2

08 **Useful language: speculating**

Exercise 1

My initial impression is that she doesn't seem too nervous, I mean, she's sitting down, not pacing round the room like I do when I'm worried about something. She seems lost in thought. I suppose she's waiting for her phone to ring, probably with news from someone. Perhaps it's a business call, something about a job offer, maybe. But then again, it looks like she's at home, so I reckon it's something more personal. She appears quite young, and I can't make out a ring or anything on her wedding finger, so maybe she's waiting to hear from a new boyfriend.

TRAINING

Speaking Part 2

09 **Keep talking**

Exercise 1

Well, it looks like she's waiting for someone to pick her up and I get the impression that they're late. It doesn't seem to be a very nice place to wait, so I reckon that it's not so much a case of not having enough time, but actually having too much time. She wants to get going. I suppose she's just got off a flight, possibly a long-distance one, so she's feeling pretty tired. Once she's been picked up, I expect she'll go home, have a shower and take a nap before she bothers with unpacking those cases we can see in the picture.

Test 2

EXAM PRACTICE

10 **Listening Part 1**

Extract One

Nathalie: David, have you read this article about watching thriller movies?
David: No, is it good?
Nathalie: Yeah, well, I'd heard before that when we're scared, our brains pump out the feel-good chemical dopamine, like when we're in love with someone. But look at this: it says that families who like nothing better than sitting together on the sofa in front of a good thriller movie are the most contented. That's news to me! Most people I know who adore thriller movies, appreciate them for the really good plot lines. You know, the stories are so rational in many ways that some otherwise very sensible people are drawn into them.
David: For me, when I watch horror movies, it's like going on a mini vacation.
Nathalie: Do you mean you can wander off into a fantasy world?
David: More that it gives me ideas, even about how to solve issues at work. And I've heard other people say the same.
Nathalie: Really? I could understand it if you said something like it's the suspense, the special effects or the thrill you get from watching them.
David: Well, it may sound odd, but they leave me feeling more excited about possibilities to do with daily life.

Extract Two

Woman: I've just been reading an article about building skyways in cities. Their effect on commerce, particularly shopping, can be considerable because when they link the upper floors of buildings, shops at ground level don't get passing trade any more. Some even go bust.
Man: Absolutely. If people are walking about on the third or fourth floor, they won't make a special trip down to the ground level to buy something, and that's why so many stores are having to close, even when they're in prime central locations.
Woman: I read they're also struggling because people are buying online. And with online shopping, deliveries are becoming more efficient. Plus centres are suffering because all those large shopping malls on the outskirts of towns were built to attract people by offering a range of activities, like movie theatres.

Man: I think the two things are different. But you know the arguments – skyways mean pedestrians can enjoy walking through a city in any weather, and there's less crime than at street level. But, to my mind, getting people away from congested roads and sidewalks has to be the winning argument. Skyways have the potential to bring life back to city centres. After all, the centre is where people not only want to shop and work, but live too.

Extract Three

Sophie: So, Gary, you're working on public information campaigns, aren't you?

Gary: Yes, Sophie, I'm actually employed by the government and the thinking behind the public awareness campaigns this year is all about encouraging participation in sports at school.

Sophie: Yes, I saw the very successful TV campaign showing the importance of doing sport for healthy growth in primary-aged children. But isn't that something that the public already knows?

Gary: Most people, yes, and that's why we started with the health aspect. What's less well understood, and what I want to get across, is how sport helps children mature socially by teaching them about teamwork and about fair play. I'd rather not focus on the discipline aspect – the idea that sports are all about learning sets of rules and sticking to them.

Sophie: Interesting. I'm looking into the effect of sport on learning performance. My first study followed a group of children from primary school right through to university level. I tracked various things like how often they were absent through illness, and their grades, and what stood out was that those who did sport were much keener to try to get good grades in maths, English, those kinds of subjects.

Gary: And did they achieve that?

Sophie: Not always, but the aspiration was there. And for me, that's what really counts.

 EXAM PRACTICE

11 **Listening Part 2**

I'm going to tell you about an archaeological site called Beni Hassan. It's located on the east bank of the Nile in central Egypt and it dates back to the 11th and 12th Dynasties of Egypt's Middle Kingdom; that's 2050–1650 BCE. The site and its decorated tombs not only tell us about the artists who worked on the tombs, but also reflect the lives of the people buried there. The tombs that interest me most are those of government officials. Their servants wouldn't have had such elaborate tombs.

In the paintings on the walls, there's a wonderful variety of fauna and flora, and you can even see some plants and animals that you don't often find in Egyptian art. Many of the tombs at Beni Hassan include full-panel representations of animals and show a keen observation of their behaviour, usually while they are out in the wild, typically in habitats such as marshes or deserts.

The paint that was used to decorate tombs has been analysed and found to be made from ground minerals; it was sometimes applied straight onto the walls of the tombs, and at other times onto a sort of base made of plaster. Although I've said that the scenes painted were very varied, you do find the same, or very similar, scenes repeated in several tombs. This could well suggest that certain images were considered an essential part of any memorial.

Some other paintings depict important annual events, such as the grain harvest and its shipment to other parts of the kingdom. I know the Ancient Egyptians also grew vegetables, but I couldn't see any in the photos of the paintings I saw. Other paintings show people wrestling. These are quite detailed, showing all kinds of different grips and holds. At first, it was thought these scenes were there to demonstrate the strength of sportsmen, but now it's believed that they are intended to illustrate soldiers during their training. And, as it was important to show admiration of the power of the kingdom in those times, I tend to agree with this latest interpretation.

Interestingly, I discovered that birds in flight, which appear in many of the paintings, are symbols of invasion, so when there's a bird being caught by a hunter, it represents victory over an enemy. Hunters are also shown using animals as a sort of tool to catch other animals. For instance, crocodiles catching birds. Cats also appear in many paintings because local people worshipped a cat goddess called Pakhet, meaning 'the scratcher'.

As in many other tombs in Egypt, there are images of creatures that are half one animal and half another. In one of the tombs at Beni Hassan, there's one creature with the head of a falcon and the body of a dog. These 'mixed' creatures express the complexity of how the afterlife was conceived and formed part of religious worship.

 EXAM PRACTICE

12 **Listening Part 3**

Interviewer: Thanks for joining us in the studio today. As you know, this is one in our series on ecology and today's programme is on sand: why people love beaches so much and how sand is being used for the construction industry. Jack, are you someone who loves going to the beach?

Jack: Absolutely, me and the vast majority of the population, I should think! A friend of mine's an artist and loves painting by the sea at sunrise. He says it's the intensity of the colours that's special for him. I'm not sure about the claims that sea air is really good for your health. I think it's mainly the unchanging quality of the coast that means people keep going back to it. What I've noticed is I fall asleep very easily when I can hear the sea crashing onto the shore again and again.

Interviewer: What about you Trisha?

Trisha: Well, I love sunbathing on a sandy beach. But I've just read an article about pop-up beaches – you know, these fake beaches that spring up each year in major cities. Truckloads of sand are brought in and dumped in open spaces. The article was extremely well-researched – the reporter had obviously looked into the subject in great depth. The conclusion was that people shouldn't support these projects because taking the sand from natural beaches causes all of problems. I'm embarrassed that I went to one in London last year, and wouldn't have gone if I'd known then what I know now. Getting cities to realise this and find alternative entertainments might be difficult, though.

Jack: Instead of taking sand from beaches, it's been suggested they should be putting new sand on some beaches because the ocean currents are washing away huge amounts of sand in some places.

Trisha: But surely the crabs, sand worms and so on on the beach can't survive huge amounts of new sand being piled on top of them?

Jack: I can't see how they could. Even doing something more permanent, like constructing a seawall, has negative consequences for the environment.

Trisha: Yeah, it can create an unnatural sort of barrier between the ocean and the land.

Jack: I think because so many people are becoming city dwellers these days, there's an enormous need for housing, and to make concrete, you need sand. And where's that sand coming from? Our beaches and rivers. You can't blame people for moving to cities because that's where the jobs, schools and amenities are. And I'd imagine that many do, in fact, realise that other parts of the country 'pay' for that in a way, but choose to turn a blind eye to it.

Trisha: Yes, the damage to the ecology of an area when sand is removed from its beaches has a knock-on effect and I don't mean things like a reduction in the income from tourism. In some places, when fish are disturbed, there's less fish for local people to catch, so they can't carry on being fishermen and have to move or try to find another job. That's a really drastic personal and economic consequence. I also wonder if the weather is affected, you know, if water flows further inland and forms pools or lagoons – that might lead to more rain.

Interviewer: So what do you think can be done to put a halt to people taking sand from beaches?

Jack: It's interesting you ask that because I went to a public lecture the other day. The lecturer was an architect and he thought it wouldn't be long before sand could be partially made from recycled materials. Some chemists are already working on that – wouldn't that be great? And that could be backed up by some initiatives, government or private sector, to try to get the message across that taking sand from beaches is not OK!

Trisha: I agree. And I think the tourist industry is already trying to promote eco-tourism and tourists are becoming more discerning.

Interviewer: Well, thank you both. You've raised some interesting points.

EXAM PRACTICE

13 Listening Part 4

Speaker 1

I've just got the results of a questionnaire which I sent out to my company's offices in eight countries. Some questions touched on customer care and how 'green' we are, but the main thrust of the questions was to find out how many face-to-face meetings we have compared to video conferencing and how people think this will change over the next five years. And, while some fears were expressed about automation and any resulting unemployment, it was clear that people were very keen to keep themselves up to date with the latest technology. I have no doubt that with the fast pace of change that we're seeing, the need for continued education is going to feature more prominently in the workplace.

Speaker 2

As I'm still only in my 20s, and in my first job ever, I'm aware that by working in a range of different companies I'll build up useful business experience. Like so many other people of my generation, I can't see myself working for large companies for long. The trend is definitely for people to set up their own small business and work from home. Having no boss sounds good! For my Master's degree I looked into how happy people who worked without a boss were, and they had more motivation, felt more sense of achievement and were more proud of what they did compared with office workers, even if they weren't living in luxury.

Speaker 3

I've just been reading about the latest financial scandal to hit a large enterprise – it's not the first and, in my view, it won't be the last. And this is only the tip of the iceberg. Any confidence people ever had in big business is going to evaporate over the next few years. The value of the company has plummeted, unsurprisingly. I've been carrying out interviews with shoppers for a paper I'm writing for a business journal, and people are smart, they see through propaganda that companies send out saying how they're helping save the planet! Companies have to realise they only have a business if people buy their stuff!

Speaker 4

I've been in business for over 40 years and will be retiring soon. I've seen many changes. For one thing, the way management treat people has improved. Workers get much more of a say now. But some things remain the same – <u>the attraction of an urban environment for workers, I'm sure will be powerful for many years to come.</u> This sort of centralisation makes sense. At present, <u>I'm involved in a study examining the carbon footprint of trade.</u> It's imperative that companies take responsibility, and also consumers. I mean, how many people really think about food air miles or where their latest gadget was made? We'll be publishing our findings in the next couple of months.

Speaker 5

I give lectures at a business school and <u>have been looking into how, as more people live on their own and families get smaller, the workplace takes on more importance as a place to make friends.</u> We can't underestimate the value of belonging to an organization from the employee's personal point of view. Loneliness among the elderly, in particular, can be a problem, but if I were to make an educated guess, <u>I'd say we'll all be in work well into our 70s, rather than 50s or 60s as is the current norm,</u> and that may go some way to solving the problem. Of course, those who have chosen to work at home may miss out on this benefit.

TRAINING

 ## Speaking Part 1

14 *Interlocutor:* How important is it for you to spend time with your friends?
Candidate 1: It's very important for me to spend a lot of time with my friends.
Interlocutor: What kind of films do you enjoy watching?
Candidate 2: I enjoy watching adventure films.

TRAINING

 ## Speaking Part 2

15 ### Exercise 1

The first picture shows a girl and a woman in a garden. It looks like the girl is explaining something about the garden to the woman. Maybe the girl is telling the woman which plants need watering or which plants are ready to pick. I suppose that if the woman doesn't listen carefully, the plants might die or might be picked too early. If the plant is picked too early, it'll be a waste.

The second picture shows a man. I think the man is talking into a microphone and it looks like the man is standing on a platform, perhaps in a station. I can't see any passengers, but passengers need to listen to the man's announcements carefully. The man may be telling them about a change to the timetable. If the passengers don't listen carefully, they may miss their train.

TRAINING

 ## Speaking Part 2

16 ### Exercise 2

The first picture shows a girl and a woman in a garden, whereas in the second one there's just a man on his own. It certainly looks like the woman is listening carefully to what the girl's saying and pointing at, but I wouldn't say this is vital information. They are probably just discussing the plants and which ones need watering. I suppose if the woman didn't listen carefully, the plants might not do well, particularly if the girl is telling her about some special attention they need. On the other hand, the information in the second picture is pretty important. It looks to me as if the man is standing on a station platform and giving an announcement, probably something about the timetable or a platform change. Announcements like these are often very difficult to hear, particularly in noisy, crowded stations – although this one appears deserted – so it's essential to listen carefully. Missing the announcement, or not hearing it correctly, could mean you end up missing your train.

TRAINING

 ## Speaking Part 3

17 ### Exercise 1

Man: Let's start with restricting traffic. I suppose if there are fewer cars, there is less pollution, so that helps improve the quality of city life. And it's safer.
Woman: It's always good to have plenty of green spaces in a city. They make the air cleaner and give people somewhere to relax. Like Central Park in New York. Lots of cities don't have that and they can be very stressful places to be.
Man: What about this point about having shops open for longer hours? I don't think that has any effect on the quality of life for residents. Unless you really enjoy shopping! And it makes it worse for shop workers because they have to work longer hours. So I don't think this is a good suggestion.
Woman: Modernising buildings can be good. These improvements mean they usually have better facilities and they can be very stylish. But it would be a shame to lose all the traditional buildings. We want to keep some of the tra-ditional style in our cities; we don't want to lose the history.
Man: Finally, having lots of celebrations and events can be

good, as that's a way of bringing people together to socialise and relax. People can make the city a place to have fun, not just a place to work and do shopping. That's a good thing.
Woman: Yes.

TRAINING

 Speaking Part 3

18 **Exercise 2**

Woman: Let's start with restricting traffic, shall we? I suppose if there are fewer cars, there is likely to be less pollution, which would help improve the quality of city life.
Man: That's a good point. It can be really difficult to breathe in the centre of some cities. And it would be safer to walk around if there weren't any cars.
Woman: Exactly! I was just about to say the same thing about safety.
Man: So, what about increasing the number of green spaces, like parks? That's a good idea, as they also help reduce pollution.
Woman: As well as giving people somewhere to relax, like Central Park in New York. Lots of cities don't have that and they can be very stressful places to be.
Man: Oh yes, I hadn't thought of that. What about this point about having shops open for longer hours? That's a good idea.
Woman: Do you think so? I don't think that has any effect on the quality of life for residents. Unless you really enjoy shopping! And it makes it worse for shop workers because they have to work longer hours. So I don't think this is a good suggestion.
Man: OK, so let's think about modernising buildings. That's not a bad idea.
Woman: I know what you mean. These improvements mean they usually have better facilities and they can be very stylish.
Man: Although that's not always the case – some of them can be really ugly and it would be a shame to lose all the traditional buildings. We want to keep some of the traditional style in our cities; we don't want to lose the history.
Woman: I couldn't agree more. We don't want all cities to look the same, do we? So the last suggestion is having lots of celebrations and events. Do you think that would help improve the quality of life?
Man: Not necessarily. It's a way of bringing people together to socialise and relax, but there may be problems with overcrowding.
Woman: Perhaps, but events like these can make the city a place to have fun, not just a place to work and do shopping. That's a good thing.
Man: Yes, that may be true. It's worth thinking about, anyway.

 Test 3

 LISTENING PART 1

19 *Extract One*

Lisa: So, Peter, how's your work on generating electricity from the oceans going?
Peter: Good, thanks, Lisa. As you know, my interest is in generating energy from ocean tides. And it's easy to talk about the obvious benefits to potential investors, like there are always tides, twice a day, so as an energy resource it won't run out. But that's not, as I see it, the main attraction – it's the fact that wherever there's a large body of water, you can generate power. Energy won't need to be imported from abroad.
Lisa: That's a really important point. And I think I'm right in saying that a whole range of new devices have been developed to harness energy from the sea, like giant blades, and paddles to power turbines?
Peter: Yes, they're the next big thing.
Lisa: But I'm still a firm believer in land-based wind turbines as a clean, renewable energy resource. The company I work for doesn't use off-shore wind turbines. To me, the possible damage to marine wildlife that can occur with generating energy from the ocean, by whatever means, cancels out any benefits.

Extract Two

Man: Hey, Nancy, you know a lot about plants – what do you think about urban foraging?
Woman: You mean people going out and picking fruit and things from public areas in cities? Well, I can understand the appeal. It'd barely make a difference to your weekly outlay on food, but I think people are so fed up with mass-produced processed food, they like the idea that it's sure to be natural – free of artificial chemicals. But I wonder how many people these days venture out into parks and forests. I mean, loads of city kids have never been into the countryside.
Man: Mmm. You know there's talk of letting people pick the fruit and nuts from the trees in the park on Main Street? Just in the area where all the trees are, so the flowers and bushes don't get trashed.
Woman: Well, as long as they offer classes so that people know what things are. Apparently, there are some blueberry bushes in the park.
Man: Really? I didn't know that. But good point – you also wouldn't want anyone getting sick because they'd eaten something poisonous! It'll be interesting to see how many of my neighbours have heard about foraging and might do it!

Extract Three

Man: Freya, do you think it's about time we did something about booking a summer holiday?

Woman: Absolutely! It seems ages since last year's holiday. Are you happy to laze about on a beach again?

Man: Perfect. Living in a city and having hectic jobs, that suits us, I think. And I'd rather not do anything too energetic like a walking holiday. Remember when we went with your sister?

Woman: Yeah, exhausting! And we don't want to book so late this year that we end up in a grotty hotel like last year. We'd even saved enough to stay in a four-star hotel, but they were all booked.

Man: I know. Anyway, we've got those new suitcases, so packing will be easy. We always seem to take more than we need, but I'd rather it was that way round than be short of things.

Woman: And you never know exactly what the weather's going to be like, so you've got to cover every eventuality! Have you still got that list you downloaded from the internet so that we don't forget anything?

Man: It's saved on my laptop. Do you want to look at it now?

Woman: Why not? I love planning everything way ahead of time; it's part of the fun.

🎧 LISTENING PART 2

20 In this talk, I'll be giving some key information about butterflies. I can only give you a brief overview here because there are known to be more than 20,000 different species, and here in North America we're lucky to have around 700 of them.

First, I'd like to draw your attention to butterflies as pollinators. They're responsible for pollinating many flowers and, even though they may not be as efficient as bees, they're better pollinators than beetles, for example. As butterflies are feeding on the nectar in a flower, the pollen sticks to their bodies and it's then transferred to other flowers.

Butterflies are attracted to plants for several reasons. As I mentioned, they're after the sweet nectar, but I've studied the effect of a plant's powerful perfume in attracting them, rather than a plant's colour or nectar content. Red and yellow flowers are known to attract butterflies.

In areas where butterflies are plentiful, it's a sign that nature is in balance because butterflies are an essential component of the food chain. They are eaten by some animals, such as bats and birds, and butterflies, in turn, eat other insects.

Farmers too can gain from some species of butterfly, such as the Harvester butterfly, which acts as a kind of pest control by eating caterpillars which damage the farmers' harvest. The detection of these caterpillars takes only seconds for these clever butterflies.

Another very important point is that scientists are aware that they can learn a lot from the movements of butterflies, in particular about climate change. Butterflies are more sensitive than many other animals, so act as a good early warning system. In North America, we've been keeping a careful watch on the Checkerspot butterfly. It's very noticeable that it's now living at higher altitudes than a couple of decades ago because of global warming. Other species too show signs of migrating away from areas at lower levels.

Moving on to a different aspect: butterflies can also give an economic boost to an area. For example, in Mexico, which is home to the Monarch butterfly, tourists come from around the world in the hope of catching a glimpse of it and of course getting the perfect photo. Hotel owners and restaurateurs do a roaring trade at certain times of the year because of them.

And my final point in this podcast is about how important butterflies can be to human health. Let me give you an example. The European Meadow Brown butterfly produces an antibiotic which scientists have been able to extract. It could mean a decrease in the need for artificial forms of treatment against bacteria if a natural treatment were available.

I think you'll agree that these small creatures are truly remarkable!

🎧 LISTENING PART 3

21 *Interviewer:* Today, in our series on the choices young people have to make, I'm talking to high school students Tamsin and Farid about whether they think it's a good idea to go to university straight after high school. Farid, there are a lot of options open to school leavers: have you been getting all sorts of ideas from friends and family?

Farid: Absolutely! My parents are very keen for me to go straight to university, but, actually, a big international company I'd contacted has just been in contact with me. They offer work for school leavers and they train you in company. That's an option. My sister did a gap year before going to university and visited about ten countries, but afterwards said she felt she wished she'd done something more useful with her time, like just going to one country and working as a volunteer for a charity. She thinks I should work for myself. I'm good at game design and she thinks I should do that for a living.

Interviewer: A lot to think about! Tamsin, what's your view on school leavers going straight to university?

Tamsin: Well, I think people have to consider every aspect of it carefully because I'm concerned that some people go to university for the wrong reasons. I don't mean that they go just because their parents and teachers say they should, more that some courses have become really cool, like social sciences, and they just want to jump on the bandwagon. However, it is true that students can sometimes make good contacts by socialising at university, which may lead to finding a job more easily later.

Interviewer: Interesting point. Do you think some people are put off going to university by the expense?

Tamsin: Well, quite a few students work while they're studying and in that way they help support themselves financially. And if they're well organised, it shouldn't mean they neglect their studies. And actually, I've heard that lots of employers like the fact that students have some familiarity with what it's really like to have a job.

Farid: And from the student's perspective, it can give you a good idea about what you do and don't like about a job. But I wonder if there's a danger when you work and study at the same time that you just get exhausted and end up ill and not able to do either well.

Tamsin: I think that's rare. Anyway, I'm pretty sure I'm going to go straight to university.

Farid: Yes, I think that's the right choice for you. After all, you've always got top grades in maths and sciences.

Tamsin: I think it'll teach me to think outside the box. Even reading details about the modules offered at some universities makes me think I'll learn to look at things from a much wider perspective. And I'm really focused on becoming an engineer – so what am I waiting for? My dad's an engineer and I've talked to some of his colleagues, and they can give me work experience during the holidays.

Farid: I wish I was as sure as you are about what I want to do. You know I went to a university Open Day a couple of weeks ago? It was great – I got to meet some students already studying Spanish, which is what I might be interested in doing, and they showed me round the Languages Faculty. What I hadn't expected was that a large number of the lecturers were available, so that you could ask them about the courses. That was really useful. There were also tours of the science labs, which are supposed to be really cutting edge, but that wasn't what interested me.

Interviewer: Right. So, Tamsin, have you written your university letter of application yet? It's very important to get that just right, isn't it?

Tamsin: Yes, I have and I asked Farid to take a look at it to see what he thinks.

Farid: It's really impressive. It covers pretty much everything that it should. The way it's written shows she's a really good communicator, and her love of engineering really comes across well. If she built up the part where she talks about what a dedicated student she is and how open to feedback she is, then I think it's ready to send. Tamsin's so lucky in that she knows exactly where she wants to be in ten years' time! I'm still not sure what to do.

Interviewer: Well, I'm afraid we have to leave it there for today. Thank you both for taking part in today's discussion and good luck with your futures.

 LISTENING PART 4

22 *Speaker 1*

The film I'd like to talk about is called *The Teller*. It's written by a comparatively new scriptwriter and, to give him his due, as the plot unfolds, you do see how the main characters grow in their understanding of themselves and others around them. However, what I find unforgivable is that I feel as though I've heard all those conversations before! If I had to sum up what the film's about, I'd say it's the value of seeing the funny side of things when life gets tough. It might be worth going to see – you never know, you may notice something in it that I missed altogether. I rather doubt it, though!

Speaker 2

If you want to know what it must be like to live in a tiny village in northern Canada, watch the movie called *Rachel*. It's about how an ageing, but fiercely passionate, aunt guides her relatives through various situations while, at the same time, teaching them the value of supporting each other. I only have one small complaint and that is, to me, the musical score didn't seem to fit the action. For example, when the main actor was saying something quite profound and serious, quite near the end, it was far too jolly. But, despite that, it's still worth seeing if you happen to come across it.

Speaker 3

I'm afraid I'm going to tell you about a film I don't think you should waste your time and money on. It's called *The Empty Jar*. Despite one of my all-time favourite actors being in it, I really had no idea what was going on from start to finish. And I'm not alone in this view. The rest of the audience were equally baffled when I went to see it. Don't get me wrong, it was obvious what the scriptwriter was getting at: that contentment can be gained from simple activities, like sharing an ice cream with your child at the beach. And to be honest, there were some fabulous panoramic shots of the landscape.

Speaker 4

You must see the film called *Sold By*. I know it's an odd title, and might actually sound more like a business documentary about how to make money, but it's not. Far from it – it's about how one small lie can result in life becoming very complicated, and how maintaining the pretence can make people very anxious. The only thing I could find fault with was little things, like one moment the main actor's holding a bag in a restaurant, but then he leaves without the bag. It's a pity such carelessness leaves a bad impression. But overall, the moral of the film, honesty, is a good one.

Speaker 5

The movie *Twice in a Row* has many strong points – the background music, to name just one. It's set in a typical, medium-sized American town and the action all takes place in a diner. However, from about ten minutes into the movie, I could have told you that in the end Bill Jenkins, that's the name of the main character, would never be able to run a restaurant with his brother as the chef and his mother as the accountant. It was a project doomed from the outset. And that's the focus really, that running a business with your nearest and dearest is no walk in the park. No wonder they all finish up hating each other!

Test 4

 LISTENING PART 1

23 *Extract One*

Nina: My view on giving praise to children is simple: approach it in the same way you'd approach rock climbing – with great caution! One false move or word can be disastrous. A child may get the wrong message if you say, for example, that poor homework is wonderful, and as for a rock climber, well, if they are led to believe that they are accomplished sportspeople when they aren't, they may find themselves in difficulty and their confidence in themselves and their instructor could be severely damaged. However, unlike rock climbing, how to praise a child in an effective way takes only moments to grasp.

Dan: I agree. And you hear so much what I call 'empty praise', when parents look absent-mindedly at their child's painting and just say 'wonderful'. It should always be followed up with 'because', for example, 'it's full of detail'. Children have very different personalities, but I've found this sort of praise is always effective, no matter whether the child is naturally self-assured or not. And when children have really worked hard at something, it's up to adults to make the praise meaningful.

Nina: That's very true.

Extract Two

Martha: Hi, Robert, are you still thinking about taking up golf?

Robert: Hi, Martha, yes, and the more I think about it, the keener I am on the idea. I know it gives you a good workout and I really need that 'cos in my job I sit in front of a screen all day long, but I'd always thought of golf as kind of dated, you know, not cool! My uncle used to play at a very exclusive golf club and had to wear what I thought were ridiculous clothes to play in. Perhaps that's where I got my prejudiced ideas from.

Martha: Probably! Well, I'm up for it if you are. I don't have a lot of extra cash to splash out, though.

Robert: You wouldn't need to if we joined the city golf club. I know what you mean, though, some private golf clubs can be pricey. I'll ask a guy I know at work about the city club – he's a golfer.

Martha: Actually, they're having an Open Day when potential members can go along. I saw a poster somewhere. We could check it out then. Interested?

Robert: You bet!

Extract Three

Man: That was the best festival ever. I mean the line-up of bands was awesome, sure, but it was the organisation as well that was first class.

Woman: I've never been to a festival where the sound was so good. Do you think it was because they'd invested in the best sound system?

Man: I think that's a given at a music festival – well, the best they can afford. What I noticed was the layout of the whole area. That had been landscaped to get the best acoustics. The importance of that often seems to be ignored or perhaps forgotten. I also liked the way the sound engineers checked everything and wouldn't let the band start until they were happy that everything was OK.

Woman: That local band held their own against some big international names.

Man: Yeah, I didn't know anything about them until I heard someone chatting about them while I was getting coffee.

Woman: And I only realised they were worth seeing when I went to the stage where they were playing and a huge crowd was gathering. I was so pleased for them, especially when one of the big names later said how great they were.

 LISTENING PART 2

24 Good morning, everyone. My name's Estelle Tinios and, as part of your series of careers talks, I'm here today to tell you about my job as a pharmacist. Pharmacists play a key role in all communities, dispensing the medication people need in order to recover from illnesses.

Let's take a look at the study path you'd need to follow to become a pharmacist. At university, you'll need to do a relevant undergraduate course, for instance, biology, chemistry … and like many other students I opted for physics. Biomedical science can also be an excellent choice.

It's a good idea to get as much experience as possible while you're studying. That way you'll be able to get to know a range of people in the industry. I suggest doing a few hours per week as a technician, rather than as a junior in a pharmacist's, because you'll come into contact with more people.

In order to become a licenced pharmacist, you'll also need to do postgraduate studies to become a Doctor of Pharmacy. During this period, you'll be required to do an internship. I found this invaluable for finding out exactly what a pharmacist does on a daily basis. And, once you've got your doctorate, you can take a specialty, for example, to become what's known as a compounding pharmacist, where you mix individual ingredients to make up a patient's prescription.

Being a pharmacist requires many and varied abilities, such as communication skills. What I hadn't anticipated, however, was the importance of memorisation skills because you'll be dealing with the names of hundreds of medications.

Towards the end of your studies, you'll start looking for a full-time job. A pharmacist may work in a retail outlet or a hospital, among other places. Medications need to be given out 24/7, so in order to have the best chance of getting a job, if you have some flexibility and you don't mind giving up your free time at weekends or evenings, you'll widen your chances of getting a job.

One of my first jobs was in research and development for an international company. The company was looking into using existing medications for different illnesses and I was working on the marketing of the medications for new uses. And a good friend of mine was working on the packaging.

I've worked in several roles as a pharmacist, and in every role there's one task that's absolutely vital to get right every time, and that's keeping records that are correct and complete. Other tasks, which you may find you have to do, could be filling out insurance claims.

I'd also like to point out that becoming a pharmacist is a great career choice. It's very interesting work, as the range of treatments is widening all the time. You will undoubtedly find work, since the population of our country is rising all the time, and, as a result, the need for pharmacists is going up proportionally.

Now, if anyone has any questions …

 LISTENING PART 3

25 *Interviewer:* Today in *Business Weekly*, I'm talking to two entrepreneurs, Charles and Betty, who both first set up companies when they were just in their teens. Charles, I read that your first company, which you started when you were 18, wasn't a success, right?

Charles: Yeah, in fact, after two years, I cut my losses and gave up! After the first year, I could already see that despite having talked to several people – for example, the local bank that had a business advisory service – the basic idea just wasn't sound. The only positive was that at 20, I had enough energy and motivation to pick myself up straight away and start on my second idea. I found it easy to put it all behind me and move on.

Interviewer: And your second company, a photo blogging platform, was a fantastic success. Betty, what is that magic something that makes a young entrepreneur successful?
Betty: Well, that's tricky. I used to think it might be as simple as putting in the hours, you know, working until all the day's tasks were done.
Charles: But that just makes you so tired it's hard to tap into your imagination. In my view, there's no doubt you have to be prepared not only to take chances, but also to seek them out sometimes.
Betty: And to realise that playing it safe is not the right approach. Occasionally, you have to completely rethink not only small things, details, but also your overall objectives.
Interviewer: And as a young entrepreneur, how did you find your first year of business? Betty?
Betty: I was selling T-shirts, and within six months I had to take on a couple of extra people, one to do the office work and the other to work on marketing. And I'd had no experience of interviewing candidates and was terrified in case I ended up with the wrong people. But it all worked out and the bank was happy to give me a loan when they saw how much the business was making and they'd been through my five-year business plan.
Charles: Did you have many competitors? There are lots of businesses selling T-shirts.
Betty: Yes, but that was a good thing, because a lot of market research had already been done and quite a lot of it was available for anyone to access.
Charles: I actually got in touch with some of my competitors to try to find out how they organised their business and they were very helpful, but what really amazed me was that they even went as far as to suggest which accountants to use and IT consultants! And now, when I think someone would be better off going to one of my competitors, I pass on their details, and my competitors do the same for me.
Interviewer: Brilliant! And Betty, you won the Young Businessperson of the Year award when you were just 20. Tell us about that.
Betty: Yes! At first, I was amazed that I'd won it. There seemed to me to be plenty of other excellent start-ups. And I felt as though I'd just been trying to live up to the benchmark they were setting for good business! Anyway, once I'd got over the shock, I felt great about it and it motivated me to grow my company much further and to try to cash in on the publicity.
Charles: That was a great time for you. I don't know how people managed to set up businesses years ago when technology wasn't so developed. I mean, it's so simple now to do some first-class courses on the internet to find out about whatever you need to set up a business. There's a lot of discussion about making contacts online, but I believe there's still an argument for doing it face-to-face. It's the same with some meetings, like with new clients.

Betty: And what about companies having websites? That's made a huge difference.

Charles: But you have to keep them up to date.

Interviewer: That's very true. Well, thank you both for sharing your thoughts with us today.

 LISTENING PART 4

26 *Speaker 1*

I finished high school and made enough money to travel before going to uni by working part time in a restaurant. My thinking behind travelling on my own was to learn to sort out any difficulties for myself – I'd always lived with my parents, but I was going to live in another city to study, so they wouldn't always be around to fall back on. My trip was amazing. I couldn't believe how many different places were so interesting. And the astonishing thing was the wide range of cuisines that I found out I loved, from spicy to delicately aromatic! Sometimes it was difficult for the waiters to explain things to me, but with a little patience we managed between us!

Speaker 2

It was great visiting Europe, but everything was so different, and at times a bit scary, from my life in a small town in the US. Going from country to country, I had to work out how to get from A to B using local and international rail routes. But the upside of that, which I hadn't thought about beforehand, was I became expert at dealing with any issue that came up, even though it was often frustrating. I'd decided to do my trip solo because a friend had been on an organised tour and said it was annoying not being able to change plans at the drop of a hat. And I knew I'd find not being able to decide things for myself aggravating too.

Speaker 3

I was really keen to go on a long trip to South America and looked at doing it in an organised group or by myself. In the end, the decision was made for me in a way when I looked at the total outlay if I went with a group. Anyway, it turned out to be the best thing because, of course, being on a budget, I had to sort out a lot of things for myself in Spanish and Portuguese and I was amazed at how fluent I became in just a couple of months. I was fortunate because people were always so accepting of my poor pronunciation.

Speaker 4

What stood out for me about my trip was that because I was on my own, I briefly spent time with loads of other travellers and locals. I hadn't considered that benefit before setting off – I'd just thought I'd have a great time trying the local dishes wherever I was – I'm a real foodie. In my free time at home I do photography and I'd chosen to travel by

myself so that I could get some new ideas for an exhibition I was going to put on. The best place for that turned out to be a national park in Spain where you're not allowed to take vehicles because they want to keep damage to the environment to a minimum.

Speaker 5

My sister had been on a great tour of Japan when she was a student, but said being in a group had lots of disadvantages. She knew it wouldn't suit me, as my main purpose was to prepare for a marathon – I wanted to be able to watch my diet and make sure I could train every day. This was the best time for me to do this – the trip and the run – because after my trip, I was starting a new job in the automotive industry. I'd been feeling a bit daunted by the prospect of this new job and I hadn't anticipated how much the trip would help me think about my future without panicking, so that was fantastic!

Test 5

 LISTENING PART 1

27 *Extract One*

David: Hi, Jeanette. How's your guitar practice going?

Jeanette: Hi, David. Well, I only started learning to play the guitar about six months ago and I'm making progress, although it doesn't always feel like that. I have good days and bad days. I wonder if great, famous guitarists have the same problem getting motivated some days. My mum keeps telling me to practise more, so I looked up on the internet what to do to spur myself into action and yes, there's loads of suggestions. But after a few futile hours browsing, I realised just reading about it wasn't the solution!

David: Still, I really think playing the guitar's a great pastime and it's certainly doing what I hoped it would for me. On my college course we were getting into some really complex work …

Jeanette: Oh, yeah, you're doing maths, right?

David: … and I was finding it hard to keep focused when I was doing these really long calculations, and I heard that learning a musical instrument can help with that.

Jeanette: And does it?

David: Without a doubt. Some of my classmates were getting a bit anxious about college work and I've recommended learning an instrument to them.

Extract Two

Man: Our company's working on some exciting new initiatives, all connected with roads – for example, making a road surface that contains magnets so that electric cars can be charged as they're driven along the road. This means electric car drivers won't have to stop and recharge their cars on long journeys. Personally, I'm involved with harnessing the wind that cars generate as they go along. This can be used to generate the required electricity for street lamps. A different department is looking at painting road markings with special paint that gets energy from the sun during the day and then the road markings light up at night.

Woman: We've been having some problems with getting the paint to shine to the same brightness along all the roads. But what interests me is that we can even put solar panels on roads – yes, roads made of glass! But don't worry, they won't be slippery. Drivers can still stop quickly, even when travelling at around 125 kilometres an hour. These 'glass roads' would also be perfect for countries with cold climates, as they can be used to melt snow and ice. That would be a real bonus!

Extract Three

Woman: I teach sociology and this week I've been talking about disagreeing. It's fascinating because I have students from all corners of the world in my classes and we've had some in-depth discussions about who you can express disagreement with and when – you know, what do you do if you're talking to someone older than you, for example. And actually, that's all quite straightforward: societies have 'rules' for that. But what makes it tricky is that disagreeing stirs up feelings, from anger to embarrassment.

Man: I think you've hit the nail on the head there. Like you, as a sociologist I've thought about disagreeing from an academic perspective. Interestingly, though, when someone at work disagreed with my proposal to introduce flexitime, I realised there's a great difference between theory and practice. I almost immediately started steering the conversation to something else. I didn't do it in a rude way, I just kept redirecting the conversation. Afterwards, I had no idea why I'd done that because I'm sure my colleague and I could have discussed it and come to a practical solution.

Woman: You were probably worried about being in an 'awkward' situation with a colleague.

Man: You're right.

🎧 LISTENING PART 2

28 Finding inspiration for fabrics to be used in the fashion industry isn't always easy. If designers go to special design galleries, the chances are that other designers are doing the same thing. I'd like to suggest that looking at everyday objects and activities might result in more imaginative designs.

Over the years, I've found watching films is a great source of inspiration for fabric design. However, in my opinion, not all films are suitable. I've had little luck with science fiction films, whereas historical films have been invaluable. It must be something about getting away from the contemporary that leads to more original ideas.

I've even been known to get inspiration in restaurants. If you really take time to examine the food on your plate, the presentation might give you a brainwave, much more so than the colours, as they are, by definition, limited in food. Even which parts of the plate have no food on them at all is worth analysing because what is left blank, without a pattern, creates certain effects.

I know that listening to music is often suggested as a source of inspiration for writing, but it also works well for me as a fabric designer. I choose the music according to the season the clothes will be worn – you could say I 'tailor the music'. So I'll listen to light music for spring, for instance. Then I conjure up what I refer to as a 'mental image' of what I'm listening to and turn it into a design.

Going out into the countryside for a walk can be a good starting place for creativity. Of course, the shapes of leaves are interesting, as are the patterns of flowers, but what inspires me most frequently are the various textures found in nature. I've also seen fabrics inspired by animals and insects.

I work alongside another designer who always has terrific ideas. I remember him bringing in some tools once that he'd found in a shed! But perhaps the most unexpected was when he used a board game for inspiration. I would never have thought of that!

An easy-to-access source of inspiration is photographs. Often the problem is that there's too much choice if you think of all the colour and black and white photos that exist. Monochrome photos can be great for getting a feeling for curves and lines because they often appear stronger than in colour shots. But, in general, make sure you look at good quality photos so that the depth of colour is there. Then, assessing the balance of colours can be really useful.

Don't forget too to look at 'big ideas', for example, styles of architecture. Modern architecture usually has simple, clean lines and reminds you of abstract paintings. But I like the Art Deco style for this reason: because it's what I'd describe as elegant, and that makes it perfect for fashion design.

Designers also have to take into account the garments that the fabric will be used for. Toys may provide inspiration for T-shirts, which can be funny or even show a puzzle that you have to work out. I've even seen jackets that have been inspired by packaging and they were spectacular. Look at some of the everyday things you've got in your kitchen cupboard – you may get ideas there.

🎧 LISTENING PART 3

29 *Tutor:* Thank you for coming in to see me today. I just wanted to check how you were getting on with your assignments on the Mediterranean diet. Bill?

Bill: Well, it took me quite a while to think through what the term *Mediterranean diet* means. I know it's generally thought of as the food eaten in Greece, Italy and Spain, etc., and it's based on using fresh, seasonal and local produce, but, in fact, there's quite a lot of misuse of the term in publicity for products that claim to keep you looking younger. I found that confusing. What's interesting is that, despite big multinational fast food chains emerging in Mediterranean countries, the basics of the Mediterranean diet are still at the heart of most family meals in those regions.

Tutor: True. And many family meals in southern Europe have bread or pasta as the carbohydrate component of the meal, perhaps more so than in some other countries. It goes back to the time when most people had physical jobs and they needed the energy these foods provide. They would then just have a small amount of fish or meat accompanied by salads and vegetables. So you have to take into account that nowadays most of us have jobs that require very little physical activity, so Mediterranean families have adapted their diets accordingly. Kelly, how are you getting on with your assignment?

Kelly: I'm really enjoying it. I've been reading a lot about olive oil, how it's an ancient food. It's been established that olive trees have been grown since around 3000 BCE and the olives pressed to extract the oil. Personally, I've never been very fond of the taste, but I think it may be because I've been using olive oil that's been heat treated during the production process. It's only pure olive oil that's never heated, just pressed, that's the best and apparently it tastes quite different. I guess it's worth paying a bit more to get good oil. Next, I'm going to read about its health benefits. Is it beneficial for our hearts?

Bill: I read that it was.

Kelly: Right.

Bill: And I think in general following the Mediterranean diet must be good for you; fresh fruit gives you some natural sugar ... but it does rely on people sourcing fresh food regularly and preparing meals properly.

Kelly: Absolutely, and not just opening a packet of some pre-prepared meal that's full of additives. But the thing is, if people don't get home from work until quite late, they don't want to spend hours in the kitchen.

Bill: Exactly – getting everything ready and then waiting for it to cook when they're really hungry! That's the problem with the Mediterranean diet. Traditionally people ate a wide range of fresh food, often taking hours over lunch, having it at home with family and friends all together. I think that must be a good mood enhancer, and it must make you feel ready to carry on working for the rest of the day. Of course, in summer in Mediterranean countries, it can be quite hot and the midday sun has to be avoided, so people have to find a shaded area if they eat outside, and resting after lunch is a quite practical way to spend the hottest hours of the day.

Kelly: Yes, I wonder if people have different routines in summer and winter. And the recipes people use must be different because different seasonal food's available; you won't get local fresh tomatoes in winter in some places, for example. But going back to the health benefits of the Mediterranean diet, I'm keen to find out whether it helps mental processes, especially people's ability to recall things. I think I saw a study by someone in one of the American universities about that. And there was another study in Japan where people of all ages had been asked to follow the Mediterranean diet. I need to read that too.

Tutor: Well, I'm glad you've both been looking into the Mediterranean diet from a wide range of perspectives. Well done.

LISTENING PART 4

30 *Speaker 1*

Traditional sports like football, tennis and golf are losing fans in their hundreds. Young people are just not getting into them. If you go back 40 years or so, when kids came home from school, they'd go and play football or something locally – often for free as long as they had a ball. But a lot of the pitches have gone, and have been used for housing in many cases. What's interesting, though, is how in years to come, with new technology, we'll be able to find out things like the player's heart rate, calories used, etc., whereas right now, we only know, for example, the speed of a serve in tennis.

Speaker 2

Well, I'm not surprised well-established sports like soccer and baseball are attracting fewer spectators. And to redress this problem, I'm sure sports will be a whole lot more exciting to watch or to take part in very soon. In fact, it's already happening if you think about the take-up rate for action sports like kiteboarding, snowmobiling and mountaineering. Then there's e-sports, where people play sports video games. And yes, these are now classified as sports – the element of competition is there, if not the physical exertion! The real explanation why regular sports are less popular is because people spend much more time alone on their computer. Being in a huge crowd at a baseball game's no longer what people want to do.

Speaker 3

My mum plays badminton at the weekend, but her club's losing members and I can understand that because I think people have become less bothered about keeping in shape. If you look at the number of hours people spend in front of a computer or TV, it's obvious. And more of us are becoming spectators rather than players. In my opinion, that's down to new sports becoming so complicated – for example, these what are called mash-up sports, where two or more sports are blended, like playing frisbee and volleyball! But that's the way sports are going, I'm convinced of it. And because these sports are new, the rules haven't really been established yet, so that's another complication.

Speaker 4

I think traditional sports like cricket and rugby have had their day. And it's not such a bad thing because when I played rugby at school, quite a few of us got injured. But that's not the cause of the drop in spectator numbers, or even players. It's more to do with the fact that now we accept that the word 'sport' can refer to many more activities, even individual sports and e-sports too. And with the increase in popularity of e-sports, a natural consequence is that players are more likely to be in their teens than their forties. And this is going to be the trend – a huge change in the demographic of who takes part in or watches sports.

Speaker 5

I can't stand traditional sports and to me it's obvious why they're no longer attracting people. I used to play hockey and, as a team, we were keen and wanted to have a good time playing, but literally every three minutes, the referee would blow her whistle and we'd have to stop because someone had done something wrong, like raised her stick too high. It's a shame because when I stopped playing, I missed being so fit. The other thing I don't like is professional sport and the amount players earn. But I think pretty soon, these mad salaries will be have to be cut because young people just don't want to support that sort of 'big business' – we're more democratic.

Test 6

 LISTENING PART 1

31 *Extract One*

Lizzie: So, have you come to a decision about taking up the keyboard or the drums? I have and I've bought a great keyboard!

Raphael: I'm still not 100% sure, to be honest. We've got a huge garage at home that'd be easy to soundproof, so my parents don't think the noise will be a problem whether I go for a keyboard or drums.

Lizzie: Are they sure about that?

Raphael: Well, anyway, on keyboards and on an electronic drum kit there's a knob to adjust the sound level. But the deciding factor might be that I'd struggle to take drums anywhere. I don't have my own car. But going back to what I was saying, our garage would make a great rehearsal space for any instrument. Why don't you come over to see it?

Lizzie: Sounds fantastic! Listen, if you went for the drums,

we'd be able to practise together at your place. And my brother's got a van, so if we got to the point where we played in a group, he'd be happy to give us and our kit a lift. What do you think?

Raphael: Oh, I don't know. I want to make sure I decide what's best for me because neither instrument's cheap to buy.

Extract Two

Man: Hi. Are you meeting our new Mexican clients next week?

Woman: Yes, I've booked the main board room for the meeting and I'm taking them out to the Clayton restaurant for lunch.

Man: Wow! That'll make a great first impression. The atmosphere's perfect for a formal lunch.

Woman: Yes, I always feel a bit tense when I meet clients for the first time, even when I don't need to put my best business suit on and I just meet them in my office – you know, a much more informal meeting. I always feel as though I've got to watch what I say and I end up not being my usual candid self.

Man: But it's interesting how relationships change over the years. Do you remember Lilly Douglas? We all thought she was wonderful when we first met her, but when she became the chief accountant, she became very distant ...

Woman: Absolutely, to the point where she was almost unfriendly. That can happen. It just goes to show that there's a very clear line between business relationships and the genuine closeness you get with your friends.

Extract Three

Woman: Nick, did you put that chocolate dessert on the menu of your restaurant – the one we often had when we were kids?

Man: Oh yeah, we'd been talking about that, hadn't we, and I thought: why not? I found the recipe and did a trial run to see what it was like. The recipe's quite complicated because there are several stages you have to go through, but anyway, I managed it.

Woman: And?

Man: Well, the honey flavour came across well, but, apart from that, it was heavy, sticky and sickly. After a couple of spoonfuls, I binned it. I didn't even dare tell the other chefs it'd been a family favourite – I just very quietly got rid of it and hoped no one would notice that I'd made something so foul.

Woman: Oh no! But it's great that you have a job where you can do that, just decide to try something out. And I think it's funny that you didn't want the others to know about it. I'm intrigued about that sense of rivalry that seems to go through everything you do at the restaurant. And I think good chefs need that drive so that they keep experimenting with new techniques and ingredients.

🎧 LISTENING PART 2

32 Good morning. My name's Diana and I'd like to talk about what it's like to be a volunteer at a riding school in Costa Rica. You never know, you may be inspired to do something similar.

Of course, one of my aims for volunteering was to become a better rider, but that's not the only skill volunteers can gain. Running a horse-riding school requires excellent management skills and I and several of the volunteers I worked alongside were there also for that reason. I had studied Spanish at school, but, for some volunteers, the fact that Spanish lessons were offered for free was very attractive.

The location of the riding school was out of this world. Although Costa Rica's famous for wildlife – it's one of the countries with the highest biodiversity in the world – it was the landscape that I found particularly awesome. If you're thinking of going, make sure you choose the dry season, between December and April.

Volunteers live at the riding school and the accommodation there was clean, comfortable and secure, with simple furniture. I could choose a single room or share. The textiles used throughout the space had all been woven in the next village. The designs were based on traditional patterns and I really appreciated that desire to promote local culture.

Now, to tell you something about my routine: every day started with a healthy breakfast prepared by the cooks. Then I had a list of jobs to do during the morning. I had to feed the horses, which was a really lovely job. But top of my list was to go through what was called the 'health checks' with a senior member of staff. Each horse had its own medical file and the records were updated every day.

The owner of the school always joined us for lunch and it was a great opportunity to get advice from him. I was keen to establish if it might be a career for me. He recommended studying Animal Science at college, even though he'd come to the business by a quite different route – he'd done a tourism course after high school.

In the afternoons, I helped out with kids' riding lessons and just one or two were a bit hesitant. I remembered my own riding instructor telling me to laugh when I was feeling tense and I passed this on to my little students. One of the instructors in Costa Rica advised children to hum a tune if they felt worried. I think these are both good techniques because you breathe and relax.

After a week's riding every day, most of the other volunteers had aching muscles, but, because I run 8k most days back home, I didn't experience that. I found my posture got better, though. I've always had good balance on a horse, but it was obvious that several volunteers improved that very quickly.

For me, the most exciting part was when a group of us went on a cross-country ride. I was on my much-loved Valetina, a young mare, and, even though I'd jumped over poles or small fences in a training ring at the school, that was the day I took my horse over a stream, or perhaps the horse took me. I'll never forget that.

Now, if anyone …

🎧 LISTENING PART 3

33 *Interviewer:* Matthew and Tracy, thank you for taking part in our series of discussions on journalism and the news. In particular, I'm interested in what you have to say about how news consumers, whether they watch TV or read newspapers, recognise if they're being presented with facts or a journalist's opinion. Matthew?

Matthew: That's a very good question and, actually, I think it's often hard for the average news consumer to know what's fact and what's opinion. As journalism students, we've spent quite a bit of our course, a whole module, on this area. In the first part of the module, we looked at how the news is changing – people get soundbites, just quick headlines online, if you like. And, of course, increasingly, people use their phones while they're travelling or waiting for something, as a way to keep in touch with the news at any time. But, unless they know and understand what has led up to an event, telling fact from fiction in the news is a challenge for them. However, on the positive side, many people get their news from several different media and that means they have a greater chance of getting a balanced view.

Interviewer: Now, I understand you put together a questionnaire to ask people if they were aware of when they were getting facts and when they were getting opinions from the news. Tell us about that, Tracy.

Tracy: Well, it was a very useful exercise because we had to really think about what we understood by the word *fact* ourselves first! Anyway, we drafted our questionnaire and tried it out on some other students on our course. We realised that asking open questions was problematic because the answers were so long, so we abandoned those and stuck to multiple-choice questions. And even then, I cut those from four choices to three to make the whole thing more manageable.

Interviewer: And I see your findings showed that most people were not that sure whether they were reading facts or opinions.

Matthew: No, so then we had to find an article that was a good example, I mean where it was clear whether it was giving facts or opinions. And, we read about a dozen before we found a really good one. I read one about the railways and even within one sentence there was a mixture of fact and opinion.

Tracy: Yes, it was puzzling, just like the one on class sizes. But one I read on plastic in the oceans was obviously factual because it gave statistics.

Matthew: And said where those data came from. I loved the one about football too, but it wasn't that well written.

Tracy: And, despite its enthusiasm, it actually said very little.

Interviewer: So, what did you do next on your module?

Matthew: We had to write a factual article. I always feel apprehensive about doing that. I got some quite negative feedback from my tutor for the first one I wrote, even though my peers thought I'd researched it thoroughly. I'm getting better at it with each one I write, but I still wake up at night concerned that I might not have checked everything carefully enough and there's some error somewhere. That can easily happen and OK, readers probably won't get hold of the wrong end of the stick because of that, but it's just not professional.

Tracy: But can I just say something about photos and video? I think that lots of people mistrust photos now because it's so easy to manipulate them. So a photo in a newspaper doesn't always support or enhance what a journalist has written. Video seems to be what most people favour when there's a choice between the two. The extent to which news has visuals depends largely on the type of publication or news channel.

Interviewer: Do you think there's more scope for developing your own style when you write opinion articles rather than factual ones?

Matthew: Definitely, I love that. I'm quite a chatty sort of person and I like it when I can write an article that stems from a conversation I've had or even sometimes just overheard. The reason I admire the author Brenda McGovern is her ability to make conversation sound so real. I heard her speak recently at a book fair and she was tremendous. You can't always write in a chatty style, though, because if the subject's something quite serious, you have to adapt so that the language is appropriate.

Interviewer: Well, thank you both …

 LISTENING PART 4

34 *Speaker 1*

Boredom's a weird thing and not something I experience often. I used to think it was a negative emotion, but, in fact, when I'm bored my brain gets time to sort stuff out, especially at work – I work as a book illustrator. I'm not saying I suddenly become more efficient or talented – just that I feel less stressed and listen to what friends and family are really saying, understand the bigger picture behind what they're saying, and I feel more empathy. Recently, I finished work on a book way ahead of schedule and I'd never felt so much at a loose end before. So I decided to go visit my brother who lives a four-hour flight away.

Speaker 2

I'm a runner, quite serious stuff, so I have a sports psychologist to help improve my performance and I sometimes go to extra lectures on technique, and that sort of thing. Anyway, the one I went to last was so dull, I thought about walking out, but decided that would look rude, so I just sat there and zoned out. Then, quite quickly, I started going over in my head how hurt I'd felt when my coach was being hard on me about my diet. And then I remembered the whole conversation and all the positive things she'd said, and I recognised that the diet bit was the only negative part. I'd just blown it up out of all proportion!

Speaker 3

I know a lot of people think of boredom – or perhaps it's better to call it daydreaming – as a good opportunity to go through every minute aspect of something they're working on, but for me it's time when I allow my imagination to wander. And as I'm a fashion designer, I need that mental space to come up with something original. Not many people would find something positive about having a bad back, but I did. On doctor's orders, I lay in bed staring at the ceiling, listening to the radio and this gave me the mental space I needed. My wife says she often comes up with answers to work issues when she's waiting at the bus stop!

Speaker 4

I'm a working mum and there are always a hundred and one things to do. In fact, there are so many that my mind goes blank and I don't know where to start. But, if I find myself doing some mindless chore again and again, like the ironing I was doing the other day, my brain seems to get things in order so that I know which is the most important thing to do first. I might have thought I needed to go to the grocery store, but, in fact, I should check my work emails, for example. If more people realised the benefits of doing monotonous things, they'd be a much more positive person to be around.

Speaker 5

I moved house a while back and it means a forty-minute commute to get to the office. Yes, very boring in many ways, but, actually, I'd been thinking about giving up teaching and going into tourism, and do you know what? That commuting time allowed me the mental space to organise how I needed to go about it. I knew I had lots of transferable skills, like people skills, so I was pretty sure it was the right thing for me. When I told a friend about my plans, he reminded me that it wasn't always a glamorous job being a tour rep – a lot of my time would be waiting at airports! But then, no job's perfect, I suppose.

Keys

Reading and Use of English Part 1

Training

Identifying collocations

1 1 make a difference / sense / an exception / trouble

   2 do your best / the shopping / someone a favour / harm

   3 have an experience / an effect / patience / a row

   4 take notice / something for granted / pleasure / turns

   5 put pressure on someone / something into practice / an end to something / your mind to something

   6 give a talk / your word / credit to someone / someone a chance

   7 set an example / a record / an alarm / fire to something

   8 keep a promise / a diary / a secret / in touch

2 1 set a/the record

   2 give (me) your word

   3 kept in touch

   4 had a row

   5 take turns

   6 puts his mind to

   7 do me a favour

   8 did her best

3 1 B 2 D 3 C 4 A 5 C 6 B 7 C 8 D

Understanding the precise meaning of words

1 C

2 B

3 C

4 B

5 D

Exam Practice

1 **C** 'safely' collocates with 'assume'. The other adverbs here don't.

2 **D** All four options can be used with 'up' as phrasal verbs. However, 'end up' is the only one that fits the meaning of the sentence – it means 'eventually finish' or 'eventually find yourself'.

3 **B** 'suggests' is the only one of these verbs which collocates with 'research'.

4 **A** The passive structure '[something] is characterised by ...' is often used to describe the most typical or noticeable qualities of something. The other verbs are not used in this way.

5 **A** 'distance' is the only one of these nouns that relates to races and measuring an athlete's win or loss.

6 **D** 'narrowly' is the only one of these adverbs that collocates with 'lose' or 'lose out'. It also collocates with 'win'.

7 **B** All these verbs mean 'think about', but 'reflect' is the only one that takes the preposition 'on'.

8 **C** 'feeling' collocates with 'happiness' and is the only noun here that can be followed by the preposition 'of'.

Reading and Use of English Part 2

Training

Useful language: relative pronouns

1 where

2 why

3 when

4 which

5 who

6 what

7 which

8 whose

Useful language: adjective + preposition

1 at
2 with
3 for
4 of
5 to
6 for
7 of / about
8 for
9 to
10 by

Useful language: verb + noun + preposition

1 of
2 from
3 in
4 on
5 of
6 for
7 for
8 of

Useful language: connecting words

1

Concession	Time	Condition
although / though despite *even though* *in spite of*	after until *ex.* *when* *before*	if even if *in case* *unless* *whether*
Comparison	Reason	Correlation
than rather than *whereas* *as ... as*	so that in order to/that *because* *so as to* *so as not to*	both ... and ... not only .... but (also) ... *either ... or* *whether ... or not* *neither ... nor*

2 1 until
   2 Not only
   3 Rather than
   4 unless
   5 Despite / In spite of
   6 whether
   7 Although /Though / Even though

Exam Practice

9 **until** If you read the whole text, you find out that scientists recently discovered where blue diamonds

come from – before that, no one knew. So the gap needs a word that indicates the period up to this recent time. We can't say 'before recently', but we can say 'until recently'.

10 **it** Impersonal passive structures like 'it is thought / said / reported / argued' are common in texts about academic research.

11 **between** When a range with two points is described, we say 'between X and Y' or 'from X to Y'. Be careful not to mix them up.

12 **as** 'known' is followed by 'as' when it has this meaning of 'called'.

13 **which** This relative pronoun refers back to '46 blue diamonds'. It's important to look further than the word(s) immediately before the gap. Sometimes the words which relative pronouns refer to can be found further away. Similar combinations with 'of' are common in more formal English, e.g. 'some of which', 'one of which', 'none of which', 'several of which'.

14 **Not** If you read the whole of this sentence, you will see that the two parts of the sentence are held together by the structure 'Not only ... but also'.

15 **than** This follows the comparative structure 'four times nearer'.

16 **according** 'according to' is a prepositional phrase which means 'as stated by'.

Reading and Use of English Part 3

Training

Useful language: identifying types of words
1 and 2

1 **professional** A word between a definite or indefinite article (*a/the*) and a noun is usually an adjective.

2 **Unfortunately** A single word at the start of a sentence which is followed by a comma will be an adverb. In this case, the rest of the sentence indicates that a negative meaning is referred to.

3 **differences** 'many' before the gap indicates that a plural noun is needed.

4 **fitness** A word coming between two nouns will be an adjective or a noun.

5 **enables** The gap between 'medical care' and 'modern footballers' needs a verb.

6 **envious** An adjective is needed to follow 'he's quite'.

7 **drawbacks** A noun is needed for the gap between 'the' and 'of'. 'One of the' indicates that a plural noun is needed.

Useful language: using prefixes and suffixes

Verb	Noun	Adjective	Adverb
create	*creation* *creator*	*creative* *uncreative*	*creatively*
intend	**intention**	**intentional** **intended**	**intentionally** **unintentionally**
originate	origin	**original** **unoriginal**	**originally** **unoriginally**
popularise	**popularity**	popular **unpopular**	**popularly** **unpopularly**
increase	**increase**	**increasing** **increased**	**increasingly**
please **displease**	**pleasure**	**pleasing / displeasing** **pleasant / unpleasant** **pleasurable**	**pleasingly displeasingly** **pleasantly unpleasantly**
	kindness	kind **unkind**	**kindly** **unkindly**

Useful language: understanding suffixes

1

Suffix	Function	Meaning	Examples
-er, -or	to make a noun from a verb	• person who does something • object that does something	*thinker, boxer, operator* *ruler, projector,*
-ist	to make a noun, often from another noun	• people in certain professions • people with certain beliefs • some musicians	e.g. **journalist, scientist** *anarchist, theorist* e.g. **pianist, guitarist**
-tion, -sion	to make a noun from a verb	for many different things	e.g. **pollution, collection,** **suspension, admission**
-ness	to make a noun from an adjective	often for feelings, qualities and states of mind	*sadness, kindness, readiness*
-ise / ize	to make a verb from an adjective	cause to have a quality	*modernise* e.g. **supervise, categorise**
-ment	to make a noun from a verb	process or result of doing something	*enjoyment* e.g. **resentment, contentment**
-ity	to make a noun from an adjective	quality or state of something	*modernity, sensitivity*
-ship	to make a noun, often from another noun	status	*friendship* e.g. **membership, partnership**
-ify	to make a verb from an adjective or noun	cause to have a quality	*notify* e.g. **mystify, simplify**
-ive	to make an adjective from a verb or noun	for many different things	*active* **e.g. talkative, pensive**

2 1 summarised / summarized

2 immersion

3 membership

4 determination

5 violinist

6 complexity

7 employment

8 identify

Useful language: adjectives and adverbs

1

Noun	Adjective	Adverb
tradition	*traditional*	*traditionally*
energy	*energetic*	*energetically*
function	**functional**	**functionally**
drama	**dramatic**	**dramatically**
politician	**political**	**politically**
essence	**essential**	**essentially**
sarcasm	**sarcastic**	**sarcastically**
athlete	**athletic**	**athletically**
emotion	**emotional**	**emotionally**
controversy	**controversial**	**controversially**
irony	**ironic**	**ironically**
nutrition	**nutritional**	**nutritionally**
enthusiasm	**enthusiastic**	**enthusiastically**
anecdote	**anecdotal**	**anecdotally**

2 1 emotional

2 enthusiastically

3 nutritional

4 anecdotal

5 Controversially

6 sarcastic

Exam Practice

17 economic An adjective is needed before the noun 'development'.

18 threatened 'are' before the gap and 'by' after it indicate that this is a passive structure, so the past participle of a verb is needed. The infinitive is 'threaten'.

19 endangered Reading the whole of this sentence carefully tells us that the trees have a serious problem. 'Dangerous' is an adjective formed from 'danger', but it doesn't fit the meaning of the sentence.

20 existence 'their' before the gap indicates that a noun is needed.

21 expansions The structure of the sentence indicates that a noun is needed. Also, 'two' indicates that it must be a plural noun.

22 moisture The structure of the sentence indicates that a noun is needed.

23 increasingly 'complex' after the gap is an adjective, so the word here is likely to be an adverb.

24 analysis / analyses Reading from the start of the sentence tells us that a noun is needed here. In this case it could be singular or plural.

Reading and Use of English Part 4

Training

How to approach Part 4

Your thinking may be something like this:

a 'A last-minute' before the gap is different from 'at the last minute'. 'Last-minute' is an adjective, so a noun should follow it.

b 'Off the match' is different from 'cancel the match'. We need a verb before 'off' to express the same meaning as 'cancel'.

c The ideas 'it was decided' and 'cancel' are missing from the second sentence.

d The key word MADE must relate to either 'it was decided' or to 'cancel'. But 'made off the match' doesn't make sense – 'made off' doesn't mean 'cancel'. So MADE must be related to the idea 'it was decided'.

e The noun 'decision' can follow the adjective 'last-minute'. But it needs to be followed by a verb: 'was MADE'. 'A last-minute decision was made' has the same meaning as 'it was decided at the last minute'. The phrasal verb 'to call off' means 'cancel'.

So, the complete second sentence is: 'Because of the heavy rain, a last-minute decision was made to call off the match.'

Applying the approach to Part 4

1 1 hasn't SEEN her cousin for

2 he had LET Maria know

3 have paid (more) ATTENTION to what

2 1 AS easy to find

2 would not/wouldn't have TURNED down

3 keeping an EYE on

Making sure sentences have the same meaning

1 A

2 A

3 B

4 A

5 B

Exam Practice

The vertical line | shows where the answer is split into two parts for marking purposes.

25 **AS hard / difficult | to visit as** 'Not as … as' is used as a comparative structure.

26 **lost TOUCH with | all (of) / fallen out of TOUCH with | all** 'Lose touch with' is the opposite of 'stay in contact with'.

27 **promotion | CAME as a surprise** After 'sudden' a noun is needed , and 'promotion' is the noun from 'promote'. '[It] came as a surprise / shock [to someone]' is a common expression.

28 **are BOUND to be | (some) complaints / is BOUND to be some complaining** 'Bound to happen' means 'certain to happen'.

29 **would NEVER have / would have NEVER | taken** 'if you hadn't suggested it' in the second part of the sentence is part of a third conditional structure; the other half must be 'would (never) have / (never) would have' + past participle. We talk about 'taking up' a sport or hobby when we start doing it regularly.

30 **in FAVOUR of | banning** 'is in favour of' means 'supports the idea of'. After the preposition 'of', the verb must be in the *-ing* form.

Reading and Use of English Part 5

Training

Identifying the ideas and feelings expressed in the text

2 Jenny Granger, lead singer of the rock band The Traces, has spent most of the last three years painting, and a book showcasing her art has just been published. As one critic recently pointed out, rock stars becoming painters has become quite a regular thing. **(A)** <u>Given that the Rolling Stones' guitarist Ronnie Wood and the great American singer-songwriters Bob Dylan and Joni Mitchell have all had high profile exhibitions of their paintings, Granger's career change is perhaps not so surprising.</u> But she has certain doubts. 'There are so many people who've been painting all their lives and they can't get their work into a gallery,' she says. 'Then I play around with some colours for a couple of years and because of who I am, there's a big fancy book of my paintings, and **(C)** <u>lots of articles and reviews in the press about it</u>! It makes me quite uncomfortable.' She may not be the most technically skilled of artists, but **(B)** <u>the portraits, landscapes and abstract images that she paints</u> have improved in quality over time. **(D)** <u>One writer has claimed that she's a phoney</u>, but that's clearly not right. In fact, she's very genuine. 'I have no problems admitting that I'm not a great painter, but I'm serious about what I do,' she says. 'But yeah, my current situation – the focus being on me – is rather embarrassing.'

3 Jenny refers to feeling embarrassed in line 8: 'It makes me feel quite uncomfortable', and in the final line 'my current situation – the focus being on me – is rather embarrassing'. Both comments are in connection with the attention her art is getting. So the correct answer is option C.

Working out the meaning of words from the context

1 'Moan' is a verb which means 'complain'. We use it in a negative way to mean 'complain too much or unnecessarily'. 'About how difficult their lives are' after 'moaning' gives a clue about what 'moaning' might mean. The rest of the sentence indicates that the writer might be using it to express disapproval.

2 'Shun' is a verb which means 'avoid something'. The information that 'Jenny is very protective of her privacy' and 'she rarely gives interviews' provides a clue to what 'shun publicity' might mean – 'avoid publicity'.

3 'Dwell on' is a phrasal verb which means 'keep thinking or talking about something'. The first sentence tells us that Jenny has an interesting past, but the second sentence tells us she prefers to talk about the future. This suggests that 'dwell on' must mean something like 'talk about or focus on'.

4 'Point-blank' here is an adverb which means 'directly and clearly'. Jenny usually says 'exactly what she thinks' (in the sentence after 'point-blank') gives a clue to what it might mean. 'Point-blank' can also be used as an adjective.

5 'Prowess' is a noun which means 'great ability or skill'. We are told that 'Jenny had no musical training', which suggests that she may not have had great musical ability.

Identifying opinion expressed in the text

1 do justice to = treat something in the right way or properly

be in awe of = feel great respect for someone/ something

conjure up = create something unexpected as if by magic

envisage = imagine what will happen in the future

with hindsight = the understanding of an event or situation only after it has happened

In her early twenties, Jenny went to art school, but dropped out before completing her degree. 'I was spending all my time playing music, and I wasn't **doing justice to** the art course,' she says. 'But I hung out with a group of young artists. I remember being very impressed with them. In fact, I was really **in awe of** how clever and cool some of them were.' Jenny also recalls that they were dedicated to self-improvement.

2   **(A)** 'They seemed to have been born with perfect technique – they could **conjure up** a brilliant painting or sculpture out of nothing almost overnight. **(D)** But they were very disciplined too – they worked at getting better.' So did Jenny **envisage** successful artistic careers for any of her friends? 'I didn't think about it at the time,' she says. 'But **with hindsight**, 20 years later, I can see that **(C)** their ideas actually weren't very radical or new. They did pretty much what they were told to do. That hasn't stopped a few of them doing very well for themselves, though. In fact, **(B)** a couple of them are now world-famous artists and their paintings sell for millions of pounds.'

3   **A** Jenny says, 'They seemed to have been born with perfect technique'. So she thought they had natural talent. There is nothing in the text which indicates that her view now is any different.

   B Jenny says, 'That hasn't stopped a few of them doing very well for themselves, though. In fact, a couple of them ... their paintings sell for millions of pounds.' So she says they have made lots of money. But there is nothing in the text to say her view in the past was, or her view now is, that they focused too much on money.

   C Jenny says, 'with hindsight, 20 years later, I can see that their ideas actually weren't very radical or new. They did pretty much what they were told to do.' So her view now is that they were rather conventional in their thinking. Earlier in the text, Jenny says she was 'in awe of how clever and cool some of them were'. This implies that in the past she thought they were not conventional – so her view has changed.

   D Jenny says, 'they were very disciplined too – they worked at getting better.' So, Jenny's view now is that the artists spent plenty of time trying to develop their skills. Nothing in the text tells us that her view in the past was any different.

4   **C**

Exam Practice

31   **A** Sentences 3–5 in the first paragraph tell us that Wilson made exaggerated claims for the game before its release and people were angry 'when features promised during development were not present when the game came out'. B: The text says Wilson's comments on *Way Beyond* were reported, but it doesn't say they were misrepresented. C: The text says that Wilson made unrealistic claims in his promotion of *Way Beyond*, not that he had an unrealistic belief in his ability to promote it. D: People were angry about the game, but the text doesn't say Wilson didn't understand what gamers wanted.

32   **D** 'Most reviewers ... praised its lonely mood, its weirdly beautiful aesthetic qualities.' A: The text says that reviewers 'unintentionally gave the critics ammunition', but this doesn't mean they exaggerated the game's weaknesses. B: The text says that 'many disappointed players moved on to other more conventional games', but it doesn't say the press encouraged comparison. C: The text says reviewers noted 'the astounding technical feat of generating an entire universe of planets, each with its own ecosystem' – this means they admired the designers' ability, rather than questioning it.

33   **C** Wilson's resentment is expressed by 'the way they did it was so unfair and over the top. We really felt that all of our hard work hadn't been recognised and some of the criticism was unreasonable.' A: Wilson was affected, but the text doesn't say he was surprised at how much he was affected. B: The text doesn't mention whether he was protected or not. D: Wilson thinks the reaction was unfair, but admits that the mistakes he and his colleagues made in the launch of the game were what sparked the reaction. So he knows what motivated the behaviour of the people who attacked them.

34   **D** The paragraph starts by saying 'Wilson and his team didn't give up. Instead, they decided to keep working on *Way Beyond* and to concentrate on what the people who were actually playing it wanted.' So the paragraph explains how he handled the situation. A: The paragraph mentions the pressure involved in trying to make a game that people want to play, but the main purpose of the paragraph is not to describe that. B: The paragraph mentions people who work in the games industry, but the main purpose is not to explain what they're like. C: Wilson refers to difficulties he faced as a child, but the main purpose of the paragraph is not to tell us about his background.

35   **A** 'one' in this phrase refers to an update. The writer goes on to describe the three updates mentioned, of which 'the key one' means that 'you can ... invite other players to explore with you, in groups of four'. B: Players could always move around easily: 'You could always fly around the universe, explore planets ...' (etc.), so there is no significant update in this area. C: The text says you can now 'construct bases' and 'colonise a planet with ever-expanding constructions', but it doesn't says this is the crucial update. D: The text makes it clear that the game now has more resources, but it doesn't say this is the crucial update.

36 B 'contrary to what one might assume, *Way Beyond* has sold extremely well right from the very start' indicates that its commercial success would surprise some people. A: Wilson mentions that the development team of six was unusually small, but this isn't what the writer says would surprise people. C: Wilson says he and his colleagues listened and responded to feedback, but the writer doesn't say this would surprise people. D: Wilson says they 'kept the feeling [they] always wanted to have of landing on a planet that no one's ever been to before', but the writer doesn't say this would surprise people.

Reading and Use of English Part 6

Training

Summarising opinions in the texts

1 A Public libraries should continue to do this.

   B It isn't sensible for libraries to do this.

   C Public libraries should continue to do this.

2 The answer is B.

Looking for paraphrases to identify opinions in the texts

1 Phrases that could be used to express views about public libraries bringing people together.

- They're places where people can meet. *Yes*
- You can make useful contacts there. *Yes*
- You can concentrate there because they're quiet. *Probably not.*
- They connect communities. *Yes*
- Anyone can go to a public library – they're not exclusive places. *Yes*

2 Text B: <u>libraries are a reminder that life is not just about ourselves, but about other people too</u>

Text C: <u>Whether it's a child looking for a fun story, an immigrant in need of language learning materials, a student wanting a place to study, or a pensioner seeking company, we can all go to one place: the local library.</u>

Text D: <u>places where we could</u> ... <u>find company with others.</u> ... <u>The internet, shopping malls, gyms and cafes are where most of us go these days.</u>

D is the answer to Question 2.

Reading the text carefully

1 *very expensive to run* = a drain on public finances

important for companies = a vital service to the business sector

2 B's opinion is that public libraries are good for the economy – 'they provide a vital service to the business sector'.

B says other people think libraries are expensive = 'It is sometimes argued that public libraries are a drain on public finances.'

3
- libraries help the economy to grow – 'libraries contribute significantly to local wealth creation' (Text A)
- it's not clear if libraries make economic sense – 'whether this is a cost-effective service is open to question' (Text C)
- libraries are too expensive to run – 'a luxury we cannot afford' (Text D)

4 A shares B's view.

Exam Practice

37 D Expert A says that home-schooled children participate in an 'array of clubs, groups and associations ... where they mix with a wide spectrum of people'. Similarly, D says: 'home educators actually go to great lengths to involve their children in an impressive diversity of cultural and social contexts'. However, B says: 'Learning how to get on with other pupils and staff ... cannot be achieved outside school'. C refers to learning 'what it takes to live alongside and communicate effectively with individuals of all kinds', but says that here 'home schooling falls short'.

38 B Expert B suggests that home schooling is likely to have a negative impact on the family unit: 'I would fear for what being in each other's company constantly would do to our relationship – and I doubt we're unusual in that respect.' A, C and D argue that home schooling would strengthen the family unit. A: 'this tends to lead to much healthier relationships.' C: 'the chances are that their close family ties will be reinforced.' D: 'The process is also likely to be immensely helpful in terms of bonding, and thus runs counter to ... the fragmentation of traditional interpersonal structures.'

39 C Expert B doesn't think parents are well suited to teach their children: 'The majority of adults are ill-equipped to provide their offspring with the in-depth cross-curricular knowledge that pupils need.' Similarly, C says: 'most [children] will gain more educationally from being in class with a trained professional than alone with a loved one who lacks the requisite skills.' A and D both think parents are likely to be suitable as teachers at home. A: 'Parents' understanding of their children and commitment to their best interests will usually make up for whatever specific expertise they may be short of.' D: 'the majority of parents who are motivated enough to tutor their own sons and daughters full time will become proficient through practice.'

40 C Expert A thinks the home is a suitable environment: 'in many ways, learning works better from a kitchen table than in an institutional setting.' B says that education in the home 'may well be a desirable alternative' for children who don't get the attention they need in a school classroom. D also emphasises the advantages of avoiding the 'peer pressure, bullying, rowdiness and other aggravations that school pupils have to deal with and which get in the way of education'. C has a very different view: 'the home is where you eat, sleep and play, and is therefore not particularly conducive to the concentration needed to absorb certain types of knowledge.'

Reading and Use of English Part 7

Training
Finding the links between the paragraphs
1 a
- a word that means people who know a lot about a specific subject = 'experts'
- words relating to the idea that something is disappearing or being destroyed = 'in danger of extinction, wiping out'

b
- a word that means sets of ideas = 'theories'

c 'the two theories' indicates that the removed paragraph is about a theory that is different from, and possibly opposed to, the one described in the first paragraph. The first paragraph refers to the banana being in danger of extinction; the removed paragraph could refer to the idea that the situation is not so serious.

2 A

In fact, that last point is relatively easy to answer. An earlier form of the disease was reported in Australia, Costa Rica and Panama in the late 19th century. It spread across Latin America, devastating production of the Gros Michel, a sweet and creamy banana that dominated the export market. But what can we learn from this?

B

What followed was mass unemployment and huge economic losses. The banana industry took several decades to recover. By the 1960s, however, the Cavendish banana, which is resistant to the fungus, had replaced the previously successful Gros Michel banana. Today the Cavendish accounts for 99% of global exports.

C

Others say such talk of disaster is exaggerated, however. They point out that bananas are as cheap and abundant as ever in our shops. The fungus causing the disease has been advancing steadily for three decades, yet global production has continued to rise. Latin America – where some 80% of exported bananas are grown – has so far managed to keep the disease away.

3 C fits best. 'Others say' links back to 'Some experts suggest'. 'Such talk of disaster' links back to 'in danger of extinction' and 'wiping out banana plantations'. Also, the second and third sentences in C emphasise that the situation of the banana isn't so bad – lots of bananas are sold and the disease hasn't yet affected Latin America. This is the second, opposing theory referred to at the start of the paragraph after the gap.

4

Reference words	Linkers	Content words / ideas
this	*however*	*points*
these	moreover	questions
he	similarly	developments
one of them	on the other hand	differences
it	as a result	issue
there	interestingly	
	later on	

5 2 F 'What researchers have discovered' in F links back to 'scientists have not yet come up with a chemical fix for TR4' in the paragraph before the gap. Also, 'It is thought to spread through infected plant parts and soil attached to shoes, tools, vehicles, planting materials and water' links forward to 'That's how plant diseases often advance' in the paragraph after the gap.

3 E 'Dr Charles Staver ... agrees' links back to '"It's only a matter of time," says Dr Miguel Dita, a plant disease specialist in Brazil. "Many banana companies have operations in Asia, Latin America and the Caribbean"'. Also, 'Banana industry technicians travel around the world, so there's also a high risk of them bringing it in. And 'it could be a tourist bringing in an ornamental plant' links forward to 'Either way, the implications are extremely serious' after the gap.

4 D 'One approach is to' links back to 'Clearly something needs to be done to combat the disease. But what?' just before the gap. Also, 'Another way to slow the spread of the disease could be to' at the start of the paragraph after the gap links back to D.

Exam Practice

41 E 'This strange peace' in E links back to 'The profound silence' and 'this isolated landscape' in the first paragraph. Also, 'a loud "boom"' that isn't bad and 'beautiful-sounding "singing" ice' that's 'scary' link forward to 'contradictions of this kind' in the paragraph after gap 41.

42 G 'Such changes affect your speed and route' in G links back to 'One day it was covered in a layer of water; the next it had a light dusting of snow' in the paragraph before gap 42. Also, 'Our guides stabbed their sticks into the ice, testing its depth. We stuck to ice that was between 10cm and 15cm thick, though 5cm would still be adequate' in G links forward to 'safety precautions like this' in the paragraph after gap 42.

43 B In the first sentence of B, 'it' refers back to 'the best ice' at the end of the paragraph before gap 43. In the second half of B, 'it was only on the third day, a Saturday, when we finally saw any other skaters … and we just glided past crying "Hej hej!"' links forward to 'Not that skating is an inherently unsociable activity' at the start of the paragraph after gap 43.

44 D 'That was the extent of my experience too' in D links back to the mention of the Australian 'who'd only been skating on a public rink' at the end of the paragraph before gap 44. Also, 'wild skating had been popular all over northern Europe' at the end of D links forward to the start of the paragraph after gap 44: 'This is difficult to imagine nowadays … rivers in Britain, France and Germany rarely freeze solidly enough for wild skating to be feasible.'

45 A 'Skating has evolved in other ways as well' in A links back to the changes ('warmer temperatures' and wild skating being limited to Scandinavian countries) mentioned in the paragraph before gap 45. Also, 'two safety "ice nails"' at the end of A links forward to 'In Sweden, these are a legal requirement' at the start of the paragraph after gap 45.

46 F 'By the fourth day, however, I had the hang of it' in F links back to the description of 'The trickiest part of being on the ice', which the writer 'needed help with … at first', at the end of the paragraph before gap 46.

Reading and Use of English Part 8

Training

Paraphrasing

1 **1** f **2** a **3** e **4** h **5** b **6** d **7** c
      8 j **9** g **10** i

2 *Suggested answers*

1 the challenge of <u>expressing ideas</u> in a <u>convincing way</u>?

2 a moment of <u>acute</u> <u>embarrassment</u>?

3 a <u>deliberate</u> <u>attempt</u> to create <u>distraction</u>?

4 the <u>pleasure</u> that can be <u>derived</u> from setting short-term goals?

5 being given <u>advice</u> of <u>doubtful value</u>?

6 the need to be <u>aware</u> of <u>your own limitations</u>?

7 a <u>difficulty</u> caused by having to <u>deal with inaccurate information</u>?

8 being able <u>to transfer skills</u> to a very <u>different activity</u>?

9 the <u>benefit</u> of <u>not taking yourself seriously</u>?

10 an <u>important distinction</u>?

Reading task

1 D 'I have to focus on engaging their interest and on getting them to believe that the point I am trying to convey is significant and correct. The complexity of the content means that it's often demanding work.'

2 B The idea of acute embarrassment is conveyed by 'there was this agonising silence which seemed to go on forever'.

3 C The examiner started shouting at him when he was trying to answer to a question to put him off.

4 A 'I might give myself a target of doing two cartoon pictures every 40 minutes. It makes the whole process more enjoyable.'

5 B '…someone suggested I put scripts under my pillow at night – I would supposedly learn the lines in my sleep. I'm sure that's just a myth'.

6 D 'I find myself working on a problem in a way that simply isn't working, even though I'm directing my full attention to it. Like many people, I don't like admitting defeat. However, I've learned from experience that rather than muddling through, it's sometimes better to abandon what I've been doing and to adopt a completely different approach.'

7 C 'Believe it or not, passengers often get into my cab without knowing the address or even the name of their destination. Getting them to the right place requires huge concentration.'

8 C 'I find mental devices like that very effective and I've actually used them to learn words and phrases in foreign languages when travelling abroad.'

9 A 'Then I caught sight of myself in the mirror and I couldn't help but laugh because, for some reason, my reflection seemed so absurd. That put everything into perspective: in the bigger picture, my talk about being a cartoonist had very little significance – and the talk went well.'

10 **B** 'The process of learning lines for a play is significantly different from learning them for a film.'

Exam Practice

47 **B** 'by the 1990s, the buses were carrying 1.5 million passengers a day. In fact, high ridership created problems, with long queues waiting to board buses and pay fares.'

48 **A** 'He created parks and gardens, and protected the city's rivers from being turned into concrete drainage canals.'

49 **D** 'BRT has become a cultural touchstone, Curitiba's answer to the freewheeling carnival spirit of Rio and the fast-paced, business-dominated lifestyle in São Paulo. As if to remove any doubt about its symbolic status for the city, the airport gift shop is built in the shape of a life-size BRT station.'

50 **B** 'A determined and clever deal-maker, Lerner persuaded private bus operators to provide the vehicles while he would pay for the new infrastructure.'

51 **C** '"There's no doubt that's where BRT systems carry the most people of any region in the world," says one planning expert. "It's probably down to the similar language and cultural context."'

52 **B** 'He called for longer buses, faster boarding through multiple doors, fares paid for before entering the bus and a single fare covering the entire network. Lerner also gave the bus stops, or "stations", a distinctive look by placing them in futuristic glass tubes. With these additions, the city gained the first bus rapid transit (BRT) network on the planet.'

53 **D** 'Contrary to what one might assume of a city known for sustainability, Curitiba has only recently begun to take cycling seriously.'

54 **A** 'They (the authorities) appointed a young architect called Jaime Lerner as city mayor, confident he would implement the planned changes.'

55 **C** 'Seeing how well the Curitiba BRT seemed to be working, the authorities in Bogotá borrowed and added to many of Lerner's concepts to build a viable larger BRT network of their own called the Transmilenio … From there, BRT's influence continued to grow, spreading as far as the United States, South Africa and China.'

56 **B** 'planners advocated the building of subway train lines. The problem with this was that construction would be costly and lengthy. Lerner instead decided to integrate dedicated bus lanes along the city's main arteries, allowing buses to run at speeds comparable to those of light rail.'

Writing Part 1

Training

Meeting the task requirements

1 1 content
   2 effect
   3 organisation
   4 range
   5 common
   6 complex
   7 control

2 1 How to improve people's health and well-being in modern society.
   2 Two.
   3 Which is the most effective measure to improve health and well-being in modern society?

3 Students' own answers

Useful language: expressing reasons

1 2 <u>We're all responsible for our own lives. No one else.</u> That's why I say it's up to us to take control.

   3 <u>Given that we spend more time alone than with other people</u>, individual choice has to be the key factor.

   4 Obviously, these days, when <u>most people spend all day sitting at a computer</u>, the media – including social media – are likely to have the biggest impact on people's choices.

   5 A further argument for not forcing people to do exercise by law is that <u>people have enough rules in their work life: they don't want them in their free time as well</u>.

2 1 Because **of** the popularity of the media, this has to be one of the best ways of influencing people's behaviour.

   2 The negative effect of modern lifestyles on our well-being is largely due **to** the popularity of technology.

   3 People spend less and less time looking after themselves because **of** they are overwhelmed by the pressures of their daily lives.

   4 **So Tempting** advertisements for unhealthy food and drink are everywhere, **so** we buy things we shouldn't without even realising. / **Because there**

are tempting advertisements for unhealthy food and drink everywhere, we buy things we shouldn't without even realising.

5 Should we look after our own health and well-being? Of course we should, **as / for / since / because** we are the ones who benefit from doing this.

6 Since **that** exercise is a key factor in keeping fit and healthy, the government should provide free, or at least subsidised, sports facilities in all towns and cities.

3 Students' own answers

Exam Practice

1 1 Examiners will look for a discussion of two of the following three areas of research which governments should spend money on: space, green energy, human eating habits. They will also look for a selection of one of these as the area of research which is more important for governments to spend money on, supported by an explanation of your point of view.

2 An essay.

3 Effective paragraphing; usually an impersonal, academic style rather than a colloquial style.

4 A neutral or formal register. You can use the first person, 'I', but avoid a conversational style.

5 Probably four paragraphs. The first can introduce the topic. The second and third will each discuss one of the points in the notes. The fourth will explain which of the two points discussed is more important. This pattern is straightforward and could help you structure any Part 1 essay.

6 You will want your reader to understand your point of view and the reasons for it.

2 *Possible answers*

1 invest in, make an investment in, fund, provide funds for, finance

2 is crucial, is vital, should be a priority, should be prioritised

3 accessing proper nutrition, having a balanced diet

3 *Possible answers*

1 Governments should spend money on researching space to continue to develop our understanding of the universe, to explore the possibility of space travel for ordinary people, to see if any other planets could support life, etc.

2 Governments should spend money on researching green energy to develop sustainable forms of energy, to protect the environment from pollution related to using fossil fuels, etc.

3 Governments should spend money on researching eating habits so that people can have a reliable source of information about what foods they should eat, so that food producers can improve their products for the benefit of consumers, etc.

4 This will be a matter of personal choice. The opinions are listed to help you start to think about the three points. You should choose two points that you think you will be able to discuss well in English, showing your command of a range of vocabulary and structures.

5 Model answer

This model has been prepared as an example of a good answer. However, please note that this is just one example from several possible approaches.

> Governments around the world spend money on research. Two areas of research that I feel deserve government investment are green energy and human eating habits.
>
> Our dependency on fossil fuels and other traditional energy sources has caused pollution and contributed to global warming. It has also had an effect on how different countries in the world work together as importers and exporters of oil and other fuels. So it is vital that governments fund research to develop other sources of energy, which are more environmentally friendly and can satisfy our growing needs for energy.

> Another area of research which deserves government investment is people's eating habits. Governments have an interest in promoting good public health and part of this is knowing what food we need for good health. Nowadays, many people claim to be nutrition experts, when in fact their claims are not backed up by reliable research. There are many short-lived diets as well, which may cause more harm than good. The general public would trust research funded by the government, which could provide trustworthy information about eating habits.
>
> While both of these areas of research are essential, in my opinion it is more important for governments to spend money on energy research. At the moment, there is plenty of information available for people to be reasonably healthy and poor public health is perhaps due to people's lifestyle issues rather than a lack of research. However, alternative green sources of energy need to be researched and developed, and so it is crucial for governments to support this.

Notes

- *The first paragraph introduces the topic*
- *The second paragraph deals with one of the points*
- *The third paragraph deals with a second point*
- *The fourth paragraph explains why one of the points is more important than the other*
- *Only two of the three points are discussed*
- *Variety in sentence structures and sentence length*
- *Good use of linking between sentences and ideas*
- *A neutral, semi-formal register, which is appropriate to the task*
- *Correct length (258 words)*
- *No language errors*

Writing Part 2

Training

Identifying the reader

1 1 an English friend
2 the advertising manager of an international wildlife organisation (Mrs Johnson)
3 the head of the council
4 the editor of an entertainment magazine
5 the college principal

2 1 informal (friendly)
2 neutral or formal (polite), but persuasive
3 formal (polite)
4 neutral or formal
5 formal (polite)

3 a 4 Inappropriate – too informal and direct. It sounds quite rude and would have a negative effect on the target reader.

Suggested alternative: I was surprised that the channel chose to show that particular series. I am afraid I lost interest after the first two episodes.

   b 2 Register and tone are fine – neutral and persuasive.

   c 5 Register and tone are fine – formal and polite.

   d 1 Inappropriate – too formal. It doesn't suggest any kind of relationship with the reader.

Suggested alternative: Don't do anything at all until you've had a chance to think about what's best for you! I like writing lists of all the pros and cons. Why don't you give that a try?

   e 3 Inappropriate – too informal, due to the short, abrupt sentences.

Suggested alternative: The young people of the town really do not have anywhere to spend time together, especially during the winter months, so I propose creating a park in which there is also some kind of shelter.

Useful language: using a greater range of vocabulary

1 be unsure, have doubts
2 downside, drawback
3 go for, opt for, select
4 enhance, upgrade
5 appreciate, get pleasure from
6 complaint, concern, dilemma, issue

Useful language: communicating ideas using complex language

Possible answers

2 Introducing a Sunday bus service would enable people to travel easily.
3 Regular maintenance of the swimming pool would have prevented it from being closed down.
4 The condition of the cycle paths varies considerably from area to area.
5 To my mind, offering more sports facilities and increasing the frequency of buses are of equal importance.
6 It's the responsibility of the council to implement a better system for keeping the parks clean.
7 If the council hadn't closed one of the car parks last year, people wouldn't have to waste time driving around in search of a parking space.

Useful language: writing with control

2 I suggest recruiting more well-known performers to attract **the** people's attention. (unnecessary determiner)
3 I'm glad you've asked my advice. Unfortunately, **it's** not an easy decision to make. (missing reference pronoun)
4 As soon as I arrived **at** university, I knew I had made the right choice. (incorrect preposition)
5 I am confident this picture would attract **a** lot of attention. (missing determiner)
6 Although I know a lot of people enjoy this programme, I **would** not say it appeals to a wide audience. (incorrect verb tense)
7 I trust the same situation won't occur **it** again. (unnecessary reference pronoun)
8 Another issue is that the canteen opening hours **are** very limited, only until 3 p.m. What about students who are studying later in the day? (verb agreement)

Exam Practice

Model answers

These model answers have been prepared as examples of very good answers. However, please note that each of these is just one example out of several possible approaches.

2 Email

Dear Students,

I'm writing to tell you about a new idea to improve the college's website and to invite you to consider participating.

At the moment, our website is quite good for factual information, but it lacks a personal touch. This is where you can get involved! We have a plan to include short videos of current students talking about aspects of college life. The idea behind this is to give visitors to the website a real taste of college life, in an authentic and friendly way. If you have a positive college experience that you'd like to share on the website, we want to hear from you. Or perhaps you could help by being involved with the actual filming and uploading of the videos. We need people to direct and edit them as well. Just get in touch with the students' union office to indicate your interest.

We think this will really benefit the college. Having an updated website is important, as most people first find out about the college through the internet. We think that having videos of people like you will help interested students get a feel for what the college is really like. If you get involved, you can use your skills in a creative way. You will also receive an official acknowledgement of your contribution on the college website, which you can list on your CV.

Getting involved is easy – simply contact the students' union office for more details and to register your interest.

Best wishes,

Marco Rossi

Notes

- *Clear organisation and paragraphing*
- *Students are directly addressed to make the email more engaging*
- *Points in the task are all directly addressed*
- *Variety in structures and sentence length*
- *Correct length (249 words)*

- *Not too formal or informal in register – too much formality would be inappropriate for an email, but too informal a style would not seem serious.*
- *No language errors*

3 Review

Quizzes for You app

As a college student studying engineering, I use a number of apps to help me. The phone app Quizzes for You is my favourite at the moment.

The app allows you to input information that you need to learn, which could be formulas, procedures or any facts and figures. Then it takes all that information and converts it into a variety of quizzes. This means that you can test yourself and see what you know well and what you need to revise more. It keeps a score for you and lets you go back to any quizzes you want and try again.

I would recommend this app to any student who, like me, has a lot of factual information to learn. Just putting the information into the app is an excellent form of revision. Then, given that you nearly always have your phone with you, the potential to revise is always at hand. You can take short quizzes at any time, such as when you are on the bus or waiting for an appointment, so it puts time that might otherwise be wasted to good use. The app has been an extremely useful tool for me in the last year.

In my experience, the app is not very complicated to use, but I do think the developers could make it more user-friendly. I had to read the instructions a number of times, but not everyone would do that. If there were more interactive instructions or samples, that would be an improvement.

Notes

- *Statement of what is being reviewed at the beginning*
- *Some basic information is given about the app*
- *The writer's opinion comes through clearly*
- *Clear organisation and paragraphing*
- *Variety in structures and sentence length*
- *Not too formal in register – formality is not necessary for a website review*
- *Correct length (255 words)*
- *No language errors*

4 Proposal

I would like to propose two ways in which we could celebrate our company's great success this year.

First, I'd like to propose that we have a party. It would be a really enjoyable and relaxed way to acknowledge the success we have had. At the party, there could be a time for recognising the particular contributions that different individuals and teams have made to the overall company success. The staff would benefit from having some 'downtime' together and also from focusing on what we've done well. The company could benefit from the good feeling this would generate.

Another suggestion I'd like to propose is that we, as a company, take an afternoon off and get involved in some sort of community project. We are lucky enough to be located quite close to the beautiful Tyrella beach, so I propose that we could participate in a beach clean-up day there. I have done this myself and it is a great cause and a very satisfying project. This would be a way for our company to give back to the community we are a part of, and also it would allow us to spend time together doing something other than work and to get to know each other better. It would help us build stronger teams within the company.

Either of these ideas would be very attractive to staff, but if only one can be implemented, I think we should have a party, as it is more of a celebration. We could look at a community project another time.

Notes

- *The reason for writing is clear in the first paragraph*
- *All points required by the task are dealt with*
- *Clearly organised into paragraphs*
- *Formal enough for a work-related proposal*
- *Correct length (258 words)*
- *No language errors*

Listening Part 1

Training

Understanding what is being tested

1 1 B 2 A 3 C 4 A 5 C

2 1 A is incorrect because if he was sure he would do well in the interview, he wouldn't be asking for help to prepare for it. C is incorrect because he says the job seems ideal for him.

   2 B is incorrect because she mentions that she had nerves in a job interview, but she doesn't suggest

difficulties the man may have. C is incorrect because she advises the man to gather information about the company.

3 A is incorrect because he has already done the background research, so this is not what he thinks is the best way to prepare for the interview <u>now</u>. B is incorrect because he wants to practise answering questions – it is the woman who is going to think about which questions to ask.

4 B is incorrect because she is impressed by the amount of useful information in the ad. Although she questions the information about the salary being in dollars, she concludes that this is probably useful for international applicants. C is incorrect because she isn't confused by the information about the salary.

5 A is incorrect because she doesn't question the man's motives at all. B is incorrect because she doesn't doubt his abilities to do the job or to do well at the interview.

Exam Practice

1 **A** B: Adam says he now has good friends in the community, but he doesn't say this is what attracted him to Montreal. C: He mentions that he and his family love celebrating Canada Day, but he doesn't say anything about the value other inhabitants put on celebrating that tradition.

2 **C** A: Although they both mention people who are moving away from their street, neither of them comments on the frequency with which people move house in Montreal. B: Only Juliet mentions that her sister would like to live in the city centre.

3 **A** B: Soraya says the opinions expressed in the press and journals now are very different from earlier ones, but she doesn't comment on their accuracy. C: She doesn't attempt to explain or clarify why people have changed their opinions.

4 **B** A: Halim expresses the opposite opinion: 'it did go into the pros and cons of the uses of plastic'. C: He also says that the documentary covered the significant points: 'it covered the main ideas we'd discussed in class'.

5 **B** A: Jane says parents cope well with their teenage children's moods, which suggests they do understand them. C: She also suggests that parents do recognise that their children's needs have changed because they adapt to giving more emotional support.

6 **A** B: Ed mentions that his son is reluctant to wake up before ten, but this is not what particularly interests

him. C: Although he is keen for his son to have a good circle of friends, he doesn't say that he's particularly interested in the influence of peers on teenagers.

Listening Part 2

Training

Making sure the answer fits the meaning of the sentence

1 Any five words for courses at university could fit here.

2 Both 'horticulture' and 'business' could fill the gap, but only 'horticulture' fits the meaning; 'business' is wrong because she chose 'the former'.

3 **2** grade

  3 proud

4 **1** In question 2, 'water' could be mistaken for the answer. In question 3, 'excited' or 'happy' could be mistaken for the answer.

  2 'water' is incorrect because, although her parents helped her understand when to water the flowers, we don't know that they praised her for it. They praised her ability to grade the flowers.

  'excited' is incorrect because it's how she felt when she was asked to deliver flowers to shops, and 'happy' is incorrect because it's how she felt about talking to the florists. When the flowers were displayed she felt proud.

Exam Practice

7 **observation** Synthetic pesticides are mentioned, but Ben doesn't use them, and he says that observation is more important than the protection of young trees.

8 **leaves** Bark is also mentioned, but it's when leaves are discoloured that the tree needs fertiliser.

9 **weather** Two factors are mentioned, but the weather is more important than the delivery dates.

10 **bacteria** Other farmers use soap, but he doesn't.

11 **irrigation** Although he mentions grass mowers and a shed, these are not systems and don't fit with the meaning of the sentence.

12 **size** He checks the levels of sugar and juice, but the sentence is about what he does <u>last</u>.

13 **scissors** Ladders and metal baskets are also mentioned, but Ben and his workers don't use them.

14 **touch the earth** He also uses the term 'intelligent food choices', but this doesn't fit the meaning of the sentence.

Listening Part 3

Training

Understanding distraction

1 **A** is the correct option.

  B is wrong because even though resources are mentioned (examples of pottery and the university's online archive of works of art), Pedro doesn't say they are what he prefers about studying at university.

  C is wrong because he says he chose a course that covers various subjects, not that having more choice is why he prefers studying at university.

  D is wrong because the well-known people mentioned are former students, not people Pedro works with.

2 **B**

3 A: In the recording you hear 'being able to get my opinion across', which implies oral communication, but Clare says she was already good at that at school.

  C: In the recording you hear 'group work' and 'collaborating', but only in connection with school. We don't know if she does team working at university or whether she has improved that skill.

  D: In the recording you hear 'giving a talk', but Clare does not say she has improved this.

Exam Practice

15 **D** A, B and C all refer to other teachers and schools and are not Amy's opinion.

16 **C** A: Only John makes the point about rules with children: 'Don't you think most parents talk about how, where and when to use phones a lot with their children before they allow them to have one' B: Only John mentions young children. D: Neither speaker says this. In fact, Amy refers to parents making rules about children's use of social media, which suggests that they do know what sites their children use.

17 **B** A, C and D are all mentioned, but John doesn't approve of them.

18 **C** A: Amy refers to a police report about the number of smartphones stolen, but there is no suggestion that the ban had any effect on this. B: Amy says students enjoyed their teachers' lessons more, but we don't know if teachers spent more time on them. D: The opposite opinion is expressed: 'It didn't go down well with some mums and dads'.

19 **A** B: John says that schools, not workplaces, should look again at their policy on the use of smartphones. C: He gives examples of workplace rules, but doesn't say these are hard to enforce. D: He says that it's a

good idea that children get used to not being able to use phones, but not that they are a valuable tool.

20 **C** A: Amy says there will always be 'heated discussions' on this subject, but not that there is disagreement between teachers and parents. B: She says 'sometimes the debate may seem trivial', but that doesn't mean that serious matters are being concealed. D: Although she mentions the speed of technological change, she isn't saying that the debate is outdated.

Listening Part 4

Training

Focusing on the message

1 Task One: F; Task Two: D

2 In Task One, some people may be distracted by A, 'to meet new people', but this is wrong because she had already started meeting new people and she doesn't say this was her reason for starting a new hobby.

In Task Two, some people may be distracted by F because the speaker mentions 'mum and dad', but she doesn't say she neglected them because of her new hobby, only that they found her choice of hobby amusing.

Exam practice

Task One

21 **G** 'a gripping read and well written' reflects G. A may be tempting, but it's wrong because it's not how she felt when she entered the competition.

22 **H** 'it'd give me the chance to get feedback on my work and I'd take it on board' reflects H. C is wrong because he had no convictions about whether he would win or not: 'whatever the result, win or lose'.

23 **F** 'I had numerous sleepless nights thinking: what'll happen if I don't win?' reflects F.

24 **B** 'I knew there'd be a big formal dinner and the winner would have to get up and come out with words of wisdom and the thought made me feel numb with fear!' reflects B. C is wrong because 'At that stage I had no idea whether I'd even win or not.'

25 **E** 'I was so hacked off by all the criteria I had to meet for the competition' reflects E. D is wrong because 'funny' refers to the amusement she feels now, not when she entered the competition and not in response to the reactions of friends.

Task Two

26 **G** 'bookshops were overwhelmed with readers suddenly wanting anything and everything I'd ever

written' reflects G. D is wrong because it was her agent who dealt with fans' emails.

27 **B** 'the mental switch I made from writing novels based on historical facts to more descriptive, character-driven stories' reflects B. C is wrong because he was travelling when he heard that he'd won the competition.

28 **E** 'I spent hours staring at a blank screen' reflects E. F is wrong because she says that being 'headline news' was 'great', not an intrusion.

29 **A** 'I was being asked to write a follow-up novel by companies in countries I knew little about' reflects A. B is wrong because there is no mention of him travelling to these countries, and G is wrong because the market interest was in a new novel, not his previous work.

30 **H** 'Winning has also made me a more assertive person, sure enough of myself to say ...' reflects H.

Speaking Part 1

Training

Focus on assessment: how your speaking is assessed

1   1 Grammatical Resource
    2 Lexical Resource
    3 Pronunciation
    4 Discourse Management
    5 Interactive Communication
    6 Global Achievement

2   1 A reasonable range of vocabulary. This could be developed, for example, by using a range of adjectives to describe the restaurant, the food and the band.
    2 Yes, it is all suitable for the topic and task.
    3 The grammatical forms are generally simple – mainly present tenses, with one example of 'used to' referring to the past.
    4 There are several errors, including use of the wrong preposition and a verb agreement error:
       Not as much as I **am** used to. I'm not so keen **on** it any more, because I have my laptop and I can **watch** movies on that. I tend to **watch** American series in the main, especially **crime** ones.
    5 Yes, it answers the question.
    6 No, the linking words are simple and limited. The candidate needs to use a wider range of cohesive devices, including more linking words / expressions and referencing.
    7 No, it doesn't answer the question.

3   Students' own answers

Speaking Part 2

Training

Useful language: speculating

1 *Alternatives to the words spoken in the recording are in brackets.*

  1 impression
  2 seem
  3 suppose (reckon)
  4 Perhaps (Maybe)
  5 looks
  6 reckon (suppose)
  7 appears (looks)
  8 make
  9 maybe (perhaps)

2 Students' own answers

Keep talking

1 To extend his talking time, the candidate talks about what he thinks might have happened before the picture was taken ('it looks like she's waiting for someone to pick her up and I get the impression that they're late; I suppose she's just got off a flight, possibly a long-distance one, so she's feeling pretty tired') and what might happen next ('Once she's been picked up, I expect she'll go home, have a shower and take a nap before she bothers with unpacking those cases we can see in the picture').

2 Students' own answers

Speaking Part 3

Training

Useful language: expressing and justifying opinions

1 1 d 2 a 3 g 4 e 5 f 6 c 7 b

2 1 due to / because of / owing to
  2 because / since / as / due to the fact
  3 due to / because of / owing to
  4 because
  5 due to / because of / owing to

Speaking Part 4

Training

Useful language: agreeing and disagreeing

1 1 couldn't
  2 agree
  3 feel
  4 Absolutely

  5 true
  6 point
  7 Wouldn't
  8 take
  9 differ
  10 necessarily
  11 sure
  12 exact

2 Students' own answers

Test 2

Reading and Use of English Part 1

Training

Review

1 Yes. It's a good idea to read the whole text through quickly to get an overall idea. To complete some gaps correctly, you need to be aware of more than just a few words before and after a gap.

2 No.

3 Yes, mainly. However, there will be some gaps where you need to look carefully at the grammar of the words before and after the gap.

4 It's best if you can find the correct answer first, but if you find it hard to do that, then you can try to decide which options don't fit, and find the correct answer that way.

5 Yes, one or two of the questions often test your knowledge of phrasal verbs.

6 Yes, it's possible.

Useful language: using the correct phrasal verbs

1 came across
2 taken off
3 cutting down
4 brush up
5 get over
6 put forward
7 cater for
8 took on

Useful language: choosing the right words in fixed phrases

1 bearing in **mind**
2 none of your **business**
3 when it **comes** to

4 at my **disposal**

5 went to great **lengths**

6 ahead of **schedule**

Exam Practice

1 B 'Rescued' means 'saved from a dangerous or unpleasant situation'. In this case, Castronovo saved the evening's performance. Although the other three verbs have meanings related to keeping something in good condition, none of them collocates with 'performance'.

2 C 'Do justice to someone' is a set phrase which means 'show the best qualities that someone has'.

3 A If something is 'of some renown', it is well known. We can't use the other three nouns in the same way following the words 'of some'.

4 D 'Applause' is the sound of people clapping to show they have enjoyed or approved of something. None of the other nouns fit with 'loud', which describes something that can be heard.

5 B 'Shed tears' is a common collocation, meaning 'cry'. We don't use 'drop', 'cast' or 'spill' with the word 'tears'.

6 A A 'turn of events' is the way in which a situation develops, especially when the change is sudden or unexpected.

7 C 'Take over' means to start doing a job or being responsible for something instead of someone else. 'Fill out' means 'complete (a form or questionnaire)'. 'Bring about' means 'make happen' (but Ian Vayne didn't make the role happen). 'Cover up' means 'hide'.

8 D 'As it happens' is a fixed phrase, which we use to introduce a surprising fact.

Reading and Use of English Part 2

Training

Review

1 No. The main focus is on grammar and common words and expressions used to hold a text together.

2 Yes, both are possible.

3 No.

4 Yes, sometimes. So don't worry if you can think of two possible answers. But make sure you only write one word.

5 No. Contractions count as two words.

6 Yes.

Useful language: using the correct verb forms

1 would / could

2 have

3 might / could

4 having

5 being

6 would / could

7 Having

8 doing

Useful language: using fixed phrases

1 order

2 According

3 by

4 far

5 so

6 few

Exam Practice

9 Although / Though / While / Whilst If you read the whole of this sentence, you will see that a contrast is being made between happy and tough times in the job. If the gap was in the middle of the sentence, 'but' would be used to join the two clauses together. The same contrast can be made by using 'Although', 'Though', 'While' or 'Whilst' at the start of the sentence.

10 as The meaning expressed in the second part of this sentence is 'and so is working shiftwork – 'as is' can be used to mean 'and so is'.

11 like Here 'like' means 'similar to'.

12 be 'There tend to be' means 'There are often'.

13 nothing / little 'There's nothing worse than …' is a commonly used phrase for talking about things that you dislike very much. 'There's little worse than …' is much less common and the meaning is less strong.

14 for When something is your responsibility, you are responsible for it.

15 whether 'Whether' is often used to introduce alternative possibilities and can be followed by a subjunctive – in this case 'be'. Here the possibilities are 'at night' or 'during the day'.

16 However 'However long' means 'It doesn't matter how long'.

Reading and Use of English Part 3

Training

Review

1 Part 3 is mainly a test of ~~grammar~~ *vocabulary.*

2 You can write ~~either one or two words~~ in each gap. *You can only write one word in each gap. If you write more than one word, you will lose a mark.*

3 ~~Sometimes the word given in capital letters can be put in the gap without any changes.~~ *You must change the word given in capital letters in some way.*

4 You need to add a prefix or a suffix, ~~but not~~ *or* both. *And sometimes you need to form a compound word.*

5 ~~Only~~ *Both* UK *and* US *spellings are accepted. But the spelling must be correct.*

Useful language: choosing the correct word for the context

1 investigation
2 unfashionable
3 electricity
4 disapproval
5 economists
6 explanation
7 interaction
8 accurate

Useful language: spelling correctly

1 successful
2 government
3 necessarily
4 negotiations
5 environmental
6 accommodation
7 exaggeration
8 advertisement

Exam Practice

17 **popularity** 'this' before the gap indicates that a noun is needed.

18 **perception(s)** The adjective 'public' before the gap and 'of' after it indicate that a noun is needed here. Both the singular form and the plural form are possible.

19 **charismatic** 'most' is used as part of a superlative form, describing animals.

20 **Ironically** This is the first word at the start of the sentence and is followed by a comma, which indicates that the missing word is an adverb.

21 **survival** 'their' before the gap and 'prospects' after it indicate that the word needed is either an adjective or a noun functioning as an adjective. 'Surviving' can be used as an adjective from 'survive', but it doesn't fit with 'prospects'.

22 **extinction** The adjective 'possible' before the gap indicates that a noun is needed.

23 **complacency** 'this may lead to' before the gap indicates that a noun is needed.

24 **unintentionally** The verb before the gap indicates that the missing word is an adverb that qualifies the verb. The sentence suggests that companies may be giving people the wrong idea about the conservation status of these wild animals. However, the problem identified earlier is 'complacency', not deliberate trickery or fraud, so 'intentionally' is not appropriate here.

Reading and Use of English Part 4

Training

Review

1 Two. The mark scheme divides the answer into two parts.

2 Three.

3 Six.

4 You will lose marks. You must use the key word unchanged.

5 Two.

Useful language: understanding phrasal verbs

1 **1** g **2** d **3** f **4** h **5** a **6** c **7** b **8** e

2 **1** catch on
2 turned down
3 stem from / stemmed from / have stemmed from
4 chill out
5 soak up
6 bumped into

Useful language: being accurate in the way you use language

1 Adam suggested ~~Jane to do~~ *that Jane do / did* a law course.

2 Don't forget to take a small ~~amount~~ *number* of coins with you.

3 Everyone should have equal ~~possibilities~~ *opportunities* in education.

4 I won't let you ~~to~~ make the same mistake again.

5 The bus stopped to allow passengers ~~going~~ *to go* to the shops.

6 We could hear some classical music ~~to play~~ *playing* in the background.

Exam Practice

The vertical line | shows where the answer is split into two parts for marking purposes.

25 **HIGHLY unlikely (that) Lily | will get** 'Highly' is often used to emphasise 'likely' or 'unlikely'.

26 **knowledge (that) Ian | has MADE up** The phrase 'it's common knowledge' is often used to express the idea that many people know / everyone knows. The phrase 'to make up one's mind' means 'to decide'.

27 **(always) USED to | get on my** If something 'used to' happen, it happened regularly in the past, but doesn't happen any more. The phrase 'get on someone's nerves' means 'to annoy someone'.

28 **she had / she'd RUN out | of energy** You can 'run out of' many things – time, energy, patience, petrol, money, ideas, inspiration. Here, the past perfect form ('had run out of …') is necessary because Silvia's energy ran out before she realised it.

29 **was SUPPOSED | to have** We use 'be supposed to' when something expected or intended doesn't happen. To refer to a past expectation, we use 'was supposed' and we can follow it with the past form of the infinitive – in this case 'to have arrived'.

30 **to be | taken into ACCOUNT** 'To take something into account' means 'to consider something'. In this case the form required is passive, with 'have to' substituting for 'must'.

Reading and Use of English Part 5

Training

Review
1 True.
2 False. Some Part 5 texts are about science and technology, but they can also be about many other topics.
3 False. The questions come in the same order as the information in the text. Also, some questions tell you which paragraph or line to refer to. Other questions contain words which make it very obvious which section of the text you should be looking at.
4 True. Some questions test implied meaning.
5 True.

Understanding attitudes and feelings
1

Positive	Negative
proud	doubtful
optimistic	uneasy
convinced	cynical
delighted	dismissive
confident	unsure
enthusiastic	hesitant
appreciative	resentful
	frustrated
	sceptical

2 1 enthusiastic
  2 optimistic
  3 cynical, sceptical
  4 frustrated
  5 doubtful, unsure
  6 dismissive
  7 convinced
  8 resentful

3 proud → pride (n) → proudly (adv)

doubtful → to doubt (v) → doubt (n) → doubtfully (adv)

convinced → to convince (verb) → conviction (noun)

resentful → resentment (n – attitude) → to resent (v) → resentfully (adv)

optimistic → optimist (n – person) → optimism (n – attitude) → optimistically (adv)

dismissive → to dismiss (v) → dismissal (n – action) → dismissively (adv)

confident → confidence (n) → confidently (adverb)

enthusiastic → enthusiast (n – person) → enthusiasm (n – attitude) → to enthuse (v) → enthusiastically (adv)

uneasy → uneasiness (n – attitude) → uneasily (adv)

delighted → to delight (v) → delightedly (adv) → delightful → delightfully

sceptical → sceptic (n – person) → scepticism (n – attitude) → sceptically (adv)

frustrated → to frustrate (v) → frustration (n – attitude) → frustrating (adj) → frustratingly (adv)

cynical → cynic (n – person) → cynicism (n – attitude) → cynically (adv)

unsure → surely

hesitant → to hesitate (v) → hesitation (n) → hesitantly (adv)

appreciative → to appreciate (v) → appreciation (n) → appreciatively (adv)

Understanding references
1 *something you wouldn't expect of someone in his profession* = they see him on his bike all around town

The structure of the sentence indicates what the answer is:

Fans say they see him on his bike all around town, which ... is *something you wouldn't expect of someone in his profession*

2 **D** – *his habit of cycling everywhere* expresses a similar idea to they see him on his bike all around town.

3 1 **A** I think Gantner has *certain limitations* as a film-maker. Although his editing is sharp and energetic, and his application of special effects can't be faulted, <u>his story-telling skills are considerably less impressive</u>. The actors he casts tend to make up for his shortcomings in this respect, though.

2 **D** Three years ago, I joined a singing group. <u>It is often said that music is an international language</u>, and despite our age differences – the youngest member is 18 and the oldest nearly 80 – and the fact that we include two nurses, a bus driver, two accountants, a student and a retired judge, we are living proof of *that cliché*. We are from Nigeria, Japan, Mexico, Korea, as well as several European countries, with the diversity of mother tongues, customs and ways of thinking that you would expect, but when we're singing, we're as one.

Exam Practice

31 **D** 'Spence is not afraid of stirring things up' suggests that he is deliberately provocative. A: The reviewer says that the book includes psychology and physics, but doesn't say that Spence is good at making science accessible. B: 'triggering much resentment among cookbook writers' means that other writers are annoyed rather than inspired. C: 'it has almost nothing to do with the practicalities of cuisine' means that the book isn't about ordinary cooking, but that isn't the same as saying that Spence is dismissive of traditional cooking.

32 **A** The reviewer expresses disapproval of dishonest practices in 'more worryingly, supermarkets label mass-produced food items with the names of non-existent farms' in order to 'exploit' their customers. B: 'Googling their guests' refers to the use of technology, but the reviewer doesn't express concern about it. C and D: The statement that chefs and food manufacturers 'have been quick to grab a slice of the action' suggests that businesses have been influenced by Spence's ideas and have been adapted to use them, but the reviewer doesn't express surprise or admiration.

33 **C** Using findings about colour to reduce the sugar content and about 'crunch' to make insect-eating more attractive are both offered as ways in which gastrophysics can make valuable contributions to society. A: 'Spence advises against giving this much publicity' does imply withholding some information from the public, but it's not the main point of the paragraph. B: Spence's belief that 'in years to come, our cuisine could be shaped by his own finding' about crunchiness is not the same as saying that future food resources will depend on people like Spence. D: Experimenting with the crunch of a crisp may seem an unlikely procedure, but this isn't the main point of the paragraph.

34 **B** 'Spence has a way with words and cheerfully leads the reader on a journey' is about communication, and the examples that follow are all about his skill in describing a variety of experiences and interesting discoveries. A: The explanation about the complaints over the chocolate bar suggest that Spence pays attention to detail, but that's not why he's likened to a magician. C: Magicians usually keep their methods to themselves but the reviewer doesn't say Spence does this. D: The reviewer mentions 'dining experiences with top chefs' and 'cinema events', but the places Spence goes to aren't what makes him like a magician.

35 **C** 'Spence's point is that there is no such thing as a neutral context for eating' tells us that 'a neutral context' is the opposite of 'a multi-sensory atmosphere'. A: 'a spoiled experience' when inappropriate cutlery is used is not the opposite of 'a multi-sensory atmosphere'. B: 'inevitable manipulations' are environmental effects that chefs create and so are part of the 'multi-sensory atmosphere'. D: 'the company we keep' are the people we eat with, who are part of 'the multi-sensory atmosphere'.

36 **D** The reviewer draws attention to a weakness in the book: 'factors that Spence pays less attention to … there is remarkably little here on the multiple ways that eating can become dysfunctional … it has less to say about what we as humans bring to the table.' A: The reviewer refers to Spence as 'addressing the growing number of people who eat alone', but doesn't say the book is suitable for these people. B: The reviewer says that Spence demonstrates 'how much the environment of the table affects our eating', which is a point made earlier, but the paragraph as a whole doesn't illustrate this. C: Most of the final paragraph is about what Spence <u>doesn't</u> deal with in the book. This is not addressed previously in the review and, therefore, the final paragraph doesn't bring together the review's main ideas.

Reading and Use of English Part 6

Training
Review
1 True

2 False. Sometimes they are reviews of books, but often they are simply four different experts giving their views on a particular topic.

3 False. There are four questions, but the answers can be any combination of letters. In fact, it is unlikely that there will be one A answer, one B answer, one C answer and one D answer.

4 True. Sometimes one of the texts will contain nothing that is relevant to a particular question. However, you should still read all the texts carefully to make sure you haven't missed anything.

5 True. It's a good idea to read them quickly before you look at the questions, so you have a general idea of what they're about.

Useful language: giving opinions

1 1 The <u>strength</u> of Smith's book lies in its organisation.

2 Smith <u>convincingly</u> demonstrates how we have severely damaged many local ecosystems.

3 Some of Smith's solutions are <u>not very feasible</u>.

4 The explanation Smith comes up with for the decline in bird numbers is <u>rather implausible</u>.

5 The <u>main drawback</u> with Smith's book lies in the way he expresses himself.

6 Smith's idea that land should be allowed to go back to being wild is <u>very attractive</u>.

7 Smith's last book <u>quite rightly</u> received some very positive comments.

8 <u>It's impossible to tell whether or not</u> Smith's forecasts are <u>valid</u>.

9 Smith's prose style in this book is its <u>biggest weakness</u>.

10 Smith makes some <u>practical</u> suggestions for dealing with the problems.

11 Smith's evidence for the environmental destruction that humans are causing is <u>compelling</u>.

12 The praise that Smith received for his previous book was <u>well deserved</u>.

13 Smith offers a <u>very credible</u> theory regarding the falling bird population.

14 As for Smith's predictions about the future, <u>the jury's still out</u>.

15 The structure of Smith's book is <u>a definite plus</u>.

16 Smith puts forward the <u>rather unappealing</u> notion that we should let parts of the country return to a completely natural state.

2 Pairs of sentences expressing similar views:

1 and 15

2 and 11

5 and 9

7 and 12

8 and 14

Pairs of sentences expressing opposite views:

3 and 10

4 and 13

6 and 16

Exam Practice

37 **D** C concludes that 'The sensible choice is to continue to build on the successes of solar, wind and thermal energy until tidal technology has reached a point where it is viable.' So for C it shouldn't be a priority. D also argues against tidal power and says that 'more traditional energy sources like oil and gas cost less and make more sense to exploit'. However, B says: 'Everything we know about global warming … points to the need to expand our ocean power resources without further delay.' A doesn't say whether or not it should be a priority, but the enthusiastic comments on the 'huge prize' to be gained and the 'colossal importance' of the environmental benefits suggest agreement with B.

38 **A** D says that 'tidal schemes can harm animal and plant life' and gives an example of the 'disastrous' effects of a French barrage on some species. B doesn't discuss marine ecosystems. C has a similar view to D: 'Noise from construction and from turbines, the corrosion of building materials and the way that turbines change water flows can all be very disruptive for flora and fauna.' However, A has a different view: 'Any new technology will inevitably affect the environment to some degree. However, the evidence suggests that barrages and underwater turbines have a relatively benign effect.'

39 **C** C thinks that appearance is a problem: 'Towering concrete barrages … are clearly unsightly, and even submerged turbines can impinge on an area. The change in the speed and height of tides as a result of these schemes … can detract markedly from the visual appeal of these places.' However, A, B and D have little concern about appearance. A: 'These structures are often not easily visible from land' and are relatively 'inoffensive'. B: 'All the evidence … indicates that these installations are minimally intrusive.' D: 'whether it offends aesthetic sensibilities is a trivial matter.'

40 **D** B says: 'Everything we know about global warming – its causes and implications for the future – points to the need to expand our ocean power resources without further delay.' A takes a similar position: '[Tidal power schemes] produce no greenhouse gas emissions, and given what we know about the severity of climate change, this is of colossal importance'. C doesn't favour tidal power, but does acknowledge its benefit for global warming: 'it has no toxic by-products ... which cause temperatures around the world to rise.' However, D takes the very different view that the building and maintenance of tidal power structures contribute to global warming: 'there's a tendency to forget the considerable energy consumption involved in manufacturing materials for them, and constructing and repairing them. This, of course, involves greenhouse gas emissions, which, in turn, play a role in higher temperatures across the planet.'

Reading and Use of English Part 7

Training

Review

1   Yes. It's good to have an idea of what the whole text is about.

2   Yes. Again, it's helpful to have a good idea of the meaning of the options.

3   No. This is probably not a good idea. There may be some words you don't know, but you can probably complete the task without knowing exactly what they mean. Also, you should have a good idea of what they mean from the context.

4   No, not necessarily. There are usually links in both directions – i.e. with the text before and after the gap. However, sometimes there is only one clear link – for example, the paragraph following the gap could be a 'fresh start'.

5   No. There are various types of links. These include linking words and phrases such as *however* and *in addition*. But there are others: personal pronouns – e.g. *the students / they*; words like *this, that, it* and *there*; related vocabulary – e.g. *football and tennis / sports*; related ideas.

6   Yes. If you find the answers for other gaps, there will be fewer options to choose from for the gap you find difficult.

Using vocabulary to link ideas

1   The thick frames of fatbikes look rather like those of mountain bikes, <u>Fatbike tyres</u>, though, are <u>wider</u> and have <u>lower air pressure</u>.
      <u>These features</u> allow them to grip snow and ice better.

2   1   facilities
      2   conditions
      3   skills
      4   misconceptions

5   attempts
6   reassurances

Exam Practice

41   **F**   'It takes the form of a pair of short beehives' at the start of F links back to 'there, in a corner, is the hotel's current use for its upper level' at the end of the first paragraph. Also, 'the stocky man next to me' and 'a pair of short beehives' in F link forward to 'Gorazd Trusnovec' and 'these twin outposts of his empire' in the paragraph after gap 41.

42   **C**   'I was sceptical about whether you could put hives at this height' at the start of C links back to 'doubts' at the end of the paragraph before gap 42. Also, 'The bees don't actually seem to struggle' at the end of C links forward to 'In fact, they've been the basis of a sweet deal' at the start of the paragraph after gap 42.

43   **G**   'Such feelings are not unusual in Slovenia' at the start of G links back to 'now I couldn't imagine doing anything else' at the end of the paragraph before gap 43. Also, the very large number of beekeepers and the statement that bees are 'valued' in G links forward to 'This national affection' at the start of the paragraph after gap 43.

44   **A**   '20 kilometres north-east of the capital, in the village of Lukovica, the focus on bees is more scientific than decorative' at the start of A links back to the description of bee decorations on buildings in Ljubljana in the paragraph before gap 44. Also, the information about the Slovenian Beekeepers' Association persuading the UN to launch World Bee Day in A links forward to 'Less global in ambition but another great champion of bees' in the first sentence after gap 44.

45   **E**   'Its busy residents are unmoved as I do so' at the start of E links back to the writer being encouraged to place his/her fingers inside the beehive at the end of the paragraph before gap 45. Also, 'The rather pessimistic mood' at the start of the paragraph after gap 45 links back to 'Bees are under threat. If bees are not here, then there is less pollination, and less food ... and then starvation' in E.

46   **B**   'Lie down on it' at the start of B links back to 'a padded bed in the added corner' at the end of the paragraph before gap 46. Also, 'gazing at these tireless creatures ... has an almost hypnotically calming effect' in B links forward to 'this concept of the bee as a purveyor of relaxation' at the start of the paragraph after gap 46.

Reading and Use of English Part 8

Training

Review

1 Having an overall idea of what the text is about will help you when you come to answer individual questions. But your first reading of the whole text should be quick – don't get stuck on details.

2 Highlighting key words in the questions will help you understand and remember exactly what you need to look for.

3 The questions often focus on ideas, feelings and attitudes, rather than simple facts, so you need to read the texts carefully to find the answers. You will probably find it easier and faster to read one section at a time, and look for the answers to all the questions you can in that section, than to look across four sections for the answer to one question.

4 Highlighting the parts of the texts where you find the answers can be useful for different reasons. Sometimes you might think that two different sections answer a particular question. When this happens, you need to compare what the two sections say and decide which one is the correct answer. Highlighting the relevant part of the text will make it easier for you to compare them. Also, you might want to go back and check your answers, and this will be easier if you've highlighted where you found them.

5 Writing the question numbers next to where you find the answers can be useful for the same reasons that highlighting parts of the texts can be useful.

6 If you think you might have found the answer to a question, but you're not sure, it's best not to spend too much time worrying about it. The correct answer to the question might be in another section. The best thing is to move on to other questions, and then go back to it later – you might also see something new that you didn't see the first time you looked at it.

Reporting verbs

1

Neutral	Attitude
describe	highlight
mention	suggest
explain	deny
state	criticise
	acknowledge
	express regret
	confirm
	dismiss
	claim
	question
	justify

2 1 denied
   2 questioned
   3 highlighted
   4 criticised
   5 suggested
   6 expressed regret
   7 dismissed
   8 acknowledged

Exam Practice

47 **D** 'so many people pour energy into their bodies when perhaps they should be trying to pour energy into the people and politics around them. Self-care is great – but what if there's no energy left to care about anyone else? ... the narcissism of the whole enterprise got to me.'

48 **A** '"What?" was all I could splutter in response to this breach in interview etiquette.'

49 **B** 'it would be dishonest not to disclose that I once secretly yearned to be one of them'

50 **C** 'putting to the back of my mind any qualms I had about the ethics of how a 5,000-year-old spiritual discipline has been turned into a profit-making machine'

51 **D** 'I kept at it for about two months before the narcissism of the whole enterprise got to me. There were other things, it turned out, that I had to do.'

52 **A** 'I ... had never managed to get beyond beginners' level. I had come to assume that was all I was capable of'

53 **C** 'My body felt looser, more pliable ... gradually I was able to keep up with the most athletic classes and my skin and hair seemed to glow.'

54 **B** 'Rich targets for satirists, these "devotees" cycle around the neighbourhood, with rolled-up yoga mats on their backs, in search of organic fruit and vegetables. Ludicrous as they are in some ways ...'

55 **A** 'I thought: "This will never take off." ... I would walk past that man's expanding chain of studios and think: "How could someone like that become so successful?"'

56 **C** 'In many respects, yoga is the perfect pastime for our age – the meditative elements give us the opportunity to find peace and stillness in a time of increasingly hectic and crowded information, the instructional bits give us moral lessons, while the stretchy, bendy, sweaty physical stuff is a great way of countering hours a day spent hunched over a computer.'

Writing Part 1

Training

Review

1 compulsory – it must be an essay.

2 compulsory – the essay must be between 220 and 260 words.

3 compulsory – you must write about two points.

4 optional – you can choose any two to write about.

5 optional – you can refer to any or all of them, or none of them.

6 optional, but it's best to avoid doing this where possible.

7 compulsory – you must give reasons to support your choice of the most important / effective / useful bullet point.

Organising your writing

1 1 family and friends, money

 2 *family and friends:* making choices based on what the family expects or by copying friends

 money: it limits possibilities, such as travelling, where to live and career choice

 3 Family and friends because we may not even be aware of their influence.

2 1 *paragraph 1:* introduction to the topic of influences on young people's choices

 paragraph 2: influence of family and friends

 paragraph 3: influence of money

 paragraph 4: the most powerful influence

 2 *paragraph 2:* This support can come from family members and close friends.

 paragraph 3: Money is also a key factor.

 Both sentences are at the beginning of the paragraph.

Useful language: linking expressions and referencing

2 The important thing is to learn from your mistakes so that the same thing **it** isn't repeated.

3 It was thanks to ~~that~~ **those** experiences / that **experience** that I was offered the job.

4 I noticed an improvement in the facilities as soon as **I** arrived.

5 As a result **of** the new measures, pollution on the streets has decreased significantly.

6 New laws are the only way of guaranteeing that the same thing **it** won't be repeated.

7 The **result** is / results **are** not only unexpected, but also impressive.

8 Teachers should find ways to develop students' learning instead **of** giving homework every day.

Exam Practice

1 The issue is ways in which people can be encouraged to have an interest in science.

2 *Possible answers:* Museums could relate to the topic because science museums provide a great range of exhibits that might interest people. School lessons could relate to the topic because most people will have had some sort of instruction in science at school. The internet could relate to the topic because people can search for any topic in science that they are interested in learning about.

3–6 Students' own answers

Model answer

This model has been prepared as an example of a good answer. However, please note that this is just one example out of several possible approaches.

Having an interest in science is important because it explains the world around us. So what can be done to encourage people to be more interested in science? I think that good science lessons at school and internet posts about science are both effective ways of achieving that aim.

Many people are, unfortunately, put off science at school due to a variety of factors. One factor may be the way they were taught, with an emphasis on memorising facts, as opposed to coming to grips with its exciting possibilities. Or science may not have been considered a 'cool' subject to study in their school. With up-to-date and effective teaching methods and enthusiastic teaching, these barriers can be overcome.

However, there still may be people who do not engage with science at school. If this is the case, those people may one day find an interesting post on the internet that gets them thinking about science with more enthusiasm. Nowadays, leading scientists and talented bloggers create content for the internet that makes difficult concepts understandable and intriguing to the general public. This content may be expensive to produce, however, and needs to compete in a crowded market – the entertainment market.

I feel that of these two ways, the best way is to engage young minds with the fascinating topic of science through interesting school lessons. If people have an understanding of science from a young age, they can develop that appreciation for the rest of their lives.

Notes

- *Appropriate introduction to the topic in the first paragraph*
- *Each of the next two paragraphs deals with one of the ways listed*
- *The final paragraph explains why one of these ways is more effective*
- *Clear organisation and paragraphing*
- *Good range of structures and vocabulary*
- *The essay is in an appropriately neutral register*
- *Correct length (248 words)*
- *No language errors*

Writing Part 2

Training

Review

1 **T** There is a choice of three questions and you have to choose one.

2 **F** There are three tasks, one of which might be a review, but it may not be. The other options are proposal, letter, email or report.

3 **T** 220–260 words.

4 **F** The task instructions specify particular points that you must include.

Identifying content

1 give an opinion on the current recycling facilities, with reasons

suggest ways to improve the recycling facilities

request to be kept informed about the council's decision

2 explain what will happen during their stay

offer to spend time helping the student

recommend how to make the most out of their stay

3 give an opinion about the good points of the attraction

suggest who the attraction would be good for, and why

recommend one improvement

Useful language: openings and conclusions 1 and 2

Reason for writing	Concluding comment
Thank you for your letter of 1st May concerning … F	Should you require any further information, please do not hesitate to contact me. F
Lovely to hear from you! I	
As requested, this report/ proposal outlines … F	If you've got any questions, drop me a line. N/I
This proposal concerns the possibility of … F	I would appreciate your immediate attention regarding this matter. F
Read on for my thoughts on the recent music festival. I	Can't wait to see you. I
I am writing in connection **with** your proposed meeting. F	Thank you in advance. F/N
	Based on the information given above, my recommendation is to … F/N
I'm writing **to** ask … N	I would have no hesitation in recommending … F/N
Sorry for the delay **in** getting in touch. N/I	I look forward to hearing from you in **due** course. F/N
With reference to your letter **of** 19th June, … F	Thank you **for** your assistance in this matter. F
	So, if you're looking for a new mobile phone, this is **the** one! I

Useful language: functional expressions

1   1   make an offer (Task 2)

      2   make a request (Task 1)

      3   give an opinion (Task 1 or 3)

      4   make a suggestion (Task 1)

      5   recommend (Task 3)

      6   recommend (Task 2)

      7   make a suggestion (Task 3)

      8   make a suggestion (Task 1)

2
  1 Have (suggestion)
  2 To (opinion)
  3 were (recommendation)
  4 if (offer)
  5 Without (recommendation)
  6 will / might / may (request)
  7 way (opinion)
  8 had (recommendation)
  9 do (request)
  10 did (suggestion)

Exam practice

1 Students' own choice

2 Factors to consider:

- Do you understand the question fully?
- Can you deal with all the aspects of the question?
- Do you have the vocabulary you need to write a good answer?
- Do you understand the conventions of the type of text required?

The answers to these questions are more important than whether or not you find the question interesting or not.

Model answers

These models have been prepared as examples of very good answers. However, please note that each of these is just one example out of several possible approaches.

2 Proposal

> <u>Proposal for an educational trip to the Museum of Modern Art</u>
>
> I would like to propose that my Art class should be funded to take a trip to the Museum of Modern Art. The museum can be reached by train from the local station in just under two hours, so the trip can take place within one school day.
>
> While books and the internet provide a chance to become familiar with the collection of the museum, there is nothing that can substitute for seeing works of art at first hand. Without visiting the museum, it is nearly impossible to appreciate the size and impact of the works of art it contains. As Art students, we need to spend time studying art and experiencing it in its original form.

> It will also be beneficial for us to see the museum as a place of work, as many of us will be completing our studies in the near future. It is important to see that museums function as workplaces for many people, as well as housing irreplaceable collections of art. In fact, we would hope to see 'behind the scenes' of the museum where the curators work. This would be very motivating for us.
>
> While at the museum, we would sketch some of the works and would be delighted to create a display of our work for other students to see. A few other students and I would also be happy to make a short presentation of our trip to the student body.

Notes

- *Use of an appropriate title*
- *Opening paragraph sets the context*
- *All the points in the question are dealt with in the answer*
- *Clearly organised into paragraphs*
- *Variety of sentence length and vocabulary*
- *Appropriate register – no informal language*
- *Correct length (251 words)*
- *No language errors*

3 Email

> Hi Suzy
>
> Thanks for getting in touch! I'm really glad to hear that you're enjoying college. But there's a lot to learn, and not just in your classes. It can be really hard to learn how to manage your money and make ends meet.
>
> As for advice, here are a few things that I do to manage my money that you may want to try. First, I set a weekly budget for all the things I need to spend money on. For me, that's mainly food and drink, transport, and entertainment. Then I also try to save a little money each week because it's very useful to have a sum set aside for unforeseen expenses.
>
> There are various ways you can save money. You should look for places where you can buy your books second-hand, or consider whether you need to buy them at all, as you might be able to borrow the ones you need from the university library. Definitely be careful with your shopping and make use of any discounts that are available for college students.

I'd really only recommend taking a part-time job if it doesn't interfere with your studies in any way. As a new college student, you have enough to get to grips with! However, if a good job comes up that will give you useful skills as well as a bit of extra spending money, you might give it a try.

Good luck and all the best,

Alison

Notes

- *The email opens and closes in an appropriate and friendly way*
- *The writer answers all the questions in the input email*
- *The answer shows a good range of vocabulary related to managing money*
- *Correct length (244 words)*
- *No language errors*

4 Report

Public speaking course

This report describes the course I attended last week to develop my public speaking skills. Overall, I feel that the course was successful.

Description
The course was at a local training centre and took place over two working days. There was a small number of attendees (8) and the focus of the two days was on developing confidence in public speaking. The course ended with each of us giving a presentation to the group. The trainer was very well prepared and the day was both useful and enjoyable.

Evaluation
Having a small group was a definite advantage to the course, as each of us got plenty of time to practise and to receive one-on-one coaching from the trainer. Over the two days, we were given a good overview of the basic principles of speaking in front of a group, including body language, voice projection, maintaining eye contact and using visual aids to good effect. Technology was used to good effect.

One weakness of the course was the venue. The room was quite small and did not provide enough space. It never felt as if we were giving a proper presentation, but only a talk among friends.

Recommendation
In my opinion, the course was too basic for anyone who is already fairly confident at public speaking, but I would certainly recommend it for people who have only had limited training or experience in public speaking.

Notes

- *Statement of what is being reported on at the beginning*
- *All the points in the task are addressed*
- *Clear organisation and paragraphing*
- *Range of vocabulary, appropriate to the topic of a work-related training course*
- *Variety in structures and sentence length*
- *Appropriate use of headings*
- *Correct length (237 words)*
- *No language errors*

Listening Part 1

Training

Review

1 three
2 two
3 three
4 detail
5 opinion
6 agree

Getting information from questions

Question 1

1 Nathalie
2 surprise
3 She has read something about thriller movies.

Question 2

1 This question is in the form of an incomplete statement, whereas question 1 is a complete question.
2 David
3 similarities

Question 3

1 Two, because the question asks what they agree about.
2 Examples could be *Yeah, Exactly, Absolutely, I do too*, etc.
3 Architects might have to design shops or shopping centres and need to be aware of the design features that work well for customers and staff.

Question 4

1 One is a man and the other is a woman.
2 the man
3 Three or more, because the question asks candidates to identify 'the greatest'.

Question 5

1 Gary

2 The future, because the question is about what he'd like to do.

3 communicate information or opinions so that the general population is better informed

Question 6

1 Sophie

2 Stated, because the question uses the word 'says'.

3 have a more probable chance (of doing something)

Exam Practice

1 **B** A: This is Nathalie's own observation, not something she's read and been surprised by. C: This is information that Nathalie has heard before – it doesn't surprise her.

2 **C** A: David says watching horror movies helps people find solutions to work problems. B: He talks about feeling excited about possibilities, but this doesn't match B.

3 **A** B: Only the woman mentions out-of-town malls, and she doesn't say they are less popular now. C: Only the woman talks about online shopping deliveries.

4 **C** 'But to my mind, getting people away from congested roads and pavements has to be the winning argument' tells us that A and B are not 'the greatest advantage'.

5 **A** B: Gary explains that there has already been a public awareness campaign about this. C: He says he'd rather not focus on rules.

6 **C** A: Sophie's first study covered students at university level, but she doesn't say that people are more likely to go to university if they do sport. B: Sophie tracked students' attendance in her first study, but she doesn't draw this conclusion.

Listening Part 2

Training

Review

1 sentence completion   **3** yes

2 1–3   **4** yes

Prediction

1 **1** B   **2** A   **3** A

2 They are all nouns. Nouns are very common as Part 2 answers.

3 **7** The answer must be plural because of 'were', and it must be concrete because 'who' refers to people.

  8 The answer could be singular or plural, and could be a concrete or abstract noun.

9 The answer must be plural because of 'various', and concrete because it must be something that can be ground up for paint.

10 The answer must be singular because of 'was', and is likely to be concrete because it is something that can be gathered.

11 The answer could be singular or plural; it must be concrete because it must be a person / people or animal(s) that can be trained.

12 The answer could be singular or plural, and could be concrete or abstract.

13 The answer must be plural because of 'Animals', and concrete because it must be a type of animal.

14 The answer could be singular and or plural, but is perhaps more likely to be singular and it is probably an abstract noun – a quality of the people's beliefs.

4 Students' own answers

Exam Practice

7 **officials** The tombs of servants were less elaborate and therefore, it is implied, of less interest.

8 **behaviour / behavior** 'show a keen observation of' reflects 'show a good understanding of' in the question.

9 **minerals** 'The paint ... has been analysed and found to be made from ground minerals' is a paraphrase of the gapped sentence.

10 **grain** 'Some other paintings depict annual important events, such as the grain harvest' is a paraphrase of the gapped sentence.

11 **soldiers** Both sportsmen and soldiers are mentioned, but it's only soldiers that Kylie links with training and it's this interpretation of the paintings that she agrees with.

12 **invasion** Birds in flight are symbols of invasion, whereas a bird being caught by a hunter represents victory over an enemy.

13 **crocodiles** Cats are also mentioned, but they appear in many paintings because local people worshipped a cat goddess.

14 **complexity** 'These "mixed" creatures express the complexity of how the afterlife was conceived and formed part of religious worship' is a paraphrase of the gapped sentence.

Listening Part 3

Training

Review

1 two or three
2 four minutes
3 four
4 The context sentence gives information about the speakers, the topic and sometimes the situation in which the conversation takes place.

Synonyms and paraphrase

1 **1** h **2** e **3** b **4** g **5** f **6** a **7** c **8** d
2   1 invigorating
    2 timelessness
    3 ashamed
    4 erosion
    5 harmful
    6 scarce
    7 concern
    8 demand
    9 financial investment
    10 rethink
    11 impose

Exam Practice

15 **A** B: Jack refers to claims for the healthy effect of sea air, but doesn't say this is the main reason people are attracted to beaches. C: The waves have this effect on Jack, but he doesn't say it's the main attraction, either for him or for people in general. D: This is Jack's friend's opinion.

16 **C** A: Trisha doesn't express surprise. B: She says the article was well researched which suggests she had all the information she needed. D: She didn't question the advice – she was immediately persuaded by it.

17 **D** A: They both say that building a seawall can have negative consequences, not that it's more effective. B: Neither of them sees adding sand as a solution because, like building a seawall, it has negative consequences for the environment. C: When Jack talks about the movement of the sea it's to explain how coastal erosion occurs.

18 **D** A: Jack says that people are aware of these issues but choose to ignore them. B: He explains why there is such a great need for sand, but doesn't say it is scarce. C: He says people move to the city for jobs, among other things, but not that money is the main concern.

19 **A** B: This is something that Trisha wonders about, but it is not a particular concern. C and D: She mentions 'a reduction in income from tourism', but says this is not her main point.

20 **A** B: Jack talks only about one particular architect and there is no mention of redesigning buildings. C: He mentions governments, but doesn't say that they should impose stricter regulations. D: He hopes for measures to 'get the message across', but as a back-up for the main solution of producing artificial sand.

Listening Part 4

Training

Review

1 five
2 five, so a total of ten for both tasks
3 eight, so a total of 16 for both tasks
4 two

Ideas and attitudes expressed about the theme by the speakers

1 Speaker 1 is probably someone working in company planning or policy.

Speaker 2 is obviously a young person who is new to business and is trying to gain experience by working in a range of companies.

Speaker 3 might be a business person who writes articles for journals or a journalist specialising in business.

Speaker 4 is an older person so he might have a senior role in the company he works for.

Speaker 5 might be an academic specialising in business or a business person who gives lectures while working in a company.

2 1, 4, 6, 7, 8, 9, 10
3 Students' own answers

Exam Practice

Task One

21 **D** 'to find out how many face-to-face meetings we have compared to video conferencing' reflects D. Some questions in the questionnaire were about customer care, but B was not the main focus of the research.

22 **E** 'For my Master's degree, I looked into how happy people who worked without a boss were' reflects E. Although the speaker makes the point that some self-employed people weren't living in luxury, C was not the focus of the research.

23 **B** 'I've been carrying out interviews with shoppers for a paper I'm writing' reflects B. Although there is mention of companies saying they want to help save the planet, G is not the focus of the research.

24 **G** 'At present, I'm involved in a study examining the carbon footprint of trade' reflects G. Although the speaker mentions consumers, B is not the focus of the research.

25 **A** '[I've] been looking into how, as more people live on their own and families get smaller, the workplace takes on more importance as a place to make friends' reflects A.

Task Two

26 **H** 'the need for continued education is going to feature more prominently in the workplace' reflects H.

27 **E** 'The trend is definitely for people to set up their own small business and work from home' reflects E.

28 **F** 'Any confidence people ever had in big business is going to evaporate over the next few years' reflects F. Although the speaker mentions a company having financial difficulties, B is not the prediction that she makes.

29 **C** 'And the attraction of an urban environment for workers I'm sure will be powerful for many years to come' reflects C. The speaker mentions how long he has been in business but D is not predicted.

30 **D** 'I'd say we'll all be in work well into our 70s, rather than 50s or 60s as is the current norm' reflects D. Although the speaker mentions people who work at home, E is not a prediction she makes about them.

Speaking Part 1

Training

Review
1 **F** You are asked questions individually.
2 **F** The assessor may say 'hello', but otherwise he or she will just listen to you.
3 **T** (The aim is to help you relax and settle into the test environment.)
4 **T**

Developing your answers
1 The answers are appropriate, but they lack development and use the same vocabulary as the question.
2 *Example answer*
Going to the cinema is one of my favourite things to do and I'm particularly keen on adventure movies.
3 Students' own answers

Speaking Part 2

Training

Review
1 one
2 three; two
3 two
4 30
5 four; six

Useful language: referencing and substitution
1 *Suggested answer*
There is no comparison of the two pictures – they are described separately. There is limited linking of ideas by linking words / expressions and referencing, so the language is very repetitive and the answer doesn't flow smoothly.
2 **1** the second one
2 this
3 They
4 which ones
5 her
6 they
7 like these
8 this one
9 it
3 Students' own answers

Speaking Parts 3 and 4

Training

Review
1 Part 3 and Part 4 are linked by topic. In Part 3, topic is specified by a question with options to discuss. Part 4 develops the Part 3 topic further.
2 Part 3: You speak to your partner.
Part 4: You speak to the interlocutor and your partner.
3 Interaction, exchanging information and opinions, justifying opinions, agreeing and disagreeing, negotiating towards a decision
4 Part 3: Initial discussion is 2 minutes (3 minutes for a group of three candidates). Discussion to make a decision is 1 minute (2 minutes for a group of three). Total time for Part 3 is around 4 minutes (6 minutes for a group of three).
Part 4: Total time is around 5 minutes (8 minutes for a group of three candidates).

Useful language: responding to and linking with contributions

1 Each candidate initiates their own contribution clearly, but there is no real interaction. They each deal with one of the prompts in turn and there is no acknowledgement or development of the points made by the other candidate.

2 1 point
   2 what
   3 hadn't
   4 more
   5 Not
   6 case
   7 so
   8 Absolutely / Exactly / Yes; about
   9 Perhaps / Maybe / Yes
   10 be

3 Students' own answers

Useful language: agreement and disagreement

1 1 partially – weak
   2 up to – weak
   3 totally – strong
   4 entirely – strong
   5 doubt – strong
   6 issue – strong
   7 goes; saying – strong
   8 coming – strong
   9 along – weak
   10 take – weak
   11 kind – weak

2 Students' own answers

Test 3

Reading and Use of English Part 1

1 B 2 D 3 A 4 C 5 A 6 D 7 B 8 C

Reading and Use of English Part 2

9   From
10 which
11 no
12 rather
13 being / becoming
14 one
15 how
16 There

Reading and Use of English Part 3

17 methodological
18 predates
19 discovery
20 primarily
21 presence
22 exceptionally
23 consumption
24 emergence

Reading and Use of English Part 4

The vertical line | shows where the answer is split into two parts for marking purposes.

25 longer | CAPABLE of playing.
26 make any / a DIFFERENCE | where
27 would / 'd GIVE | her dance class a
28 comes ACROSS as | lacking
29 RESULTED in | the train being / getting
30 of | having BEEN told / advised / warned / instructed

Reading and Use of English Part 5

31 C 32 B 33 D 34 A 35 A 36 C

Reading and Use of English Part 6

37 A 38 C 39 B 40 B

Reading and Use of English Part 7

41 F 42 G 43 A 44 C 45 B 46 E

Reading and Use of English Part 8

47 D 48 C 49 A 50 D 51 B 52 D 53 C
54 B 55 A 56 B

Writing Part 1

1 Essay

Model answer
This model has been prepared as an example of a very good answer. However, please note that this is just one example out of several possible approaches.

Learning about another culture is very important in today's society and there are possibly more ways to do this than ever before. I would like to discuss visiting a place in person to learn about a culture and taking a course.

First, while seeing a culture and experiencing it first-hand can be invaluable, this depends on the type of visit. For instance, a quick weekend in the capital city of a country might give a hint of what life is like and the forces that shaped that city, but it would not provide a deep understanding of the reality of living there, nor would it explain the history of the culture. However, if someone has an opportunity to spend longer in a place, perhaps studying or doing some voluntary work, this will definitely provide a chance to develop a better understanding of its culture.

Some people prefer to learn about a culture by signing up for a course. A good course, and a good teacher, can give an overview of the history of a culture. However, the risk of any course is that the teacher may present material in a dull fashion, or that it may be biased or only informed by the teacher's point of view. Also, it may not focus on the aspects of the culture that most interest you.

Overall, I would say that the most effective way to learn about a culture is to visit it yourself, as long as the visit is substantial enough and there is some effort made to interact with local people.

Writing Part 2

2 Proposal
Model answer

Proposal for increasing shopping in the town centre

This is in response to the town council's request for proposals to deal with the decrease in shopping in the town centre.

Reasons for the decrease
There is a general trend towards internet shopping and away from making purchases in physical shops. Further, a new out-of-town shopping centre has opened up, which is popular with people from the town.

Impact on the town centre
As a result, the town centre is a less welcoming place for people, as there are a lot of empty shops and, consequently, fewer reasons for people to visit.

Suggestions for increasing town centre shopping
There is little that the town council can do about internet shopping. Individual shops may be able to combine their

online sales better with their in-store offer, but that is for them to consider. However, there are several things the town council can do to help the shops in the town.

First, parking in the town centre is expensive. While public transport is a good option, people who are planning to shop will often want to drive if they have a lot of purchases to make. For this reason, I would recommend reducing the cost of parking in the town centre shopping area.

In addition, the current regulations require town centre shops to close at 6 p.m., whereas the new shopping centre is open until 10. Town centre shops should be allowed to stay open later.

These measures should help the town centre shops to become more competitive and bring back customers.

3 Review
Style
The style can be formal or quite informal as long as it is consistent throughout the review.

Content
Your review should give some information about person who was the subject of the film, expressing clearly what the film highlighted and the extent to which you think it was accurate. Readers will also probably want to know whether you think they should see the film.

Organisation
Write in clearly defined paragraphs.

4 Report
Style
Neutral to formal – appropriate for writing a report for the college principal

Content
Your report should explain what activities you organised for the student's visit, say how successful you think the activities were and recommend ideas for future visits. The college principal should feel fully informed.

Organisation
Write in clearly defined paragraphs. Include a title and sub-headings.

Listening Part 1
1 C **2** B **3** B **4** B **5** B **6** C

Listening Part 2

7 bees
8 perfume
9 food chain
10 pest control
11 climate change
12 higher altitudes
13 tourists
14 antibiotic

Listening Part 3

15 B 16 D 17 A 18 B 19 C 20 B

Listening Part 4

Task One
21 D 22 B 23 G 24 C 25 F

Task Two
26 G 27 A 28 D 29 E 30 F

Test 4

Reading and Use of English Part 1

1 D 2 C 3 B 4 A 5 B 6 D 7 C 8 A

Reading and Use of English Part 2

9 up
10 no / little
11 how
12 whether
13 which
14 against / from
15 Whatever / Whichever
16 if / though

Reading and Use of English Part 3

17 unknown
18 compositions
19 diversity / diverseness
20 liken
21 genetically
22 handful
23 comparable
24 continuously / continually

Reading and Use of English Part 4

The vertical line | shows where the answer is split into two parts for marking purposes.

25 WISH I had / I'd | talked
26 no MATTER what / which | promises
27 no CHANCE | of it (whatsoever / at all)
28 was ONLY when | Sam turned
29 HAD his wallet | stolen
30 couldn't / could not TELL the difference | between

Reading and Use of English Part 5

31 D 32 B 33 D 34 C 35 A 36 D

Reading and Use of English Part 6

37 A 38 C 39 D 40 A

Reading and Use of English Part 7

41 C 42 F 43 A 44 G 45 E 46 D

Reading and Use of English Part 8

47 D 48 C 49 B 50 D 51 C 52 A 53 B
54 C 55 A 56 B

Writing Part 1

1 Essay

Model answer
This model has been prepared as an example of a very good answer. However, please note that this is just one example out of several possible approaches.

Choosing a college course is one of the biggest decisions that a young person might make, and many factors will influence that choice. While it is wise to consider a variety of factors, cost and the reputation of the course are two matters which deserve particular consideration.

There is no doubt that the cost of college courses is on the rise in my country. Many students go into debt in order to study at college level. Even though grants are available, the competition for them is very tough and not every deserving student receives one. However, a college degree is indispensable for jobs in many fields and people generally regard the cost as a necessary expense, or an investment. Also, students often get part-time jobs while they study and this is a way of getting some valuable work experience.

The reputation of the course is also worth considering. This is because courses build a reputation for quality over many years and this gives you some assurance that you have chosen a well-run course. Of course, some new courses may actually be very good and you might be pleasantly surprised by the quality. However, future employers will be more impressed with you if you have a degree from a top college. This will, in the end, bring you many benefits.

Therefore, I think that overall it is more important to prioritise getting the best degree you can from a course with the best reputation possible.

Writing Part 2

2 Email

Model answer

This model has been prepared as an example of a very good answer. However, please note that this is just one example out of several possible approaches.

Dear Ms Taylor,

I'm writing to you because I'm interested in the opportunity to do a placement in another city.

My current role involves developing software to improve internet security for a variety of customers. While I am based in London, I have been working closely with a team that is based in Rome, Italy. There is only one hour of time difference between us, so it is easy enough to conduct meetings using internet conferencing.

However, I would very much appreciate the opportunity to spend some time in Rome with the team. I think this would strengthen our working relationship much more than working at a distance can.

For me, this would provide the opportunity to experience how another branch of our organisation works and to gain an appreciation for working in a different place.

My Italian is quite basic, which might be a problem socially, but most of our work is conducted in English. I am studying Italian online and would be more than willing to take an evening course before the placement begins.

I also believe that we would be able to make much quicker and better progress on the project we are currently working on, which would benefit the organisation. This team and I have also discussed ways we could develop the work we're doing for different markets. If we were working more closely, I believe we could progress with that work more effectively.

Thank you for considering my application for the placement.

Sincerely,

Joanna Simpson

3 Review

Style
The style can be formal or quite informal as long as it is consistent throughout the review.

Content
Your review should consider one online shopping experience and one in-person shopping experience. They should be compared for the choice they offered, how convenient they were and the service you received. Your review should make it clear which experience you preferred.

Organisation
Write in clearly defined paragraphs.

4 Report

Style
Neutral to formal

Content
Your report should describe how the funding you received supported the activities of the club you help to run. It should explain how the club's activities made a positive contribution to the life of the college and make a case for the funding to continue in the year to come.

Organisation
Write in clearly defined paragraphs. Include a title and sub-headings.

Listening Part 1

1 C **2** B **3** C **4** A **5** B **6** C

Listening Part 2

7 physics

8 technician

9 internship

10 memorisation / memorization

11 flexibility

12 marketing

13 records

14 population

Listening Part 3

15 B **16** C **17** B **18** A **19** D **20** D

Listening Part 4

Task One
21 F **22** G **23** A **24** D **25** H

Task Two
26 G **27** A **28** F **29** D **30** B

Test 5

Reading and Use of English Part 1

1 C **2** B **3** D **4** A **5** B **6** A **7** C **8** D

Reading and Use of English Part 2

9 Although / Though / While / Whilst
10 makes
11 As a rule
12 ago
13 other
14 whatever
15 only
16 even

Reading and Use of English Part 3

17 findings
18 participants
19 preference(s)
20 unimpressed
21 talkative
22 predictably
23 regardless
24 correlation(s)

Reading and Use of English Part 4

The vertical line | shows where the answer is split into two parts for marking purposes.
25 no idea | WHOSE fault
26 have been ABLE to | sort / work
27 did not / didn't take (very) LONG | for
28 impressed by | HOW committed
29 has GIVEN up | dreaming / his dream of
30 can't / cannot be BOTHERED | to

Reading and Use of English Part 5

31 C **32** B **33** B **34** C **35** B **36** A

Reading and Use of English Part 6

37 C **38** D **39** D **40** A

Reading and Use of English Part 7

41 G **42** D **43** A **44** F **45** C **46** E

Reading and Use of English Part 8

47 B **48** D **49** A **50** C **51** D **52** B **53** C
54 D **55** A **56** B

Writing Part 1

1 Essay
Model answer
This model answer has been prepared as an example of a very good answer. However, please note that this is just one example out of several possible approaches.

There are many qualities that contribute to people having a successful life. The ones that I would like to discuss are ambition and honesty.

For many people, ambition is the key to their success. Having clear goals and plans to achieve them gives motivation and direction to people. This can help when choosing a career path. For example, if your ambition is to be very wealthy, then you might decide to study a subject that leads to a well-paid profession. However, that is not always the case. Many famous billionaires gave up on their education in order to start a business. The key here is to be determined to follow your ambition.

Of course, everyone can decide for themselves what the definition of a successful life is. For some, it will be having a lot of money or material possessions, but for me, success in life should be judged by the quality of the relationships that people develop over their lives. And in order to develop strong relationships, people need to have honesty and strong principles. I personally do not consider people who build their wealth on dishonesty or immoral practices to be 'successful'.

An ambitious person without honesty may be tempted to push themselves forward at the expense of others, which is not fair. Therefore, it is my opinion that honesty is more important than ambition to consider oneself successful in life.

Writing Part 2

2 Proposal

Model answer

This model has been prepared as an example of a very good answer. However, please note that this is just one example out of several possible approaches.

Work experience proposal

This proposal is for an element of work experience to be included in the college's Business Studies course.

The course

I am currently enrolled in the two-year Business Studies course. The work we do in the college provides an excellent background for understanding how businesses function. Our instructors all have a background in business, which they use to inform their lectures with examples from their real-life experiences.

Benefits of a work experience element

Many of us on the course feel that our learning would be improved if we could spend a period of time doing work experience in a business environment. A number of us have done part-time jobs, but these are generally jobs that are low-skilled and, while it is good to have the experience, it doesn't develop our skills in the same way that a work placement would. Such a placement would allow us to put our knowledge into practice and build confidence, which, in turn, would further motivate us in our studies. It could also help us to make useful contacts and would provide us with a welcome addition to our CVs.

Recommendation

I would suggest that the college contacts local businesses to set up work experience placements that support the studies we do. I think that a short placement could take place during term breaks, or else longer ones could take place over the longer summer break. Some students may even be willing to extend the course by a term because work experience is so valuable for us.

---

3 Report

Style

Neutral to formal – appropriate for writing to a manager in a work environment

Content

Your report should say how your colleagues get to work, but this should be brief and serve as background for the main issue, which is the impact of commuting. You should make suggestions based on what you say the impact is; for instance, you could suggest working from home one day a week to save commuting time for some colleagues.

Organisation

Write in clearly defined paragraphs. Include a title and sub-headings.

4 Review

Style

The style can be formal or quite informal as long as it is consistent throughout the review.

Content

Your review should focus on a place of natural beauty that you know well enough to write convincingly about. Your review should capture the attention of the reader with expressive language. You must evaluate the significance of the place, which could be personal, local or national significance depending on the place you choose to describe. You must suggest how accessibility to the place could be improved without damaging its beauty.

Organisation

Write in clearly defined paragraphs.

Listening Part 1

1 B **2** C **3** B **4** A **5** A **6** C

Listening Part 2

7   historical

8   presentation

9   mental image

10   textures

11   board game

12   balance

13   elegant

14   packaging

Listening Part 3

15 B **16** A **17** D **18** A **19** B **20** C

Listening Part 4

Task One

21 C **22** H **23** E **24** F **25** B

Task Two

26 G **27** F **28** B **29** D **30** H

Reading and Use of English Part 1

1 B **2** A **3** D **4** C **5** A **6** C **7** D **8** B

Reading and Use of English Part 2

9 which
10 rather
11 making
12 for
13 without
14 in
15 did
16 how

Reading and Use of English Part 3

17 Admittedly
18 dramatically
19 inactivity
20 worsening
21 wellbeing / well-being
22 overdo
23 tiredness
24 addiction

Reading and Use of English Part 4

The vertical line | shows where the answer is split into two parts for marking purposes.

25 were PREVENTED | from leaving
26 doesn't / does not STRIKE me | as (being)
27 making an EFFORT | to cut down
28 in mind | the changes BEING
29 to RAISE | teenagers' awareness / awareness among teenagers
30 who / that OBJECTED | to having to work / to working

Reading and Use of English Part 5

31 B **32** C **33** B **34** A **35** D **36** B

Reading and Use of English Part 6

37 D **38** C **39** A **40** A

Reading and Use of English Part 7

41 E **42** B **43** G **44** A **45** F **46** D

Reading and Use of English Part 8

47 D **48** C **49** A **50** D **51** B **52** A **53** C **54** D **55** A **56** B

Writing Part 1
1 Essay

Model answer
This model answer has been prepared as an example of a very good answer. However, please note that this is just one example out of many possible approaches.

Many people these days are not as active as they should be and this is having a big effect on their health. Taking part in sport is one way to counteract the inactive lifestyles that many of us lead. Which factors might influence people's decision to take part in sport? I would like to discuss education and facilities.

One way is certainly through education. Young people can be taught about the health risks of inactivity and all the benefits that taking part in sport can bring to people. They can also be taught and given the opportunity to practise the skills needed to participate in a variety of different sports.

However, many young people are actually turned off sport at school if they are not particularly good at it. For this reason, I would argue that the best way to motivate people is through having really good facilities. This means that they should be up to date, accessible to everyone and affordable. People who are good at sport don't generally require extra encouragement to increase their participation, but access to high-quality facilities would make taking part in sport more appealing for those people who do need motivation. For example, no one really wants to swim in a small, dark pool, but one that is pleasant and spacious would definitely be more tempting to the reluctant swimmer.

Therefore, I believe that good facilities would motivate people to take part in sport more effectively.

Writing Part 2
2 Report

Style
Neutral to formal

Content
Your report should describe the main ways in which the college's official social media accounts are used. It should then make recommendations about a few ways in which the accounts could be used more effectively and how these improvements would benefit both the college and the students.

Organisation

Write in clearly defined paragraphs. Include a title and sub-headings.

3 Email

Style

Neutral to formal – appropriate for writing to the editor of a website.

Content

Your email should describe what the criticisms of young people in the original article were. It should then go on to address those criticisms and express your view of them clearly. You should end by persuading the editor that publishing your email would be a good idea.

Organisation

Write in clearly defined paragraphs. Use appropriate opening and closing phrases for an email to a professional person.

4 Review

Model answer

This model has been prepared as an example of a very good answer. However, please note that this is just one example out of several possible approaches.

> Do you love listening to music as much as I do? If you do, then you won't be surprised to find out that I have tried quite a few paid music streaming services. There are many competing services available at the moment, and many offer short-term free trials, so you can sample what they have to offer. At the moment, I am using Firefly and am really enjoying its features and functions.
>
> First, the strengths. The main thing is the vast music library that is available. This even includes a few artists who share their music only on Firefly. Also, in my opinion, the interface is easier than most others to use and attractive as well. Like many other services, Firefly allows subscribers to download tracks to listen to offline, which I think is great for times when Wifi is not available.
>
> The main weakness I have found is the way that Firefly 'suggests' music for me to try based on what I have already listened to. I find that this leads me to be always listening to the same sort of artists, when what I really want to do is explore that vast library they have.
>
> Firefly is available at two different subscription rates. I think the lower rate provides surprisingly good value for money, but you have to be prepared to listen to ads between tracks of music every now and then. While the higher rate is ad-free, it is quite a bit more expensive.

Listening Part 1

1 C **2** A **3** B **4** C **5** C **6** A

Listening Part 2

7   management skills
8   landscape
9   textiles
10 health checks
11 tourism
12 laugh
13 posture
14 stream

Listening Part 3

15 D **16** A **17** B **18** B **19** D **20** C

Listening Part 4

Task One
21 C **22** G **23** D **24** F **25** B

Task Two
26 H **27** F **28** A **29** E **30** D

Sample answer sheet for Reading and Use of English

53114

Cambridge Assessment English

Candidate Name	
Centre Name	
Examination Title	
Candidate Signature	

Candidate Number	
Centre Number	
Examination Details	
Assessment Date	

Supervisor: If the candidate is ABSENT or has WITHDRAWN shade here ○

Advanced Reading and Use of English Candidate Answer

Part 1

	A	B	C	D
1	○	○	○	○
2	○	○	○	○
3	○	○	○	○
4	○	○	○	○
5	○	○	○	○
6	○	○	○	○
7	○	○	○	○
8	○	○	○	○

Instructions

Use a PENCIL (B or HB).
Rub out any answer you want to change using an eraser.

Parts 1, 5, 6, 7 and 8:
Mark ONE letter for each question.
For example, if you think A is the right answer to the question, mark your answer sheet like this:

0 | A ● | C

Parts 2, 3 and 4: Write your answer clearly in CAPITAL LETTERS.

For parts 2 and 3, write one letter in each box.

0 | EXAMPLE

Part 2

Do not write below here

9																	9 1 ○ 0 ○
10																	10 1 ○ 0 ○
11																	11 1 ○ 0 ○
12																	12 1 ○ 0 ○
13																	13 1 ○ 0 ○
14																	14 1 ○ 0 ○
15																	15 1 ○ 0 ○
16																	16 1 ○ 0 ○

Continues over ➡

53114

Photocopiable

Sample answer sheet for Reading and Use of English

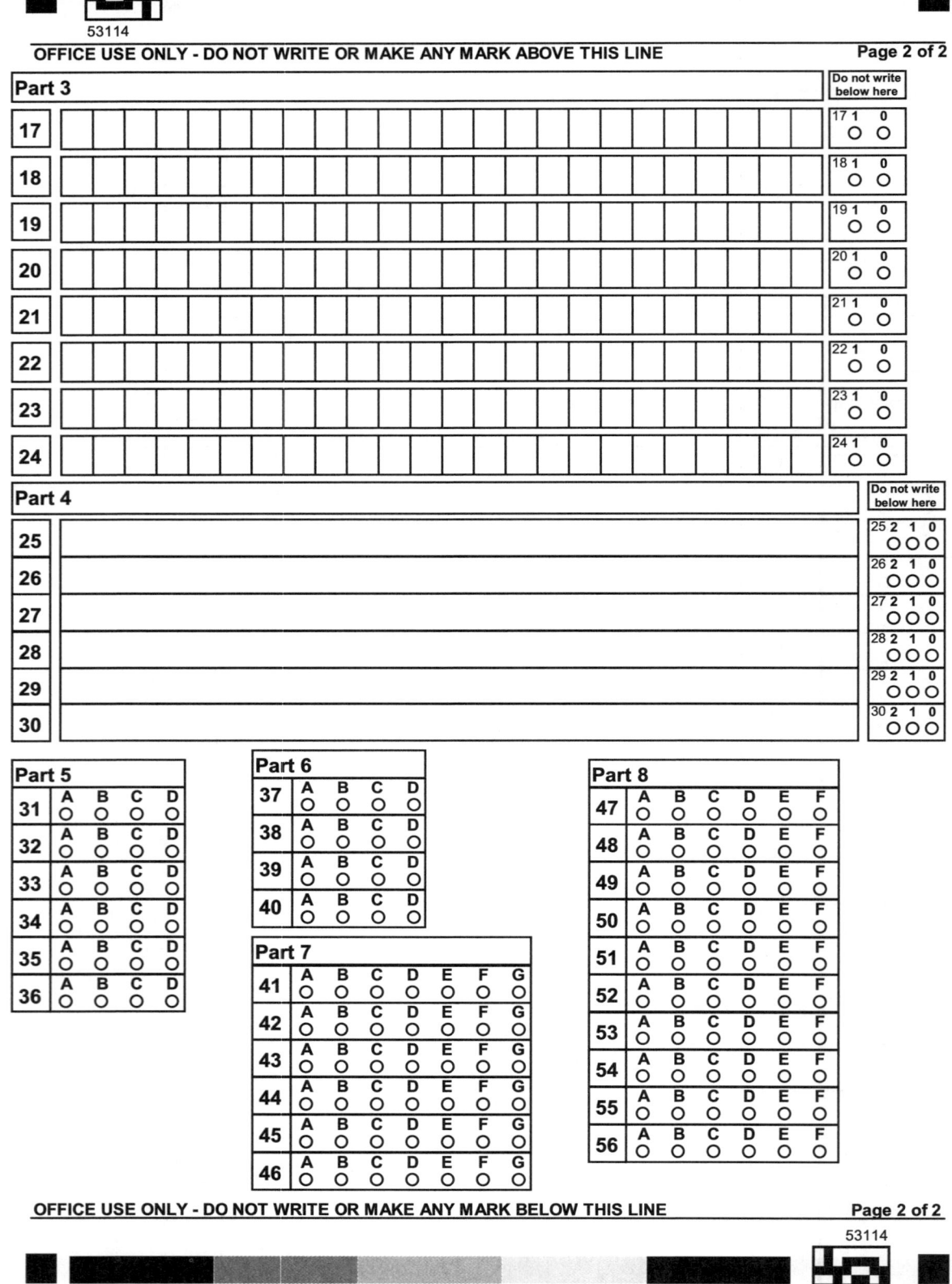

258   Sample answer sheets

Sample answer sheet for Listening

Cambridge Assessment
English

Candidate Name		Candidate Number	

Centre Name		Centre Number	

Examination Title		Examination Details	

Candidate Signature		Assessment Date	

Supervisor: If the candidate is ABSENT or has WITHDRAWN shade here ◯

Advanced Listening Candidate Answer Sheet

Instructions
Use a PENCIL (B or HB).
Rub out any answer you want to change using an eraser.

Parts 1, 3 and **4:**
Mark ONE letter for each question.

For example, if you think **A** is the right answer to the question, mark your answer sheet like this:

Part 2:
Write your answer clearly in CAPITAL LETTERS.

Write one letter or number in each box.
If the answer has more than one word, leave one box empty between words.

For example:

Turn this sheet over to start

Sample answer sheet for Listening

Part 1

	A	B	C
1	○	○	○
2	○	○	○
3	○	○	○
4	○	○	○
5	○	○	○
6	○	○	○

Part 2 (Remember to write in CAPITAL LETTERS or numbers)

Do not write below here

7		7 1 ○ 0 ○
8		8 1 ○ 0 ○
9		9 1 ○ 0 ○
10		10 1 ○ 0 ○
11		11 1 ○ 0 ○
12		12 1 ○ 0 ○
13		13 1 ○ 0 ○
14		14 1 ○ 0 ○

Part 3

	A	B	C	D
15	○	○	○	○
16	○	○	○	○
17	○	○	○	○
18	○	○	○	○
19	○	○	○	○
20	○	○	○	○

Part 4

	A	B	C	D	E	F	G	H
21	○	○	○	○	○	○	○	○
22	○	○	○	○	○	○	○	○
23	○	○	○	○	○	○	○	○
24	○	○	○	○	○	○	○	○
25	○	○	○	○	○	○	○	○
26	○	○	○	○	○	○	○	○
27	○	○	○	○	○	○	○	○
28	○	○	○	○	○	○	○	○
29	○	○	○	○	○	○	○	○
30	○	○	○	○	○	○	○	○

> • Why might the people be feeling nervous in these situations?
> • What could they do to overcome their nerves?

- Why is time important in these situations?
- How difficult would it be for people to manage without sufficient time?

CANDIDATE A

- What might have caused the people to laugh in these situations?
- Where do you think they are?

CANDIDATE B

- How difficult might it be to teach others these things?
- How much preparation might the teachers have made?

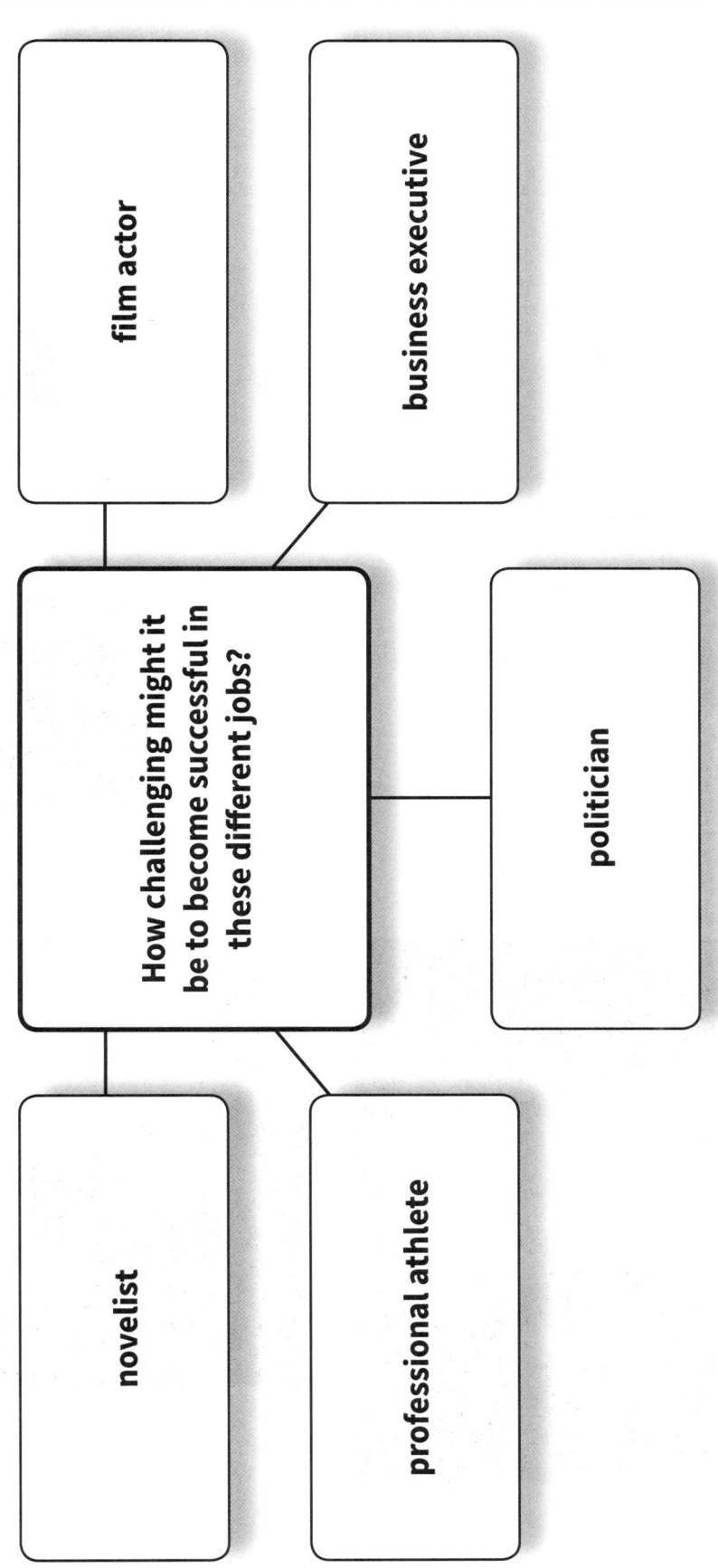

film actor

business executive

How challenging might it be to become successful in these different jobs?

politician

novelist

professional athlete

EXERCISE 1

> - Why might the people need to listen carefully in these situations?
> - What might be the consequences of them not listening carefully?

EXERCISE 3

CANDIDATE A

- What might these people be preparing for?
- How do you think they're feeling?

CANDIDATE B

- Why might the people be showing these things to others?
- How interested might the others be in what they're being shown?

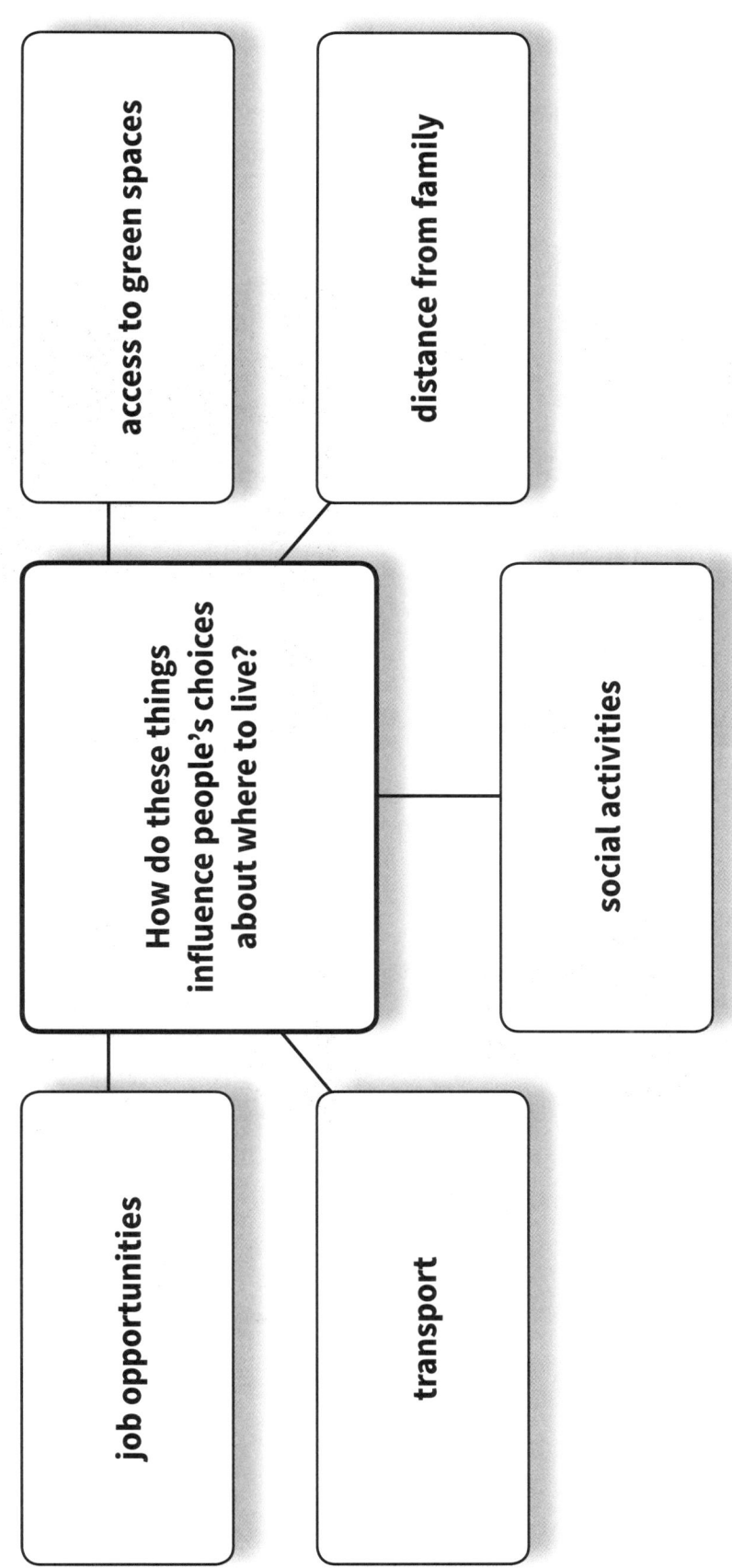

access to green spaces

distance from family

How do these things influence people's choices about where to live?

social activities

job opportunities

transport

CANDIDATE A

- Why might the people be feeling tired?
- How long do you think this tiredness might last?

CANDIDATE B

- How long might the people have taken to prepare for these events?
- How might they be feeling?

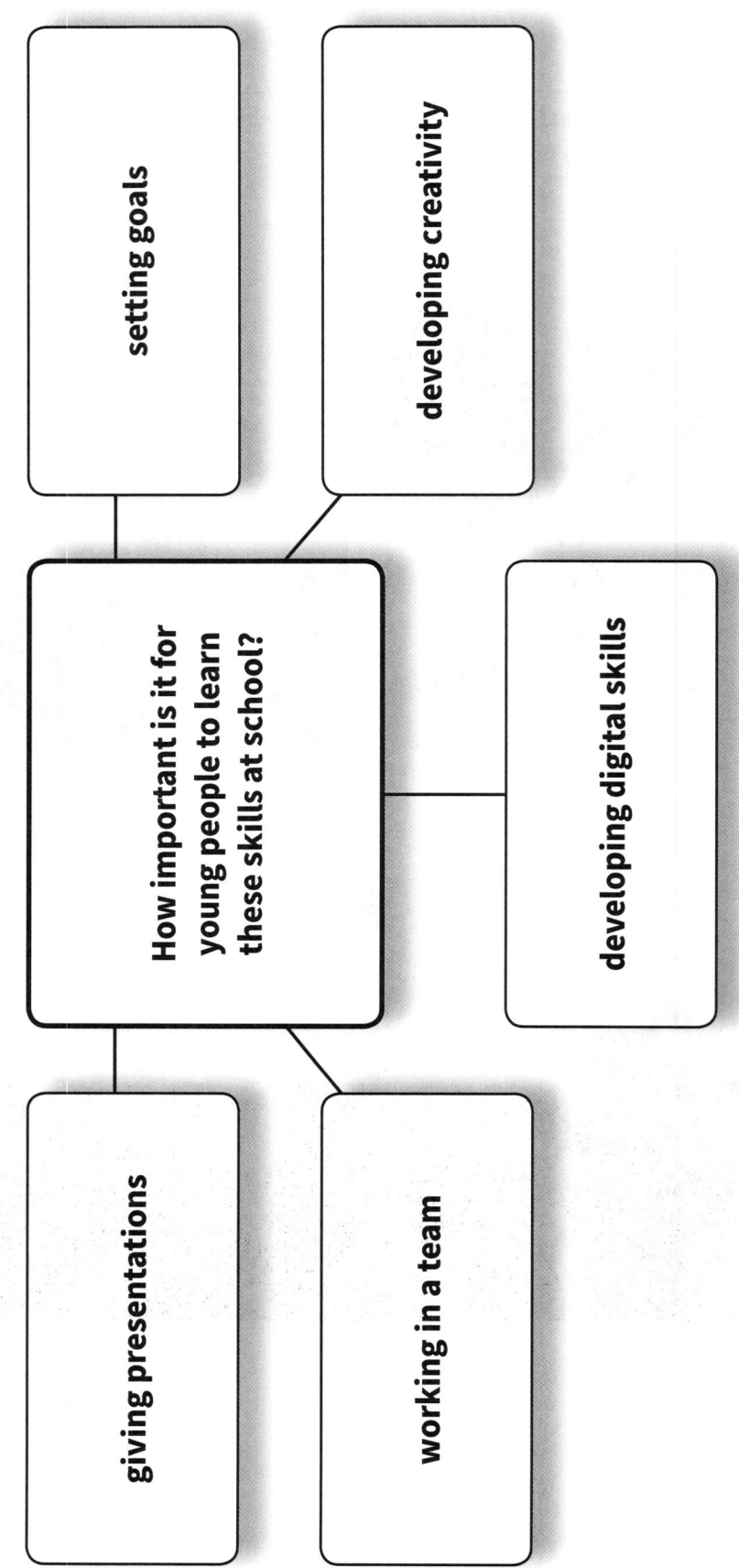

setting goals

developing creativity

How important is it for young people to learn these skills at school?

developing digital skills

giving presentations

working in a team

CANDIDATE A

- Why might the people be using the screens in these situations?
- What problems might they experience using them?

CANDIDATE B

- Why is good weather important in these situations?
- What might the people do if the weather changed?

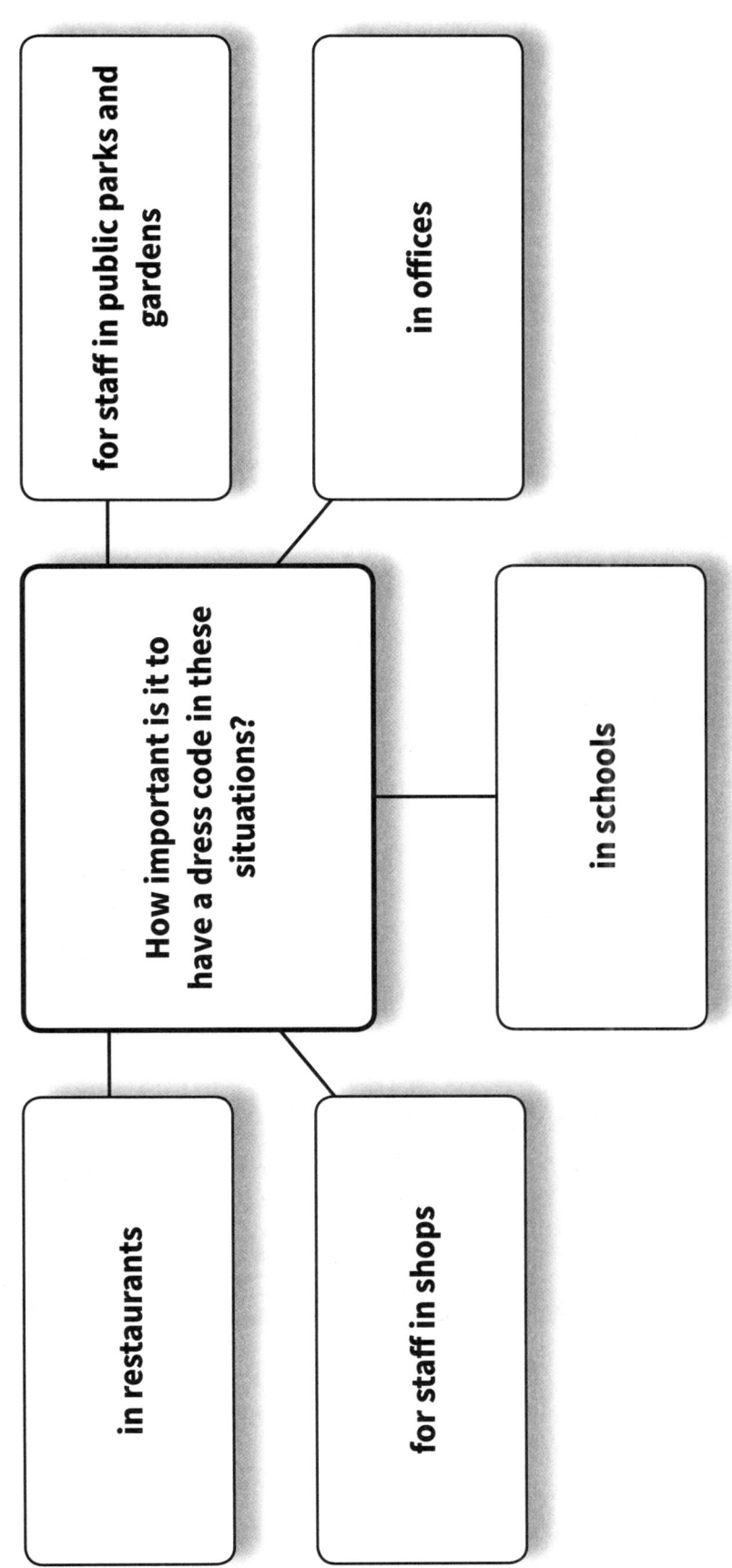

for staff in public parks and gardens

in offices

How important is it to have a dress code in these situations?

in schools

in restaurants

for staff in shops

CANDIDATE A

- What might have inspired the people to paint in these situations?
- How might they feel when they have finished painting?

CANDIDATE B

- How might the people benefit from sharing these experiences?
- How long do you think they might remember them?

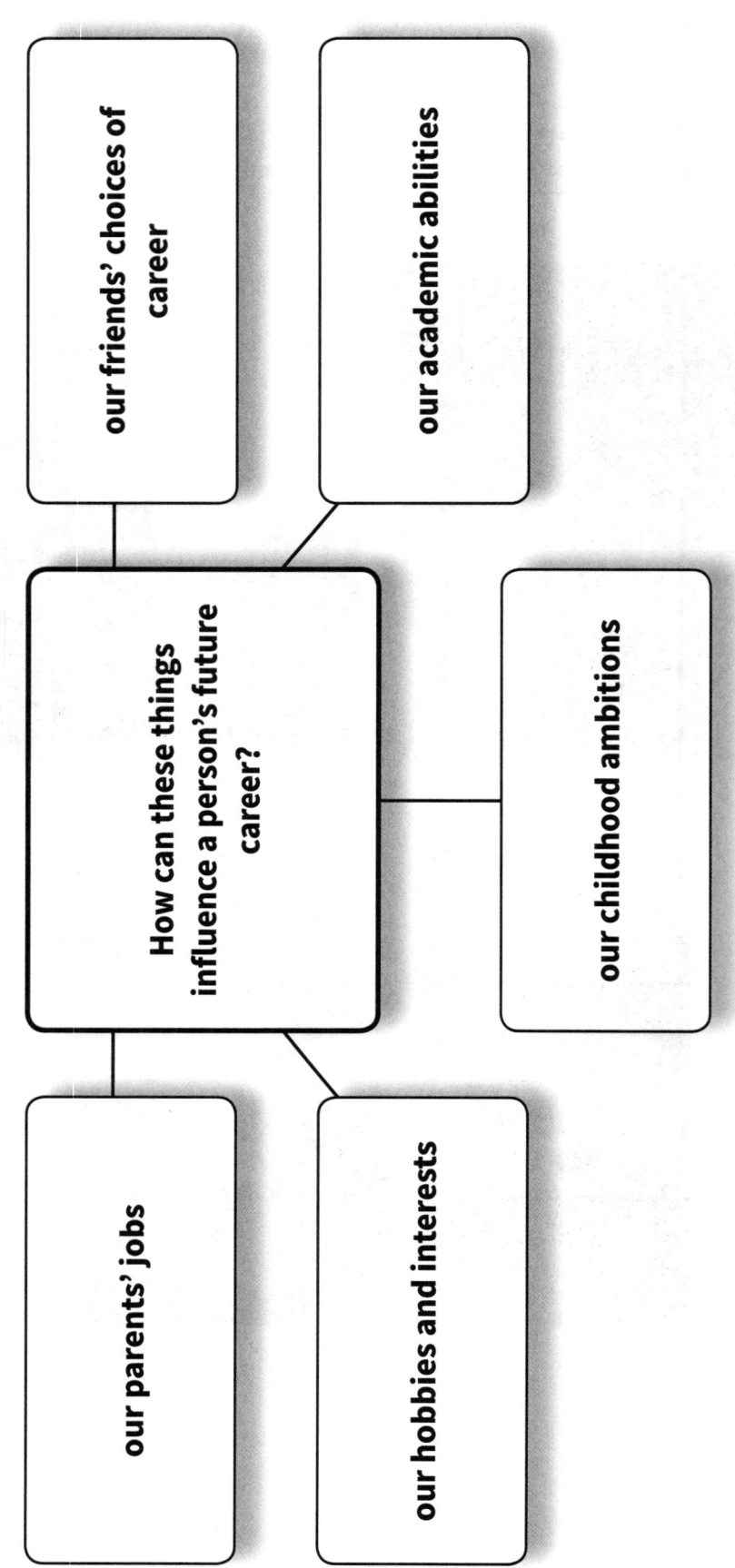

our friends' choices of career

our academic abilities

How can these things influence a person's future career?

our childhood ambitions

our parents' jobs

our hobbies and interests

CANDIDATE A

- Why is confidence needed in these situations?
- How might the people feel when the event is over?

CANDIDATE B

- What skills are important for these people when they deal with customers?
- How rewarding might the jobs be?

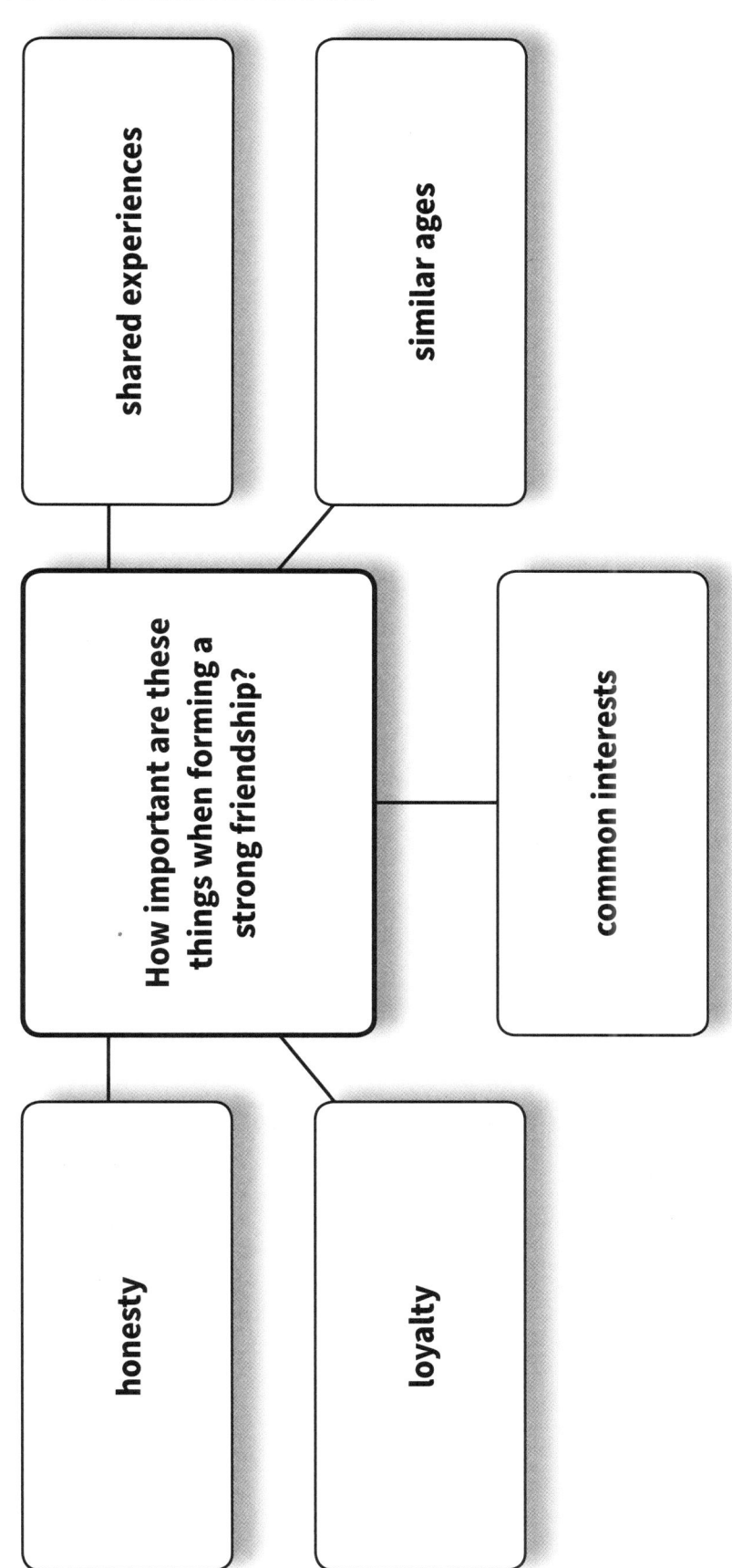

shared experiences

similar ages

How important are these things when forming a strong friendship?

common interests

honesty

loyalty